Doing Research in Business and Management

Visit the *Doing Research in Business and Management* Companion Website at **www.pearsoned.co.uk/saunders** to find valuable **student** learning material including:

- Multiple-choice questions to test your learning
- Tutorials on Excel, NVivo and SPSS
- Updated research datasets to practise with
- Updated additional case studies with accompanying questions
- Smarter Online Searching Guide – how to make the most of the Internet in your research
- Real-life examples of good and bad research

Doing Research in Business and Management

An Essential Guide to Planning Your Project

Mark Saunders and Philip Lewis

Financial Times
Prentice Hall
is an imprint of

Harlow, England • London • New York • Boston • San Francisco • Toronto
Sydney • Tokyo • Singapore • Hong Kong • Seoul • Taipei • New Delhi
Cape Town • Madrid • Mexico City • Amsterdam • Munich • Paris • Milan

Pearson Education Limited
Edinburgh Gate
Harlow
Essex CM20 2JE
England

and Associated Companies throughout the world

Visit us on the World Wide Web at:
www.pearson.com/uk

First published 2012

© Mark Saunders and Philip Lewis 2012

ISBN: 978-0-273-72641-8

British Library Cataloguing-in-Publication Data
A catalogue record for this book is available from the British Library

Library of Congress Cataloging-in-Publication Data
A catalog record for this book is available from the Library of Congress

10 9 8 7 6 5 4
15 14

Typeset in 9/13pt Stone Serif by 30
Printed and bound in Great Britain by Ashford Colour Press Ltd, Gosport, Hampshire

Brief contents

About this book   xi
About the authors   xv
Acknowledgements   xvi

1 Choosing your research topic   1

2 Reviewing the literature   30

3 Managing the research process   57

4 Using secondary data   84

5 Choosing your research design   102

6 Collecting data   131

7 Analysing data   164

8 Writing and presenting the research proposal   201

Bibliography   227
Index   229

Contents

About this book   xi
About the authors   xv
Acknowledgements   xvi

1 Choosing your research topic   1
1.1   Why you should read this chapter   1
1.2   Why choosing the right research topic is so important   2
1.3   Why choosing a research topic is difficult   4
1.4   Ten ways to generate ideas for a research topic   5
1.5   How to refine research topic ideas   11
1.6   What makes a good research topic?   15
1.7   How to turn a research idea into a research project   18
Summary   28
Thinking about your research topic   29
References   29

2 Reviewing the literature   30
2.1   Why you should read this chapter   30
2.2   What a literature review is   31
2.3   Why it is important to review the literature   33
2.4   The types of literature available to you   36
2.5   Searching for and obtaining literature   38
2.6   Evaluating the usefulness of literature to your research   45
2.7   Reading, noting and correctly referencing useful literature   46
2.8   Writing your literature review   51
Summary   54
Thinking about your critical literature review   55
References   56

3 Managing the research process   57
3.1   Why you should read this chapter   57
3.2   Getting access to your research organisation and your respondents   58
3.3   What about access to information?   60
3.4   Six strategies for making sure that you get the organisational access you want   61
3.5   Managing yourself   68
3.6   Managing your supervisor   70

3.7   Managing your university   73
3.8   The ethics of doing research   74
Summary   82
Thinking about your research process   83
References   83

4 Using secondary data   84

4.1   Why you should read this chapter   84
4.2   What forms does secondary data take?   85
4.3   Why you should use secondary data – the potential?   90
4.4   What are the pitfalls of using secondary data?   94
4.5   Assessing the suitability of secondary data   96
4.6   Where and how to find secondary data   98
Summary   99
Thinking about using secondary data   100
References   101

5 Choosing your research design   102

5.1   Why you should read this chapter   102
5.2   The importance of research philosophy   104
5.3   Differing approaches to research: deduction and induction   107
5.4   Differing types of studies: exploratory, descriptive and
      explanatory studies   110
5.5   Differing strategies   114
5.6   Making sure your research conclusions are believable   125
Summary   129
Thinking about your research design   129
References   129

6 Collecting data   131

6.1   Why you should read this chapter   131
6.2   Selecting samples   132
6.3   Collecting data using questionnaires   141
6.4   Collecting data using semi-structured or unstructured interviews 151
Summary   161
Thinking about collecting data   162
References   162

7 Analysing data   164

7.1   Why you should read this chapter   164
7.2   What are different types of data?   165
7.3   Analysing data quantitatively   168
7.4   Analysing data qualitatively   187
Summary   198

Thinking about analysing data   199
References   200

8 **Writing and presenting the research proposal**   201
   8.1   Why you should read this chapter   201
   8.2   Why is the research proposal so important?   202
   8.3   When should I write my research proposal?   206
   8.4   What should I include in my research proposal?   206
   8.5   In what style should my research proposal be written?   216
   8.6   How will my research proposal be judged?   220
   Summary   225
   Thinking about your research proposal   226
   References   226

   Bibliography   227
   Index   229

Supporting resources

Visit www.pearsoned.co.uk/saunders to find valuable online resources:

Companion Website for students
- Multiple-choice questions to test your learning
- Tutorials on Excel, NVivo and SPSS
- Updated research datasets to practise with
- Updated additional case studies with accompanying questions
- Smarter Online Searching Guide – how to make the most of the Internet in your research
- Real-life examples of good and bad research

For instructors
- Complete, downloadable Instructor's Manual
- PowerPoint slides that can be downloaded and used for presentations

Also: The regularly maintained Companion Website provides the following features:

- Search tool to help locate specific items of content
- E-mail results and profile tools to send results of quizzes to instructors
- Online help and support to assist with website usage and troubleshooting

For more information please contact your local Pearson Education sales representative or visit www.pearsoned.co.uk/saunders

About this book

It is now fourteen years since we collaborated in the writing of our first research methods book. In 2009 the fifth edition was published (Saunders et al., 2009).* The success of that book suggests that research methods is a popular subject with business and management students. This may be so. But we think that it has more to do with the fact that research methods is a complex area – one where it is easy to do things, but much less easy to do things right.

When we planned the first book we had one overall mission in mind. That was to write a book in a way that came as near as possible to the way in which we taught our students. By this we mean that we wanted to be clear and straightforward, and explain things in a way that lost none of the complexity, or academic rigour of the subject. Over the years this mission has not altered. We feel just as passionate about clear communication as we did back in 1997.

However, things in the world of business and management education have changed since 1997, and this book reflects those changes. In 1997 the normal requirement was for undergraduate students in their final year to undertake a large piece of research, which involved them in collecting their own data and was assessed by means of a written project report. This is now often not the case. Although some degree programmes still require students to complete an assessed research project, they may be told that, rather than collect their own data, they should use only data that have already been collected for some other purpose (secondary data) or, alternatively, write an extended review of the literature. For a second category of students on undergraduate programmes the extent of their research work is a research methods module which is assessed by a research proposal. There is a third category, those business and management students who opt not to do a research project at all.

We have written this book to cater for all three categories of student. For those undertaking research to be assessed by a written project report, we aim to help in all aspects of the research process: from thinking of a topic through to writing the final submission. We therefore include material, in Chapter 3, on managing the research process, as well as chapters on using secondary data (Chapter 4) and reviewing the literature (Chapter 2). There are also two chapters (6 and 7) on collecting and analysing data, as an understanding of these is important for all types of research projects as well as preparing a research proposal. If you're taking a research methods module which is assessed by a research proposal, you will find that there is considerable emphasis on the preparation of a research proposal. Indeed, Chapter 8 deals specifically with writing the research proposal.

* Saunders, M., Lewis, P. and Thornhill, A. (2009) *Research Methods for Business Students* (5th edition), Harlow: FT Prentice Hall.

It may sound strange, but we think that business and management students in the third category, those who opt not to do a research project at all, can gain just as much from this book as those in the other two categories. As a student you will spend much of your time studying material which is the result of careful research that has been scrutinised by the research community prior to publication. This scrutiny is a guarantee of good quality: that you should put your faith in what you have read. However, some of what you read may not have been through quite such a rigorous process. Knowing something about the research process enables you to ask the right questions of the material you are studying. It gives you the sense of healthy scepticism that is the hallmark of a university education.

How you might use this book

We don't anticipate that you will read this book progressively from Chapter 1 through to Chapter 8. In fact, you may not read all the chapters, although we certainly hope that you will! The reason, we suspect, is that you will choose those chapters that meet your own needs. This may be because you are in one of the categories we mentioned earlier, have specific questions about the research process you need to answer, or it may be that your research methods lecturers specify certain chapters. We've written the chapters in such a way that they stand alone. To some extent, they draw inevitably on material from other chapters directly. Where this is so, we have cross-referenced to the relevant chapter. But the point remains that you can pick up any chapter in isolation and make sense of it.

This book is not a self-study text in the truest sense; there are no questions with model answers! However, we have included points in each chapter which facilitate an element of independent learning. Each chapter begins with a summary of content which we call 'Why read this chapter?' This gives you some idea of the chapter content and the approach we have taken on the topic being discussed. Each chapter contains a small number of examples of research called 'Research in practice'. These serve to illustrate in a practical manner some of the points being made in the chapter, in much the same way as a lecturer would give practical examples in a research methods lecture. Every chapter ends with a summary of the main points in the chapter and a section called 'Thinking about …' Here we make suggestions as to how you may test and reinforce the learning you have achieved during the reading of the chapter. Throughout the book, key research terms we use are isolated and placed in 'Definition' boxes to make it easy for you to refresh your understanding of these terms as you read through each chapter.

What's in the book?

Chapter 1 deals with the first issue you will encounter in the research process: choosing the right research topic. We suggest some novel ways in which you may decide upon your topic, offer guidance in deciding what constitutes an effective research topic, and consider some topics which may be problematic. In the latter part of the chapter we deal with the issue of defining suitable research questions and objectives. The chapter ends with a discussion on what is meant by the all-important term 'theory'.

In Chapter 2, we approach the subject of the literature review. We offer some practical suggestions on the way you may go about approaching your literature review and actually conducting it, particularly through the use of information technology. The chapter also explains what constitutes an effective critical literature review and offers guidance in how it may be structured.

Chapter 3 is concerned with practical issues regarding gaining access to organisations from which you may collect your own research data. In this chapter we also consider the issues of self-management you may face in conducting your research, particularly the effective use of resources such as time. The management of other aspects of the research process is also discussed, such as your supervisor, university and those from whom you collect your data. We also help you to think about the ways in which you adhere to the code of research ethics that you will be required to observe.

In Chapter 4 we consider the use of secondary data. We discuss the valuable role which secondary data may play in your research and the reasons you may use secondary data. The ready availability of a wealth of secondary data, particularly as a result of the growth of the Internet is considered. We also warn you about some of the pitfalls inherent in the use of secondary data and how to assess its value to your own research project.

The subject of Chapter 5 is research strategy. This involves a consideration of the main philosophies you may adopt and the ways in which they affect choice of strategy. We discuss the different types of research strategy, with an emphasis on the possibility of mixing strategies in one research project. We end the chapter with a discussion of the importance of validity and reliability: ensuring that your research results and conclusions are believable.

Chapter 6 gets to the heart of the research process: the collection of data. We explain how to choose a sample; draft an effective questionnaire and conduct effective interviews in their various forms, including electronic means.

In Chapter 7 we deal with the process of data analysis. We discuss the two types of data: quantitative and qualitative and the ways in which these data may be prepared for analysis and actually analysed. The use of statistics in both the presentation and analysis of data is explained with particular emphasis on the use of different software packages. We also discuss ways in which qualitative data may be prepared for analysis and analysed. As with the analysis of quantitative data, we emphasise the way in which you may develop theory from the analysed data.

Chapter 8 is devoted to the writing of your research proposal. We explain how the process of writing clarifies your ideas, and we emphasise the importance of treating the research proposal as an item of 'work in progress' by constantly revising it. The chapter also includes a discussion on what content the proposal should contain; how it may be structured and the appropriate writing style to be adopted. Finally, we suggest some of the criteria against which the quality of your research proposal may be assessed.

We hope you will learn a lot from this book: that's why it exists! But we also hope that you will enjoy reading it. Doing your research project should be fun!

Mark and Phil

About the authors

Mark N.K. Saunders BA, MSc, PGCE, PhD, FCIPD is Professor in Business Research Methods and Director of PhD programmes, The Surrey Business School at the University of Surrey. He was formerly Professor of Business Research Methods and Assistant Dean (Director of Research and Doctoral Programmes) at Oxford Brookes University Business School. He holds visiting professor roles at Newcastle Business School, University of Northumbria and at Worcester Business School, University of Worcester. He currently teaches research methods to master's and doctoral students as well as supervising master's dissertations and research degrees. Mark has published articles on research methods, service quality, and trust and organisational justice perspectives on the management of change. He is co-author with Phil Lewis and Adrian Thornhill of *Research Methods for Business Students*, currently in its fifth edition, and of *Employee Relations: Understanding the Employment Relationship*; with Phil Lewis, Adrian Thornhill, Mike Millmore and Trevor Morrow of *Strategic Human Resource Management*; and with Adrian Thornhill, Phil Lewis and Mike Millmore of *Managing Change: A Human Resource Strategy Approach*, all published by Financial Times Prentice Hall. He has co-authored two books on business statistics, the most recent being *Statistics: What You Need to Know* co-authored with Reva Berman-Brown; and co-edited *Organizational Trust: A Cultural Perspective* with Denise Skinner, Graham Dietz, Nicole Gillespie and Roy Lewicki. He undertakes research and consultancy in public, private and not-for-profit sectors. Prior to becoming an academic, he had a variety of research jobs in local government.

Philip J. Lewis BA, PhD, MSc, MCIPD, PGDipM, Cert Ed began his career in HR as a training adviser with the Distributive Industry Training Board. He then taught HRM and research methods in three UK universities. He studied part-time for degrees with the Open University and the University of Bath, from which he gained an MSc in Industrial Relations and a PhD for his research on performance pay in retail financial services. He is co-author with Mark Saunders and Adrian Thornhill of *Research Methods for Business Students*, currently in its fifth edition, and of *Employee Relations: Understanding the Employment Relationship*; and with Adrian Thornhill, Mike Millmore and Mark Saunders of *Managing Change: A Human Resource Strategy Approach*; and with Mark Saunders, Adrian Thornhill, Mike Millmore and Trevor Morrow of *Strategic Human Resource Management,* all published by Financial Times Prentice Hall. He has undertaken consultancy in both the public and private sectors.

Acknowledgements

We are grateful to the following for permission to reproduce copyright material:

Figures

Figure 2.2: Emerald screenshot from www.emeraldinsight.com, reproduced with permission; Page 91: unnumbered screenshot from www.statistics.gov.uk/. Crown Copyright material is reproduced with the permission of the Controller, Office of Public Sector Information (OPSI); Figures 5.1 and 5.2: Adapted from *Research Methods for Business Students*, 5th Edition, Pearson Education, (Saunders, M., Lewis, P. and Thornhill, A., 2009); Page 175: unnumbered figures adapted from www.statistics.gov.uk/statbase/tsdownload.asp?vlnk=224. Crown Copyright material is reproduced with the permission of the Controller, Office of Public Sector Information (OPSI); Figures 7.7, 7.8 and 7.9: SPSS screenshots reproduced courtesy of International Business Machines Corporation. Copyright © 2011 International Business Machines Corporation.

Tables

Table 3.5: from 'Ethical standards for research involving human participants: code of practice' (Oxford Brookes University, (2010)) www.brookes.ac.uk/res/policy/ethics_codeofpractice.pdf

Text

Page 44: extract from 'Affective and continuance commitment in public private partnership', *Employee Relations*, 32, 396–417 (Wang, C.L., Indridason, T. and Saunders, M.N.K, 2010); Pages 112–13: extract adapted from *UK Children's Media Literacy*, OFCOM (OFCOM, 2009); pages 196–97: extract from 'UK managers' conceptions of employee training and development', *Journal of European Industrial Training*, 34, 609–30 (McDowall, A. and Saunders, M.N.K, 2010); pages 209–10: extract from 'Hofstede's model of national cultural differences and their consequences: A triumph of faith – a failure of analysis', *Human Relations*, 55, 89–118 (McSweeny, B. 2002). Copyright © 2002 by SAGE. Reprinted by permission of SAGE.

In some instances we have been unable to trace the owners of copyright material, and we would appreciate any information that would enable us to do so.

Chapter 1

Choosing your research topic

1.1 Why you should read this chapter

This is a big moment in your life! You are about to embark on a voyage of discovery. You will discover a lot about the research process, the topic you are going to research and, we hope, a lot about yourself too. For many of you the research project is the one part of the course where you have an opportunity to choose what you are going to study and the way in which you study it. We hope that you see this as an exciting opportunity because we believe strongly that's what it is. It's your chance to express your individuality, your ingenuity and imagination, your resourcefulness and, above all, your personal organisational skills. These attributes have always been important. But in the twenty-first century they are more important than ever. Why do we say this? It's because we think that all the social, economic and technological changes of the past few years have empowered us all to take charge of our own lives to a greater extent than ever before. So take charge of your research topic now!

The overall purpose of this chapter is to enable you to get your research project off to a good start by choosing a research topic that will give you the best chance of succeeding and passing this important component of your course. It's worth bearing in mind that, however good you may be at all the relevant skills that go into producing a good research project, you will give yourself a better chance of succeeding if you have chosen your topic wisely.

In this chapter we talk about why choosing the right research topic is so important. We then go on to explain why for many of us the choice of topic is so difficult. The choice is made easier if this decision-making process is tackled in a systematic way. In the chapter we outline some of the procedures for adopting a systematic approach. Then, having got to the stage where you have chosen a topic, we examine ways in which the topic you have chosen can be refined in such a way that it is acceptable to your assessors and will provide you with the maximum amount of satisfaction. We end the chapter with a consideration of what makes a good research topic, and some help on writing research questions and objectives.

1.2   Why choosing the right research topic is so important

It is possible, of course, that you may be constrained in your choice of research topic. Your university may define strict limits outside which you may not stray. Alternatively, it is possible that an employer has asked you to undertake a piece of research. In either case some of the points in the next two sections on choosing the right research topic and generating research ideas may not apply to you directly. However, we encourage you not to ignore the points made. It may be that, although you may not have a free choice of the general topic, the way in which you approach it may be entirely your decision.

Now let's look at some of the reasons why choosing the right research topic is so important.

You have to live with it

The decision about which research topic to choose is something you will have to live with, maybe for as long as a year or more. We mean this in two senses. First, it is a topic you will become intimately familiar with so it makes sense to choose something that you will enjoy. Ask yourself: what am I really interested in? OK, so it may be that football is your passion. Well, football nowadays is big business, particularly in the major leagues in Europe such as the English Premier League. So if your passion has a business dimension then maybe there is a research topic to be pursued. One of our student's undergraduate project explored the reasons why attendances at matches were generally lower when the match was screened live on television. This led into interesting areas such as the affiliation aspect of motivation theory where some people, for example a football team's fans, have a need to be affiliated with like-minded people and are motivated towards interaction with these people. This posed a question about the extent to which a comfortable armchair and the economic benefits of not attending the match in person overrode the need for affiliation!

The second sense in which we mean that the decision about which research topic to choose is something you will have to live with is that when you have chosen it, normally there is no going back. You will make life much more difficult for yourself if you find out after one half of the time period allotted to your research that you have chosen the wrong topic. It may be possible to change even at that stage, but you spend the rest of the allotted time playing catch-up. We talk later in this chapter about problems in choosing a research topic, and the consequences of making the wrong choice. So it is better to spend the time at the outset making sure it's right for you. It is a time-consuming process. Many students have remarked to us in the past that they thought that choosing their topic would be easy. It may be easy to choose one that you are interested in, but turning it into a viable proposition for your course may take much longer than you thought.

● It will be better choosing a topic that will both exploit and develop your knowledge and skills

As well as choosing a topic that you will enjoy, it obviously makes sense to choose a topic that you are capable of doing well. Making a list of your skills and knowledge seems a good starting point. Here are a few questions you can ask yourself to help you prepare the list.

What are your personal strengths and weaknesses?

We are all better at some things than others. You may have discovered strengths on your course that you may want to exploit. These may relate to your background experience or particular skills that you can practise in the data collection and analysis stages of the research. The knowledge gained in previous or current work experience is a good knowledge source for many students. You are more likely to know your way around some of the areas that need specialist knowledge. In addition, this specialist knowledge will lead more easily to an informed research question that needs answering. Alternatively, you may be keen to learn about an industry that's new to you. For example, you may be fascinated by software design and want to learn more about that industry with a view to possible employment. In this case you will need to ask yourself whether locating a research project in that industry will give you an equal chance of success compared to an industry with which you may be familiar. It's also a good idea to think about the modules you have studied and those in which you have had success. This will give you a confident start.

The data collection and analysis methods you adopt offer slightly different options. Here, you may be experienced at interviewing but less so at designing questionnaires. Do you exploit your expertise or decide to learn the skill of questionnaire design? Of course, you can include an element of both. The choices you make may be based on practical as well as personal development considerations. It's not much good having learned a lot but not passed the module!

What knowledge and skills do you think you will need in the future?

This may be quite a difficult question to answer for many of us. Few of us could have predicted twenty years ago the extent to which we all now need information technology skills in both our work and home lives. Yet it may be possible for you to predict some of the generic skills you may need to equip you for effective personal performance. Some of these, such as influencing others and conducting meetings, you may have encountered during your course. The opportunity may present itself in your research to practise some of these skills, particularly in the data collection stage. In the same way, your choice of topic could help develop your specialist knowledge of an aspect of your chosen area of employment.

What resources can you draw upon to help?

Perhaps the value of this question is most evident when it reveals the absence of resources! Most of you will have access to key people such as lecturers, managers and colleagues. The degree to which these can be of assistance will, of course, vary. It will be very valuable to be able to consult an 'expert' in the subject area you are studying for your research but, if you have chosen a fairly specialist field, the absence of such assistance may be a considerable block to your progress. You will, of course, have access to information technology but such issues as the processing of questionnaire answers and the analysis of questionnaire data is a complex and demanding affair if you have no experience in this. Don't be afraid to ask for help!

Your choice of topic may help you pass the whole course?

Although we have put the emphasis here upon self-development, the point remains that you must choose a topic that will allow you to meet the assessment requirements and will give you the best possible chance of ultimate success. If there is one fundamental lesson that we have learned as a result of supervising many research projects over the years it is this: the earlier you start deciding upon your topic the more likely you will be to choose the right one and ensure final success!

1.3   Why choosing a research topic is difficult

There is no question that for many of us choosing the right topic is one of the most difficult aspects of the whole research process. At this stage you are on your own! It has to come from you, and making decisions which have important consequences is often a difficult business for most of us. So, what are some of the reasons why this one may be particularly difficult? Let's have a look at some of them.

There is simply too much choice

It's wonderful living in an age when there is so much information available to all of us at the end of our fingertips. But this leads us to think that there is no question that has not been asked and no problem which has not been solved. Whatever it is we are interested in, there appears to be a vast amount of information available, much of which there is never enough time to read. This leads to the inevitable feeling that whatever it is you have in mind will have been done before. Well, it probably has, but not in the way you intend to do it. But that doesn't mean that you can't tackle it. One of the most popular undergraduate research topics is worker motivation. 'What is it that workers value most about their working lives?' is a frequently asked question. The textbooks are full of generic answers to this question. And your university library will be full of project reports which have asked the same question. Yet there are lots of managers in organisations who need to know the answer in respect of their own employees. In other words, the application of even the most familiar topic can be applied to many different, specific situations.

The fear that it will be too difficult

The research process is challenging enough without making it more difficult by choosing a topic that stretches you too far. How will you know if that is the case? Have a look at the literature on a topic that interests you as a possible choice. Maybe the way in which the topic is covered has an overly theoretical approach which makes it too difficult for you to 'think your way in'. The motivation of people to work has a distinctly practical feel. But researching the way in which the brain operates to direct our enthusiasm to one interest rather than another seems to emphasise the biological aspects, rather than the business perspective for which your course has prepared you.

The fear that it will be insufficiently theoretical

It's quite understandable that you should feel a mild sense of panic when you go to your supervisor to explain with great enthusiasm your choice of research topic only to be greeted by 'Yes, very interesting, but what role will theory play?' This is where it starts to get tricky. But don't despair because theory has a role to play in all project reports. It's just a question of how you use it and where you use it. Later in this chapter we explore the role of theory in writing research questions and objectives. And in Chapter 5 we explain that theory can be used as a 'way in' to your research by setting up theoretical propositions which can be tested. It can also be used as a lens through which you can study your data, or a structure against which you can perform your data analysis.

In case you are unconvinced, just consider this statement: 'Students read research methods textbooks in the hope that they perform more effectively in their research module'. That's a theory, and what you are doing right now is evidence that it is accurate!

The temptation to reuse work you have already done

It is tempting to take the easy way out and use an assignment which you have written for a previous purpose and just enlarge it to make it into a research project. There is a similar temptation for part-time students who perhaps have produced a research report at work. The trouble is that it never quite 'fits'. It's a bit like fitting a wheel to a bike that's not quite the right size. It may be OK, but it's never more than that. You are likely to spend more time getting it to fit than thinking through a purpose-made topic.

1.4   Ten ways to generate ideas for a research topic

Having given you some general guidelines on choosing a suitable research topic, let's look at some techniques for deciding on the topic itself. We have listed our favourite ten of these in Table 1.1. They are in no particular order.

Table 1.1 Ten techniques for generating research ideas

1	Thinking
2	Looking at past project titles
3	Using past projects from the university library
4	Using past course assignments
5	Using relevant literature
6	Following the news media
7	Brainstorming
8	Concept mapping
9	Making a note of ideas
10	Discussion with others

Thinking

We are bound to start with this one, because there is no escaping it! By thinking we mean really thinking. Keep the need to select a topic in your mind all the time; when you watch TV, read a newspaper, browse relevant web pages, talk to colleagues, talk and listen in seminars, discuss issues with your lecturers. Probably, like us, questions often go through your mind when you are in stores, airports, buses – questions such as 'How are the work rotas for these people organised?' or 'How can the cost of delivering this service be reduced while maintaining quality of service?' This is what you may call 'background thinking'. Now let's look at a series of more specific techniques for generating ideas.

Looking at past project titles

You are not the first person to have trodden the path, so it's a good idea to look at what those before you have attempted. You should find a list of past research project titles for your course in your university library. This will give you an idea of the sort of topic that may be suitable. It will also fire your imagination and help you to start thinking about how that title may relate to something that you have thought about. Don't worry about what you think may not be a particularly well-written title. And do bear in mind that in some universities all past projects are placed in the library whether they are bare passes or distinctions. So the fact that a project is in your library does not necessarily mean that it's a good piece of work. The point is to generate ideas for your project, not work out what makes a good project.

Using past projects

Having delved into the university library to look for past project titles, why not spend some more time checking the projects which have caught your attention? Raimond (1993) suggests a useful method for generating research topic ideas this way.

Table 1.2 Four steps for generating research topic ideas using past projects from the university library

1 Select six projects that you like.

2 For each of these six projects note down your first thoughts to answer these three questions (if responses for different projects are the same this does not matter):
   (a) What appeals to you about the project?
   (b) What is good about the project?
   (c) Why is the project good?

3 Select three projects that you do not like.

4 For each of these three projects note down your first thoughts to answer these three questions (if responses for different projects are the same, or cannot be clearly expressed, this does not matter; note them down anyway):
   (a) What do you dislike about the project?
   (b) What is bad about the project?
   (c) Why is the project bad?

Having completed these four steps you will have a note of the things that you like and dislike about projects and, of equal importance, what you consider makes good and poor projects. What's more, that list will be personal to you. It's your opinion, and that is what you can use to guide your choice for your own research topic.

Using past course assignments

Many students find that past course assignments serve as a good starting point for research topic ideas. It seems logical to develop the work of an assignment in which you have had some choice of topic, particularly when you have enjoyed it and received a good grade. However, do bear in mind the maxim that 'all research ends with ideas for more research'. Look hard at what you have done and ask yourself: 'Are there questions posed by my work which I have not answered?'

Beware of developing the assignment because you got a good grade! There must be scope for development, and it must meet the assessment criteria. For example, many universities have rules to prevent students reusing work that they have already submitted as an assignment.

Using relevant literature

Since what you are going to tackle should use the literature relevant to your topic, it seems sensible to start by examining that literature. Let's assume that you have decided to look at a possible research topic that is a development of a module you have enjoyed. Go back to your lecture notes and course textbooks on that topic and make a note of the names of relevant authors. This will give you a basis on which to undertake a preliminary search. This should help you to produce a list of articles, books, reports and other items.

A particularly valuable literature source of research topic ideas is academic review articles. They are valuable because they contain both a thorough review of the state of knowledge in that topic area and pointers towards areas where further research needs to be undertaken. Recent journals in your field are also a good source of possible research ideas. For many subject areas your project supervisor will be able to suggest possible recent review articles, or articles that contain recommendations for further work.

Books, by contrast, are less up to date than journal articles. But they do often contain a good overview of research that has been undertaken, which may suggest ideas to you. Reports may also be of use. The most recently published are usually up to date and, again, often contain recommendations that may form the basis of your research idea. An example of such a report is shown as Research in practice 1.1.

Research in practice 1.1

Using reports to generate research topic ideas

A report by the British Library's Business & IP Centre (2009) has recommended that newly established small firms should be given some form of tax exemption for their first year or two of business. It also suggested that a fast-track scheme should be created to help firms to patent ideas, and that broadband speeds must rise.

Former BBC television programme *Dragon's Den* panel member Doug Richard, who was one of the business experts questioned in compiling the report, said tax relief was the best way to provide incentives to aspiring entrepreneurs. He said 'it takes a good 18 months of solid work before a new business starts to really establish itself. If the government is serious about encouraging enterprise in the UK, then they need to avoid gimmicks like the VAT cut, and offer start-ups a genuine exemption from tax until they get their businesses up and running.'

Other suggestions put forward by the British Library's report include an increase in maternity leave subsidies, the creation of a subsidised national internship scheme, and a plan to make it more straightforward for small firms to apply for government contracts.

Sources: BBC News (2009) *New small firms need tax break*. November 15. Available at: http://news.bbc.co.uk/1/hi/business/8358688.stm.

British Library (2009) *Enterprising voices: supporting the drive for recovery*. London: The British Library Business & IP Centre.

Table 1.3 lists some useful questions to ask when searching articles and reports for possible research topic ideas. The answers to these can help progress your choice of topic.

Following the news media

We would always encourage you to go to the academic literature as your first port of call, but don't ignore the value of keeping up to date with items in the news. News media can be a very rich source of ideas. The stories which occur everyday in the 'quality' newspapers (e.g. *The Times*, the *Financial Times*, *The Guardian*, *The*

Table 1.3 Useful questions to ask when searching articles and reports for possible research topic ideas

---

- What did the authors conclude?
- What alternative conceptual models, explanations, or hypotheses did the authors consider?
- What methods did the authors use to approach the problem?
- Do you accept the authors' conclusions? If not, are there other methods that could allow you to test their conclusion?
- Do the authors' research suggest new ways to interpret a different problem?
- Are there other problems that could be studied using the same methods?

Independent and *The Daily Telegraph*) in both print and online versions may provide ideas which relate directly to a possible research topic. Don't forget there may be other ideas which flow from the main story. On the morning of writing this section in 2010, customers have been waiting all night outside Apple's UK stores to be the first to buy the iPad. This suggests a research topic exploring the extent to which global companies can use their expertise to obtain maximum impact.

Brainstorming

Brainstorming can be a useful and fun way of generating research topic ideas. It is particularly valuable when you brainstorm with a group of people, ideally those who really understand why you are doing this. However, you can brainstorm on your own – but it's much less fun!

To brainstorm, you start off by defining the general field you are interested in. Try to make this as precise as possible. It may be that in the early stages of formulating a topic you have to be pretty imprecise, such as 'I am interested the effects of the weather on food retailing but I am not sure how I can turn this into a research topic'. The next stage is to ask the other members of the group for suggestions, relating to the imprecise topic you have suggested. It's a good idea to arm yourself with a pen and a large sheet of paper and note down all the suggestions you receive. The following five rules are very important:

1 Do record as many suggestions as possible.
2 Do record all suggestions, however 'wacky' or 'off the wall' they may appear at first sight.
3 Don't criticise or evaluate any ideas until they have been considered.
4 Do consider all the suggestions and explore the precise meaning of each of them.
5 Do analyse the list of suggestions and decide which appeal to you most as research ideas and why.

> **Definition**
>
> **brainstorming**: a technique that can be used to generate and refine research ideas. It is best undertaken with a group of people.

Concept mapping

Having completed your brainstorm you may move on to use another technique which we find very useful in many contexts – **concept mapping**. This is a process which moves from a general idea which may have been the outcome of a brainstorm, or other idea-generating technique, to the creation of a map which represents visually the organisation of your thinking. Concept maps may be elaborate or simple; indeed they may start out very simple and end up quite detailed. The purpose is to help you organise your thinking about a topic and get them into a coherent state. Concept maps are very useful in helping you to recognise where you have gaps in your knowledge. This can help with planning further searches in the literature. They are also a good base from which you can move on to develop research questions and objectives.

Figure 1.1 A simple concept map showing representation of competitive advantage
Source: Institute for Manufacturing (www.ifm.eng.cam.ac.uk/csp/news/05april/4.html)

> **Definition**
>
> **concept map**: a map which represents visually the way we organise our thoughts about a set of related ideas.

Making a note of ideas

Many of you will look at this title heading and say: 'That's all very well for them but I never get any ideas!' You do, all of us do. Think positively and forget any notions that ideas are reserved just for the creative few rather than the rest of us. That's often enough to have ideas start flowing! It's perfectly normal to go through several days without having any ideas at all. Then, perhaps when you are thinking of something else entirely, an idea will come to you followed by more ideas. Sometimes, the ideas will come pretty quickly so you will have to make sure you capture them before they are forgotten. When you start getting ideas you will learn not to worry about the times when the ideas are not coming. It's just important to take full advantage of those idea flows when they happen.

So what about capturing those precious ideas when they come? It's important to keep a notebook of ideas, or, perhaps, voice record ideas in a device such as your mobile phone. All you need to do is to note any interesting research ideas as you think of them and, of equal importance, what started you thinking of the idea. You don't have to go as far as Mark who takes his notebook on holiday with him so he can jot down any flashes of inspiration that occur to him while sitting in the café!

Discussion with colleagues, friends and lecturers

Don't forget the more usual sources of ideas and advice: your colleagues, friends and university lecturers. Project supervisors will often have ideas for possible student projects which they will be pleased to discuss with you. These may be based upon work done by other students which may be developed, or taken in a different direction. One of our students conducted an analysis of a food manufacturer's advertising strategy for launching a new brand with a view to discovering the optimum advertising expenditure level. We suggested a similar project using an insurance company. Each of the two students tackled the project in a different way. Both delivered very successful pieces of work.

You can also pick up useful ideas from talking to practitioners and professional groups. Find out if your local professional association has a students' evening. Here you can meet local managers who will be more than willing to discuss ideas with you. Most professional groups are pleased to welcome students to meetings where, often, interesting presentations are given which may spark off your ideas. Once again, do bear in mind the value of discussing possible ideas and make a note of them.

1.5   How to refine research topic ideas

Refining topics given by your employing organisation

The choosing of a research topic may be less problematic than we have suggested above, at least on the face of it. We say this because you may be given a topic. This may apply particularly to you if you are a part-time student and you have been given a topic to research by your manager. The problem here is that it is not 'your' topic, and you may not be wildly enthusiastic about it. If you find yourself in this situation, you will have to weigh the advantage of doing something useful to the organisation against the disadvantage of a potential lack of personal motivation. Aim for a balance.

One of the problems in this situation is that the research project your manager wishes you to undertake is larger than that which is suitable for your course. This may not be an insurmountable problem. Within the larger project there may well be a smaller element on which you can concentrate for your university research project.

In such cases, it may be possible to complete both by isolating an element of the larger organisational project that you find interesting and treating this as the project for your course.

Peng, a student of Phil's, worked for a large manufacturing organisation which felt it had a problem with communicating with its employees. She was asked by the HR manager to carry out an employee survey to establish what employees felt about the way in which managers communicated with their staff, and the way the company in general delivered important news to employees. One of the motives behind this managerial initiative was the feeling of the HR director that the company should have a regular newsletter. (Not the least reason for this motive was the thought that this would promote the profile of the HR function!) This project was not one which Peng would have chosen. However, she was interested in the theoretical proposition that employees would feel more committed to the company if they felt trouble was being taken to communicate effectively with them. Peng talked this over with Phil and, with the approval of the HR manager, included some questions designed specifically to test this theoretical proposition.

Peng decided to treat the company research as one major piece of work with a separate element which was 'hers' for her university research project. This involved writing a large report for her employer and a smaller report for her university work.

Peng was very aware of the political dimension to her work. She knew that the HR director had a vested interest in the outcomes of her work. Phil advised her to keep this in mind, but not let it compromise the element of the work she was doing for her university course. Peng and Phil agreed that it was important to have a clear stance with regard to her personal objectives, and to stick to them.

One final point about the potentially tricky job of 'serving two masters' – the biggest potential problem may be one of your own making: to promise to deliver research outcomes to your employer and not do so. After all, don't forget that in this situation, as an employee, you get paid for what your employer asks of you.

The preliminary study

Even if you have been given a research idea, it is still necessary to refine it in order to turn it into a research project. This is often called a **preliminary study**.

For some research ideas, this study need only be an initial review of some of the literature. This is similar to 'using relevant literature' and 'following the news media'

Definition

preliminary study: the process by which a research idea is refined in order to turn it into a research project.

in the 'ten techniques for generating research ideas' section above. You may think of this as the first run at your critical literature review, a topic we deal with in detail in Chapter 2. Other research ideas may benefit from revisiting the techniques discussed earlier in this section, in particular looking at past project titles, using past course assignments and using past projects from the university library. Discussions with lecturers and managers may also be very valuable.

Your university may require you to complete a research project which restricts you to collecting secondary data, data which already exists (see Chapter 4). If so, it is important that you establish that the data you require are available.

If your research is going to be conducted in an organisation, it is essential to gain a good understanding of that organisation. One good way of doing this is to shadow employees who are likely to be important in your research. They will usually provide useful insights into the way the organisation works, as well as specific guidance for your research. Whatever way you choose to familiarise yourself with the organisation, don't forget that the underlying purpose is to gain a greater understanding so that your research question can be refined.

At this early stage you will be testing your research ideas. However, it may be that after a preliminary study, or discussing your ideas with colleagues, you decide that the research idea is no longer viable. Don't despair too much if this is the case. It is much better to revise your research ideas at this stage than to have to do it later, when you have undertaken far more work.

The Delphi technique

Another approach you may use for refining your research ideas is the **Delphi technique**. This technique involves using a group of people who are either involved or interested in the research idea to generate and choose a more specific research idea. To use this technique you need to:

1 explain your research idea to the members of the group (they can make notes if they wish);

2 encourage group members at the end of the briefing to seek clarification and more information as appropriate;

3 ask each member of the group, including the originator of the research idea, to generate independently up to three specific research ideas based on the idea that has been described (they can also be asked to provide a justification for their specific ideas);

4 collect the research ideas in an unedited and non-attributable form and distribute them to all members of the group;

Definition

Delphi technique: a technique which can be used with a group of people who are either involved or interested in the research topic to generate and select a more specific research idea.

5 conduct a second cycle of the process (steps 2 to 4) in which individuals comment on the research ideas and revise their own contributions in the light of what others have said;

6 undertake subsequent cycles of the process until a consensus is reached. These either follow a similar pattern (steps 2 to 4) or use discussion, voting or some other method.

People generally enjoy trying to help one another, so this technique can be very effective. It is also very good for forging team spirit among groups of people.

Research in practice 1.2

Using a Delphi group

Mishal explained to the group that her research idea involved understanding the decision-making processes associated with bank and building society mortgage applications. She briefed the four other members of her group about her idea and they asked her questions for clarification. Her briefing generated a number of useful ideas, among which were:

- the extent to which prior saving with the bank and building society by potential borrowers impacted upon the decision process;
- the past financial history and present financial circumstances of the potential borrowers;
- the degree to which personal discussion between potential borrowers and potential lenders affected the decision outcome;
- the extent to which factors concerned with the property to be purchased influence the decision outcome.

The group then moved on to generate a number of more specific research ideas, among which were the following:

- the factors that influenced potential first-time property purchasers to deal with particular banks or building societies;
- the extent to which mortgage applicant identification with a particular bank or building society affects the mortgage application decision-making process.

All five group members considered and commented upon the various ideas put forward. At the end of the second cycle Mishal had, with the other students' agreement, refined her research idea to this – the potential property buyer's decision to apply to a specific bank or building society: what factors contribute to this decision and what effect this decision has upon the bank or building society's mortgage application decision-making process.

Mishal had found this process very helpful and she proceeded to the next phase of her research, a preliminary search of the literature, with great enthusiasm!

Narrowing down

The Delphi technique illustrates what is perhaps the most difficult aspect of refining your research ideas – the move from the general to the specific. Many of us start out with some idea of what we want to do for our research but find it tricky to narrow down.

One useful way of moving from the general to the specific is to think of research ideas as developing through a process which goes through three stages of idea classification:

1 the general area;

2 the more specific field;

3 the precise focus of the research.

One of our students recently was following the marketing route through his degree. He was also very interested in environmental issues. These can be termed his general area of interest. More specifically, he was also very enthusiastic about learning the different ways in which marketeers can learn about 'greener' ways of conducting marketing for their organisations. After much thinking and discussion he developed the research questions: 'What methods do marketeers use to learn about "greener" ways of conducting marketing for their organisations?' and 'Why do they decide upon the methods chosen?'

1.6 What makes a good research topic?

The next section draws together some of the thoughts in the section above 'Why choosing the right research topic is so important' as well as introducing ideas about what goes into making a good research topic choice. Some of the most significant of these ideas are listed below.

It is a topic about which the researcher is enthusiastic and it matches their career goals

Let's start by repeating two of the points we made earlier. A good research topic is one in which you have a genuine interest because, as we said earlier, you have to live with it for possibly a few months or more and you want to give yourself the best chance of success. A well-chosen topic is also one that matches your career goals.

There are resources available, particularly data and time

We also referred to the question of resources, in particular those of your skills and knowledge and individuals, such as lecturers, who may be able to help you. But there are two other key resources to think about. The first of these is data. It is all very well thinking up and precisely defining an intriguing research idea if you can get access to the data to explore it. You may, for example, be very interested in the effect on patients of specific management initiatives in the UK National Health Service. However, getting primary data from patients may be far from easy for all but researchers appointed by the Service. Secondary data may be available, but will it answer precisely the research question you have set?

The second question to ask yourself is: 'Is the research topic achievable within the available time?' This may be quite a difficult question to answer at the beginning of your research project because you cannot anticipate the potential delays. If you are dependent on data from other people, such as managers, customers or colleagues, it is reasonable to say that this will not be as high a priority for them as it is for you. It is always a good idea to be realistic (or even pessimistic!) in your assessment of the timescale necessary to gather data. Even the collection of secondary data may be less straightforward than you envisage, particularly that from non-official sources. The more realistic you are in setting your timescales at the beginning, the less stressful you will find the latter stages of the research process.

The subject is topical

The attraction of choosing a topical subject relevant to current business concerns is obvious. But there is a danger that if the subject is too topical it may be much less so by the end of the project period. Consequently, what seemed a great idea at the beginning of the academic year may not be so at the end of it. In January 2010 Google announced that it was considering withdrawing its presence from China as a result of the alleged intrusion into the Google email accounts of Chinese human-rights activists by Chinese authorities. Analysts previously expected Google to make about $600m from China in 2010 (BBC News Online, 2010). (In the event the dispute was resolved some months later.) This raises an interesting question about the extent to which moral concern outweighs profit in business. In a few months' time this particular issue may well be resolved and almost forgotten. Yet the issue it raises about moral concern versus profit is an interesting one which may be worth exploring in a research project. Google in China may have been the catalyst for this project and serves as a useful example. It is a question of getting the balance right between the specific and the general.

Whatever the outcome, you still have a worthwhile project

Let's say that you develop a research question such as 'How do severe winter weather conditions affect retail food supermarket trading patterns?' On the face of it, this sounds a reasonable question. It could be expected that there would be an effect, not only on the volume of trade but also on the type of food purchased. However, it is possible that the answer may be 'There is no effect'. The consequence of the 'no effect' result for you is not only rather dispiriting, but also you don't have an interesting story to tell in your project report.

The trick is to define a research question that gives you results of similar value whatever you find out. In the above example – 'To what extent does the weather affect retail food supermarket trading patterns and why?' – the question is a much wider one, and one that will guarantee that you have the scope to write an interesting project report, whatever the outcome.

The topic fits the specifications and meet the standards set by the examining institution

Your lecturers are likely to issue you with a set of guidelines to help you with completion of your research project. This will give you general ideas of what constitutes a successful project. A good place to start in your study of this is the assessment criteria. It's good idea to check through these criteria to make sure that your choice of research topic will enable you to meet those criteria. So, for example, if there is a criterion that your research must aim to solve an organisational problem, it's of little use pursuing a study that analyses consumer expenditure data over a given time period. Similarly, if the assessment criteria state that you should only use secondary data, you should not design a questionnaire or interview people.

It is taken for granted that the chosen research topic should match the content of the course being undertaken. Yet we have seen a number of cases where this is questionable. An interest in the under-representation of women in management, for example, could easily develop into a study of the role of women in society in general, rather than in organisations specifically. This is an easy trap to fall into. One of the problems with a study chosen by you, and pursued by you, is that you become so close to it that you lose sight of the fact that you are wandering away from the initial brief. That is why talking to people is such an important part of the process.

As with all concerns you may have about the progress of your research, talk to your lecturer if you are not sure about the appropriateness of your topic choice.

There is a clear link to the relevant literature

It is almost certain that your assessment criteria will specify the need to link your work to the relevant academic literature. It is essential here to ask yourself: 'Why am I doing this?' Too often the literature chapter in project reports we read is of the 'he said this, she said that and they said the other' variety (section 2.2). You should use the literature. An alternative way of thinking about the review of the literature is to call it a 'review of previous research on my topic'. From this you can extend this work. This can be done, for example, by setting your study in the context of the literature reviewed. A student of Mark's, for example, reviewed studies of workers who have some autonomy over the way their work is organised and applied this to her project on the work organisation of courier drivers. As well as locating your study in a different work context to that which has been covered in your literature review, you can set it in a different time context or national culture. Many of the classic management theories are several decades old. You may well ask the question: 'Does this still apply in the twenty-first century post-industrial age?'

Fresh insights into the topic are provided

We hope it will have occurred to you that the previous points about the extension of your literature search will guarantee that your research will be able to provide fresh insights into your chosen topic. A fresh context leads to fresh insights. What is less easy to guarantee is the degree to which your project report's discussion conclusions are insightful.

Research question(s) and objectives are capable of being stated clearly

Perhaps the best test of the clarity of your research question(s) and objectives is the extent to which those who know nothing about your topic can understand what it is you plan to do. If you pass this test, and the others listed in Table 1.4, you are well on your way to developing a successful research topic. We say more about writing clear research questions and objectives in the next section of this chapter.

Table 1.4 Summary: what makes a good research topic?

- It is a topic about which you are enthusiastic and it matches your career goals.
- There are resources available, particularly data and time.
- The subject is topical.
- Whatever the outcome, you still have a worthwhile project.
- The topic fits the specifications and meets the standards set by the examining institution.
- There is a clear link to the relevant literature.
- Fresh insights into the topic are provided.
- The research question(s) and objectives are capable of being stated clearly.

1.7   How to turn a research idea into a research project

Settling on a suitable research idea is a great step forward in the research process. It is challenging, and time-consuming. But the early stages are not complete yet. The task of turning your big idea into precise and meaningful research question(s) and objectives is vital if you are to end up with reliable and valid data from which you can draw valid conclusions.

Do you need research questions and objectives? Well, we think that you do. We see them as a progression – from research questions you then move on to define objectives. Perhaps this is clearer if we define what we mean by these two key terms. Research questions are those questions that the research process will address. They are often the forerunner of research objectives. On the other hand, research objectives are clear, precise statements that identify what you wish to accomplish as a result of doing the research. And research objectives are vital. Why? You've guessed it. Because, if you don't know where you're going, you're likely to end up somewhere else!

Developing research questions

Rather like generating research ideas, defining **research questions** is not a simple, straightforward matter. Here, again, we come up against what is a suitable research question? For the answer to this we go back to the last section: 'What makes a good research topic?' A suitable research question is one that reflects the fact that you have thought about what fits the specifications and meet the standards set by the examining institution; provides a clear link to the relevant literature, and promises fresh insights into the topic you have chosen. Let us concentrate on that word 'insights'. Here we raise the point about two types of questions – those questions that are too easy and those that are likely to provide insights. An example will illustrate the difference. Let us say that your research idea involves examining the impact that Internet banking has had upon local bank branch closure. Asking the question 'How many local bank branch closures have there been in the period since Internet banking became widespread in my country?' would be too simple. It would merely describe a situation and not provide insights into the link between the growth of Internet banking and local branch closures. Questions that would promise more insights would be 'What effect has the growth of Internet banking had upon the uses customers make of branch facilities?' and 'Why do customers prefer to bank online in preference to visiting their local branch?' The answer to these questions may give some clue to the eventual effect on branch closures of Internet banking. If, for example, you found that the overwhelming response to the question 'Do you still value your local branch?' put to Internet banking users was negative, then the obvious conclusion would be that the future for local bank branches is bleak.

One way of ensuring that you do not ask unsuitable research questions is to avoid asking easy questions that promote descriptive answers; another is to avoid asking questions that are too difficult. Earlier in this chapter we cited the example of a research interest that many researchers have had in recent years in the under-representation of women in management. There are several ways you may be able to gain insights into the research question 'Why are women under-represented in senior management positions?' but it is a difficult question to answer definitively. In this case, as with most research questions, there is a simple response to the question of how to find out the answer – ask those who select the appointees to senior management positions. But the reality here is that it would probably be very difficult, if not impossible, to gain access to those key decision makers in large organisations. Without such access it would not be possible to get a good understanding of the subtle 'unofficial' processes that go on at staff selection which may favour one type of candidate over another. Overreaching yourself in the definition of research questions is just as big a danger as asking simple, descriptive questions.

Definition
research questions: this may be one overall question or a number of key questions that the research process will address. These are often the precursor of research objectives.

To end up with a research question that is suitable, try subjecting it to the 'Goldilocks test'. This is what Clough and Nutbrown (2008) used to decide if research questions are either 'too big', 'too small', 'too hot' or 'just right'. By 'too big' they meant those that probably need significant research funding because they need too many resources. Questions that are too small are like those that we mentioned above – the ones that just promote descriptive answers. The 'too hot questions' are so called because they stray into sensitive areas, rather like our example of asking senior managers why they tend not to recruit women to senior management positions. There are other reasons why the context may be too sensitive. Many of these are likely to involve issues of status and power among subjects whom you wish to play a part in your research. Alternatively, it may be that the timing of the research is inappropriate. One of our students was conducting research on redundancy. His requests to organisations were often met with refusals because the organisations that refused to participate were going through difficult times. Outside people talking about redundancies would have sparked off suspicion among employees that these organisations were planning redundancies. On the other hand, research questions that are 'just right' (Clough and Nutbrown, 2008:38) are those that are 'just right for investigation at this time, by this researcher in this setting'.

Another useful metaphor to help you think about clarifying your research question is Clough and Nutbrown's (2007) Russian doll principle. Here your research can be broken

---

Research in practice 1.3

Defining the research question

Zihan was studying for a BA in Business Studies and taking his placement year in a high-technology electronics company. The company's overall mission was 'to focus on our customers' market challenges and needs by providing excellent communications network solutions and services in order to consistently create maximum value for customers'. One of the company's strategic objectives was 'to provide high-quality, excellent service, low operating costs, and give top priority to meeting customer requirements to enhance their competitiveness and profitability'.

During his degree Zihan had become particularly interested in corporate strategy. His particular fascination was with how the often rather grandiose mission statements were turned into reality by organisations. In the case of his placement company, Zihan's interest was sparked by the potential contradiction between the twin objectives of high-quality customer service and low operating costs. He wanted to see how this potential contradiction was reconciled in reality.

Zihan realised that this was potentially too big a question and he was worried about 'biting off more than he could chew'. He talked this worry over with his supervisor, Dr Sheng, who suggested narrowing the question in order that it should relate only to one small part of the organisation. Eventually Zihan decided on the following research question: 'How does [organisation's name] meet the twin strategic objectives of high-quality customer service and low operating costs in relation to its Radio Access Network business in the UK?'

down from the original statement to something which strips away all the complicated layers and obscurities until the heart of the question can be expressed, in the same way as the Russian doll is taken apart to reveal a tiny doll at the centre. Table 1.5 has some examples of research ideas and the general focus research questions they suggest.

Table 1.5 Examples of research ideas and the focus research questions they suggest

Research idea	General focus research questions
1 The marketing of security in credit cards	To what extent does a credit card company market the measures it takes to ensure consumer security in order to gain competitive advantage?
2 Organisations' employee newsletters	How effective are organisations' newsletters at gaining employee identification with the organisation in geographically diverse organisation structures?
3 The use of shelf display point-of-sale material in retail supermarkets	In what ways does the use of shelf display point-of-sale material in retail supermarkets affect buyer behaviour?
4 Sustainable accountancy	How are organisations ensuring that environmental and social performance is better connected with strategy and financial performance?

In the examples in Research in practice 1.3 and Table 1.5 there is one general focus research question generated from the central research idea. Of course, this may lead to several more detailed questions or the definition of research objectives. In the next section we deal with the development of research objectives.

Developing research objectives

Having written your research questions, you may be asking yourself why it's necessary to develop **research objectives**. The answer is that it may not be. Your research project assessment brief may state that it's acceptable to write research questions or research objectives. In our view it's better to do both. Why? Because we think that research objectives add an element of precision to research questions. In Table 1.6 below we illustrate this point by showing research objectives alongside the research questions from which they have been developed. In general, research objectives tend to be more acceptable to the research community. Research in practice 1.4 is a good example of how an official research report prepared by the UK government expresses an overall research aim, then expands this to three specific areas. Table 1.6 comes from research we did on organisations' employee communication schemes. This was

> **Definition**
>
> **research objectives**: clear, specific statements that identify what the research process seeks to achieve as a result of doing the research.

the forerunner of research on the scheme of a particular organisation that wanted to establish if their scheme was 'working'. This prompted us to explore a highly debatable question to which the literature offered no satisfactory answers.

Research in practice 1.4

Developing research objectives from an overall research aim

Here is a good example of how an official research report prepared by the UK government expresses an overall research aim, then expands this to three specific areas

Attitudes towards investment choice and risk within the personal accounts scheme

Background

The UK Government Pensions Act 2008 sets out the government's reforms introducing, from 2012, a duty on employers to automatically enrol all their eligible employees into a qualifying workplace pension scheme. Employers will also have to provide a minimum contribution towards the pension saving for those employees who participate.

Employees will be able to opt out if they do not wish to participate. The Pensions Act also sets out plans for the establishment of the personal accounts scheme, which will be a trust-based, occupational pension scheme for employers that do not have, or wish to use, a qualifying scheme of their own. The pension scheme will be run at arm's length from the government by a body corporate acting as an independent not-for-profit trustee. The aim of these reforms is to overcome the decision-making inertia that currently characterises individuals' attitudes to pension saving, and to make it easier for individuals to save for their retirement.

The personal accounts scheme will be required to offer a default fund into which the contributions of members who do not make an active investment choice will be automatically invested. It may also offer a limited choice of investment funds for those who do want to make an active choice.

This study contains the findings from qualitative research undertaken by the Personal Finance Research Centre (PFRC) and ECOTEC Research and Consulting Limited on behalf of the Department for Work and Pensions (DWP). The research was conducted with individuals who would be eligible for automatic enrolment.

Aims and objectives

The overall aim of this research was to explore attitudes to investment choice and risk within the personal accounts scheme among those who fall into the eligible group for automatic enrolment. The research considered three main areas:

1 individuals' understanding of, and appetite for, financial risk, both generally and in relation to saving for retirement;

2 reactions to, and preferences for, potential investment fund choices within the personal accounts scheme, and reasons for these reactions and preferences;

3 the likelihood of individuals making an active choice of investment funds, the factors they would consider, and what would enable or hinder active choice.

Source: Developed from Collard, S. and Breuer, Z. (2009).

Table 1.6 Phrasing research questions as research objectives

Research question	Research objective
1 Why have organisations introduced employee communication schemes?	**1** To identify organisations' objectives for employee communication schemes.
2 How can the effectiveness of employee communication schemes be measured?	**2** To establish suitable effectiveness criteria for employee communication schemes.
3 Has employee communication been effective?	**3** To describe the extent to which the effectiveness criteria for employee communication have been met in published studies.
4 How can the effectiveness of employee communication be explained?	**4a** To determine the factors associated with the effectiveness criteria for employee communication schemes being met.
	4b To estimate whether some of those factors are more influential than other factors.
5 Can the explanation be generalised?	**5** To develop an explanatory theory that associates certain factors with the effectiveness of employee communication schemes.

Writing research question 1 as an objective prompted a consideration of the objectives of the organisations. This was useful because it led to the finding that there often were no clear objectives. This in itself was an interesting theoretical discovery (how often management initiatives are introduced with no clear objectives in mind!).

Objectives 2 and 3 operationalise the matching research questions by introducing the notion of explicit effectiveness criteria. This is particularly important if measurement of success is to be attempted. Similarly, objectives 4a and 4b and 5 introduce an element of precision about factors that lead to effectiveness in question 4. The most significant difference between these questions and objectives is illustrated by the way in which question 5 becomes objective 5. Although similar, they differ in the way that the objective makes clear that a theory will be developed that will make a causal link between two sets of variables: effectiveness factors and team briefing success.

You may find it easier to write specific research questions than objectives. But, as Table 1.6 demonstrates, research objectives add a further level of precision. Our view is that research objectives require more rigorous thinking, which derives from the use of more formal language.

We make one final point on the development of your research objectives. Think about adding personal objectives to those specific research objectives. These may be concerned with your specific learning objectives from your research or more general personal objectives such as enhancing your career prospects. You will be familiar with the SMART test, listed in Table 1.7. Try this when you have thought about your personal research objectives.

Table 1.7 The SMART test

Check that the objectives are:	
Specific	What precisely do you hope to achieve from undertaking the research?
Measurable	What measures will you use to determine whether you have achieved your objectives?
Achievable	Are the targets you have set for yourself achievable, given all the possible constraints?
Realistic	Given all the other demands upon your time, will you have the time and energy to complete the research on time?
Timely	Will you have time to accomplish all your objectives in the time-frame you have set?

The part that theory plays in developing research questions and objectives

There is no more misunderstood word in the research vocabulary than 'theory'. Below we clarify what **theory** is by explaining what it is not. It's important that you get this clear. In Chapter 5 we explain the importance of theory in research design. We emphasise that the role of theory will play a key part in your study as all projects will need to link to theory in some way. The most likely link will be to an existing theory explained in the literature relevant to your research topic.

Theory may be broadly defined as an explanation of the relationship between two or more concepts or variables. So, for example, the fact that you are reading this book is based (we hope!) on the theory that the outcome will be that you are better equipped to pursue your study.

We said we would clarify what theory is by explaining what it is not. Sutton and Staw (1995) help here. In their view theory is not:

- lots of data;
- lists of variables;
- numerous hypotheses;
- pages of references;
- frequent use of diagrams.

Theory is not lots of data

We warned earlier in this chapter about developing research questions that are too easy. They often only allow for description of phenomena. Such questions lead to project reports which are full of **data**, and little else. Data only describe what you

> **Definitions**
>
> **theory**: an explanation of the relationship between two or more concepts or variables.
>
> **data**: facts, opinions and statistics that have been collected together and recorded for reference or for analysis.

have found out and, possibly, reports on the patterns observed: theory explains the relationships between these patterns. As Sutton and Staw (1995: 372) say, 'data do not generate theory – only researchers do that'.

Theory is not lists of variables

You may be tempted to list a series of **variables** in an attempt to explain the determinants of a given process or outcome. But simply listing variables which may predict an outcome is insufficient. For example, in a study of effective management decision-making merely listing those factors which seem to be associated with effectiveness is insufficient. What is required for theory development is an explanation of why the factors associated with effectives are likely to be strong predictors of effectiveness.

Theory is not numerous hypotheses

In section 5.5 we explain the role of hypotheses in a research design and in section 7.3 we talk about **hypothesis** testing. Predicting possible relationships between variables certainly has a part to play in setting up research projects. But they do not clarify why phenomena have happened and therefore do not constitute theory.

Definitions

variable: individual element or attribute upon which data have been collected.

hypothesis: a testable proposition stating that there is a significant difference or relationship between two or more variables.

Theory is not pages of references

'How many references should I include?' is a question you have probably been asked by student colleagues; you may have asked it yourself. It's as if the more references you include, the more 'theoretical' your work will be. OK, so it may (only may) indicate that you have done lots of reading, but that isn't theory. Theory is present when you outline *why* the things you describe occur.

Theory is not frequent use of diagrams

Diagrams, boxes and arrows may help in clarifying patterns and causal relationships between variables, but they don't usually explain why the relationships have occurred.

So, to sum up, the keyword to stress in establishing the presence of theory in your project report is 'why'. Why do certain things happen when particular variables are present and others absent? Why does A happen and B does not? Why do people behave in this way rather than the opposite way?

We made the point earlier that the fact that you are reading this book is based on the theory that it better equips you to complete successfully your research study. In that case every purposive decision we take is based on theory: that certain consequences will flow from the decision. So, if your decision to read this book is theory-based, then so is, for example, every managers' meeting that is devoted to decision-making. Yet managers are unlikely to realise this. They are equally unlikely to want to acknowledge this! After all, theory is something that belongs in the university; it is not something which is part of the 'real world'. Yet, as Kurt Lewin (1945:129) said, 'there is nothing as practical as a good theory'.

So, if theory is something that plays an important part in our everyday lives and it's implicit in the decision-making processes which go on, it's not something which you should be too scared about. What is important is that the element of theory in your research is made explicit, not left implicit.

How 'grand' does my theory need to be?

Still feeling a bit scared about the idea of theory development? Well, let's try to put your mind at rest by looking at a three-type categorisation of theory developed by Creswell (2008). Creswell talks of of 'grand theories', 'middle-range theories' and 'substantive theories' (Figure 1.2).

Grand theories are those that are so significant that they make a major contribution to the way in which we understand the world around us. We have just passed the 150th anniversary of a book which publicised one such grand theory, Darwin's theory of evolution. Don't worry, there is no need for you to think about following in Darwin's footsteps! Neither is there the need for you to be so ambitious as to be thinking of **middle-range theories**. These are not as world-changing in their scope as grand theories, yet they are clearly of great importance in their particular field of study. You will have studied many of these in your course. Examples are those concerned with motivation, leadership or creative thinking. Of course, you may apply one of these to your particular situation. But you wouldn't be expected to come up with an original theory of such significance, which could be generalised to many other contexts.

However, most of us are concerned with developing rather more modest theories – **substantive theories**. These are restricted to a specific context: a particular time, research setting, population or problem. So you may be concerned with a study of the reason why, for example, the introduction of a new computer system in a particular organisation proved to be a failure. The conclusion you draw would be prefaced by the word 'because' – a term which serves as a 'trigger word' for a theoretical statement, for example 'it failed because there was too little of A and not enough B and C'. Alternatively, 'it failed because management did not explain the reason for the introduction to staff concerned which led to staff discontent'. Either of these theoretical explanations may stand alone, or you may link them to well-established middle-range theories developed by other researchers.

Definitions

grand theories: theories that make a major contribution to the way in which we understand the world around us.

middle-range theories: theories which are not as world-changing in their scope as grand theories but are of great importance in their particular field of study.

substantive theories: theories which are restricted to a specific context: a particular time, research setting, population or problem.

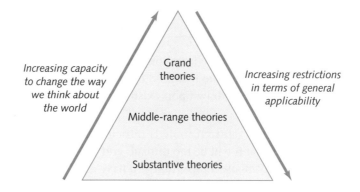

Figure 1.2 Grand, middle-range and substantive theories
Source: Saunders et al. (2009), developed from Creswell (2008).

Substantive theories may be more modest, but they may lead to 'middle-range theories'. And by developing substantive theories we are doing our bit as researchers to develop our understanding of the world about us.

Research in practice 1.5

Writing a research question based on a middle-range theory

Julian was a final-year business undergraduate who wanted to base his research project on the theory of situational leadership. This theory advocates that there is no single 'best' style of leadership. Effective leadership is task-relevant and the most successful leaders are those that adapt their leadership style to the particular task in hand. Therefore, effective leadership varies, not only with the person or group that is being influenced, but it will also depend on the task, job or function that needs to be accomplished.

Julian wanted to apply situational leadership theory to the work of the three project managers in the organisation in which he had completed his second-year placement. He had noticed that the level of effectiveness of these managers seemed to vary considerably. The variance was not on a uniform basis in the sense that manager 1 was more uniformly more effective than manager 2, etc. The level of effectiveness seemed to Julian to vary according to the particular project that was being handled by the managers. He did not really understand the reason for this pattern of variance and thought that situational leadership theory may provide the answer.

Julian intended to study the work of one of the managers on three of the projects for which that manager had responsibility. He had yet to define 'effectiveness' but felt that a range of measures such as prompt task completion, team morale and effective resource usage would feature in his definition. The great thing about his proposed research was that he had the cooperation of all three managers who were anxious to enhance their level of competence.

Julian discussed his ideas with his supervisor who was enthusiastic and full of encouragement. The research question that Julian proposed was: 'To what extent does situational leadership theory help to explain differing levels of management effectiveness in project managers managing multiple projects simultaneously?'

Summary

- Choosing the right research topic is important because: you have to live with it for a considerable period of time; it should exploit and develop your knowledge and skills, and enable you to draw upon existing resources and help you to pass the course you are studying.

- Choosing an appropriate research topic is difficult because: there is too much choice; there are fears that it will be too difficult and insufficiently theoretical and there is a temptation to choose a topic that you have done before for another purpose, resulting in repetition.

- Ten techniques for generating ideas for research topics are: thinking; looking at past project titles; using past course assignments; using past projects from the university library; using relevant literature; following the news media; brainstorming; concept mapping; making a note of ideas and discussion with helpers.

- Pursuing a research topic assigned to you by your employer poses its own problems. In such cases you should aim for a balance between the competing demands of your employer and your university by, for example, isolating an element of the larger organisational project that you find interesting and treating this as the project for your course.

- Research topic ideas may be refined by the conduct of a preliminary study, application of the Delphi technique and a process of narrowing down.

- A good research topic is one: that you are enthusiastic about and it matches your career goals; for which resources are available; that is topical; that, whatever the outcome you still have a worthwhile project; where the topic fits the specifications and meet the standards set by the examining institution; that links to the relevant literature; that provides fresh insights into the topic and for which research question(s) and objectives are capable of being stated clearly.

- The next stage after choosing the research topic is the development of research questions and objectives. A suitable research question is one that reflects the fact that you have thought about what fits the specifications and meet the standards set by the examining institution; provides a clear link to the relevant literature and promises fresh insights into the topic you have chosen. Research objectives add an element of precision to research questions.

- All projects will need to link to theory in some way. The development of a 'grand theory' or 'middle-range' is unnecessary; 'substantive theory' development is sufficient.

Thinking about your research topic

→ Look again at the ten techniques available for generating research ideas (Table 1.1). Choose those that appeal to you most. Use these to try to generate a research idea or ideas. Once you have got some research ideas, or if you have been unable to find an idea, talk to your project supervisor.

→ Evaluate your research ideas against the checklist 'What makes a good research topic?' (Table 1.4).

→ Choose a research report contained in an article in an academic journal relevant to your topic. Revisit the useful questions to ask when searching articles and reports for possible research topic ideas (Table 1.3) and apply these to the article.

→ Write a general focus research question related to your research topic. Try to ensure this is a 'why?' or 'how?' rather than a 'what?' question.

→ Use the general focus research question to write more detailed research questions and your research objectives.

→ Go back to the research report contained in an article in an academic journal relevant to your topic that you used to ask the questions in Table 1.3. Assuming that the research question and objectives are not made explicit, try to establish from the content of the article what the research question and objectives may have been.

References

BBC News Online (2010) Google 'may pull out of China after GMail cyber attack'. 13 January. Available at: http://news.bbc.co.uk/1/hi/business/8455712.stm [Accessed 14 January 2010].

Creswell, J. (2008) Qualitative, Quantitative, and Mixed Methods Approaches, 3rd edn, Thousand Oaks, CA: Sage.

Clough, P. and Nutbrown, C. (2008) A Student's Guide to Methodology, 2nd edn, London: Sage.

Collard, S. and Breuer, Z. (2009) Attitudes towards investment choice and risk within the personal accounts scheme: Report of a qualitative study. Department for Work and Pensions, Research Report No. 565, London.

Lewin K. (1945) The Research Centre for Group Dynamics at Massachusetts Institute of Technology, Sociometry, 8(2): 126–36.

Raimond, P. (1993) Management Projects, London: Chapman & Hall.

Saunders, M., Lewis, P. and Thornhill, A. (2009) Research Methods for Business Students, 5th edn, Harlow: Pearson Education Ltd.

Sutton, R. and Staw, B. (1995) What theory is not, Administrative Science Quarterly, 40(3): 371–84.

Chapter 2

Reviewing the literature

2.1 Why you should read this chapter

Since you started your programme your lecturers have expected you to read textbooks and academic journal articles as part of your studies. Sometimes your lecturers will have told you exactly which book chapters and articles they want you to read. At other times, such as when undertaking an assignment, you will have been expected to find at least some books and articles yourself, deciding whether or not they were relevant. This will have meant you looking in your university's library catalogue to see if there were any potentially useful books, as well as searching one or more of your university's online databases of academic journal articles. You will also have probably searched the Internet for relevant reports and articles using a general search engine such as Google or Bing. Having found some books and articles you would then have read them quickly to work out whether or not they were relevant before reading them more carefully and using them in your assignment. Well done! You have already started to develop some of the skills you need to review the literature!

The overall purpose of this chapter is to help you further develop the skills and understanding you need to review the literature so that you can complete your research project. We explore these by looking at reviewing the literature as an iterative process consisting of four activities which you will need to go through a number of times to develop your literature review chapter (Figure 2.1).

However, before we do this, it is important that you understand what a literature review is, why you need to review the literature for your research project and are aware of the variety of literature available to you.

In this chapter we therefore start by talking about what a literature review is and its purpose. We then go on to explain why it is important that you review the literature as part of your research project and describe the variety of literature available to you. Next we consider the skills and understanding you will need to conduct a literature review. First we look at how you will search for and obtain the literature using your university's

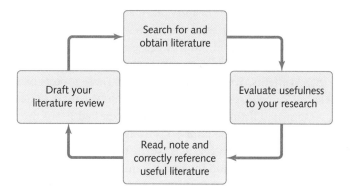

Figure 2.1 The process of reviewing the literature

online databases of academic articles. As part of this we also consider briefly your use of the general search engine Google and the online encyclopaedia Wikipedia. Next we talk about how you can evaluate the usefulness of the literature you have found for your own research project. We then explain how to read, note and correctly reference this useful literature, emphasising the importance of not passing off others' work as your own by mistake and so being accused of plagiarism. We end this chapter by talking about how you can structure and draft your literature review.

2.2 What a literature review is

You will find that, although there are numerous definitions of a **literature review,** these usually emphasise four aspects. In particular, a literature review:

- offers an overview of significant literature available in your chosen topic;
- includes relevant items such as academic journal articles, books and other sources;
- provides a discussion and critical evaluation covering each of these, the level of detail reflecting the significance of each item to your research questions;
- develops a clear argument to contextualise and justify your research.

This means your literature review is not like a book review, or series of book reviews simply describing and summarising what each book or article is about. Firstly, it only includes significant literature published on your research topic. You will therefore have to decide what is significant to your research topic and why it is significant.

> **Definition**
>
> **(critical) literature review**: a detailed overview of the significant literature available about your chosen topic, providing a discussion and critical evaluation, and using clear argument to contextualise and justify your research.

This will involve you in assessing how relevant, if at all, each item you read is to your research and, on the basis of your assessment, deciding whether or not to include it. We talk about this more in section 2.6. For those items (mainly articles and books) you decide to include, you then need to ensure that your review is more than just a description of their contents. You will need to discuss those aspects of what has been said that are relevant to your research, and within your discussion you must be critical. We would be surprised if this was the first time you had heard the term 'critical'. It, or something similar such as the phrase 'critically evaluate', is often used in assignments and exam questions! However, it is worth pausing for a moment to explain what is meant by 'critical' in relation to your literature review. This word is crucial as it summarises what you must do when writing your literature review.

Within your literature review, being critical simply means you providing clearly justified reasoned judgements about what you have read and are now writing about. To do this, you need to have a good knowledge of the literature on your topic that both supports and opposes your ideas, and show through your writing that you have this knowledge. This is often referred to as 'demonstrating familiarity with the topic' in assessment criteria and means that you also need to show you know who the recognised experts in your topic area are. When you read and note the items that relate to your research topic, you will need to do so with some scepticism, questioning what you read. If you think an author's arguments, ideas or research findings are unclear, biased, poorly justified, inconsistent or need to be tested further, this may well mean that they are. However, it is not enough for you to just write that her or his arguments are unclear, biased, poorly justified, inconsistent or need to be tested further. In your critical literature review you must also include clear reasons why you think this. By justifying the points you make, you are showing your critical judgement. In doing this, you will also provide a reasonably detailed justified analysis of the key literature in your research topic area, including research that both supports and opposes your ideas.

Table 2.1 What a critical literature review does and does not

A critical literature review does...	A critical literature review does not...
• identify and include the most relevant and significant research to your topic	• include all research that is possibly relevant to your topic
• discuss and evaluate this research	• just summarise and describe this research
• identify the recognised experts	• fail to mention recognised experts
• contextualise and justify your research questions	• fail to justify or mention your research questions
• consider and discuss research that supports your ideas	• only consider and discuss research that supports your ideas
• consider and discuss research that opposes your ideas	• ignore research that opposes your ideas
• justify points made logically with valid evidence	• make unjustified or poorly justified points
• distinguish between fact and opinion	• mix up fact and opinion
• include up-to-date relevant research	• miss out recent relevant research
• reference all items referred to fully	• fail to reference all or some items referred to

2.3 Why it is important to review the literature

Now you know what a critical literature review is, it is important to understand why you need to undertake one and include it in your project report. While we have already provided you with some hints about the reasons for this in the previous section, we still believe it is worth talking about these and others in more detail.

Provides the base on which you will build your research project

Reviewing the literature is one of the first things you need to do when you start your research as it will provide the base on which your research project is built. By reviewing the literature, you will be able to develop a good understanding of what research has already been undertaken on your topic area. This means that you will be clear about what is known about your topic and also the context in which it is known and will be able to write about this in your literature review chapter or chapters. Let's say your research topic is viral marketing. As you review the literature, you will begin to find out not only how viral marketing is used by some organisations but also the reasons why these organisations are using viral marketing. You will also become aware of the countries and industry sectors in which this research was conducted, in other words the context of the research. Eventually you will have sufficient knowledge from what you have read to discuss the broader context of your own research on viral marketing. You will also be able to explain and justify your own research questions in relation to what is already known (and what is not known!) about viral marketing and in what contexts (section 1.6).

Helps you decide on the topic you want to research for your project

You will have read about how reviewing the literature can help you decide on your research topic in section 1.4. In that section you read about the importance of academic review articles in providing a thorough review of the state of knowledge in a topic area and in providing you with pointers towards areas where further research needs to be undertaken. You also read how browsing peer-reviewed journals could provide you with a good source of possible research ideas. You will find that such research ideas are often introduced under the heading 'Directions for future research' or with the phrase 'Further research is needed...' These articles are useful not only for the ideas, but also because they give you a justification for undertaking your research to which you can refer. It is also likely that the theories these articles identify will be those you will explore further in your own research.

Although books are often less up to date than journals, they may also suggest research topics to you. In particular, edited books based on papers given at a conference or seminar often contain a final chapter that summarises the key findings from the earlier chapters and draws out key themes, including future directions for research (Research in practice 1.1).

In addition to reviewing academic journal articles and textbooks, you will also be reading trade and professional magazines. Reviewing this type of literature will provide you with an indication of whether your research topic is 'hot'. Returning to our example of viral marketing, if this has been discussed in recent issues of marketing magazines such as *Marketing Today,* it is newsworthy and likely to be a 'hot' topic. This can be helpful, particularly if you are going to collect your own data. People are often keener to be involved in research they believe is topical and that will have immediate benefits for them or their organisation (section 3.2).

Can give you insights into the secondary data that are likely to be available

It is likely that you will make at least some use of data that have been collected by others for some other purpose in your research project. Such secondary data are useful, not least because they give you access to far larger data sets than you could collect yourself and can also provide you with comparative and contextual data (section 4.3).

As you review the literature, you will become aware of the data that other researchers looking at your topic have used. In some articles and reports (and occasionally books) the data collected will be presented as tables. You can use these as secondary data for your own research, providing of course you reference the article, report or book as the source of the data! In other articles, reports and books the authors will explain how they have used data sets collected originally by someone else for some other purpose. Where these data sets are in the public domain, you will also be able to find, download and use them in your research, providing of course there is a full reference to the source of these data!

Can give you insights into possible ways of collecting your own data

The literature you review will also give you ideas about how you might collect your own data. This is important because, if a method has been used before to collect similar data and worked, it will hopefully work if you decide to use it. In particular, articles and book chapters that report research using data that the researcher has collected will nearly always describe how those data were collected in a section headed 'Method' or 'Methodology'. While you would hope that the description is in sufficient detail for you to be able to understand fully and repeat the same method, unfortunately this is not always true. However, even if the description is not particularly detailed, it can still provide you with an indication of how you might collect your own data. In addition it is likely to include references to other items which you can read to find out more about the method used.

Let's say that you read an article on your research topic that has used a questionnaire to collect the data. This article provides both a detailed description of the method and, as an appendix, a blank copy of the questionnaire that the authors used to collect their data. This gives you a clear idea of the questions you need to ask if you decide to also use a questionnaire to collect your own data. If you think the questions are suitable for the people you are intending to collect your data from, you may decide to use the same questions. However, if you do this you must give credit to the people who originally designed the questions and include the full reference to their article in your methods chapter. If you do not do this, you may be accused of plagiarism as you are passing off the work of others as your own.

Alternatively, you may read an article in an academic journal that focuses on research methods, such *Organizational Research Methods* or *Field Methods*, which explains the use of a particular technique for collecting data such as a particular form of interviewing or observation or a particular use of questionnaires. Such articles will provide you with helpful insights about how to conduct your own research and what to avoid. They are likely to contain more detail about particular techniques than we have been able to include in Chapter 6. Where you use the ideas from one of these articles for your own method, you should refer to that article in your methods chapter (Research in practice 2.1).

Can give you insights into possible ways of analysing your own data

Academic journal articles can provide insights into how to analyse both data you collect yourself and secondary data. The techniques used to analyse data are usually named in the 'findings' or 'results' sections. Where these are widely used techniques, in particular statistical tests, it is likely that although the test is named it will not be explained in any detail as it will have been assumed that the reader (you!) will already be aware of and understand the technique. In addition, you will not see a

---

Research in practice 2.1

Insights into research methods from the literature

An article by Mark (Saunders, 2012) in *Field Methods* concludes by offering a series of recommendations about the use of web-based questionnaires for organisational research which may be helpful for your research. These include:

1 For research in organisations, the use of web-based questionnaires should be considered only where respondents are IT-literate and have ready access to the Internet at work.

2 Web-based questionnaires should be designed to allow the impact of people not responding to be assessed.

3 Caution should be exercised regarding the inclusion of questions on topics related to the use of the Web or associated technologies.

4 Care should be taken when comparing responses to open (write in) questions from web-based questionnaires with those from questionnaires delivered using other methods, owing to the impact of the technology on response length.

reference to a journal article or a statistics textbook. This is not a problem as you will almost certainly be able to find sufficient information about the test in your own statistics textbook or by using the Help feature of a statistics software programme such as IBM SPSS Statistics.

Where an academic journal article uses data analysis techniques that are not widely known, it is likely that the author or authors will have explained how to use the analysis technique. Hopefully, this will be in sufficient detail for you to be able to understand fully and use the same technique, although unfortunately this is not always true. However, even if the description is not particularly detailed, it can still provide you with an indication of how you might analyse your own data. In addition, it is likely to include references to other books and articles which you can read to find out more about the technique. Such articles are likely to contain far more detail than we have been able to include in Chapter 7, and where appropriate should be referred to in your method or findings chapter.

2.4   The types of literature available to you

The amount of literature available to you is expanding rapidly as more sources are made available via the Internet. In addition to the library catalogue, your university library's web pages will provide a comprehensive list of the other sources you can access and the types of literature they contain. Most of these other sources accessed are online databases, so your library web pages will usually include direct web links and details of any passwords needed.

We have listed the main types of literature you are likely to access through your library catalogue and online databases for your literature review in Table 2.2, along with a brief description of their contents and an indication of the likely use for your literature review. Textbooks, such as those that have been recommended to you for your modules, will be very helpful as you start your literature review, providing an overview of your research topic and the recognised experts. However, academic journal articles which have been **peer-reviewed** will be the most useful to you in your literature review and will form the majority of items you use. These articles will have been read and evaluated by other academic experts, called peer reviewers, to ensure they meet the quality criteria of the journal before they are published. Peer reviewers are usually anonymous and ensure quality by both detecting errors which may have to be corrected before the article is published and providing a detailed assessment of the article. Where peer reviewers consider the quality is not sufficient or there are too many errors, the article will not be published.

Definition

peer review: the process of evaluating an article by experts to ensure the article meets quality criteria before being accepted for publication.

Table 2.2 Main types of literature available to you

Type	Contents	Use for your literature review
Textbooks	Written specifically for audiences such as students or professionals. Material usually presented in an ordered and relatively accessible form. Often draw on a wide range of sources including peer-reviewed academic journal articles.	Useful, particularly as an introductory source to get an overview of your research topic and find out who are the recognised experts.
Peer-reviewed (refereed) academic journal articles	Provide detailed reports of research. Articles written by experts in the field and evaluated by other academics (peer reviewers) to assess quality and suitability. Pay rigorous attention to detail and verification of information. Usually contain extensive list of references. Before publication, have usually been revised in response to comments. Not all academic journal articles are peer-reviewed (see below).	The most useful type for your literature review.
Non-refereed academic journal articles	Articles may provide detailed reports of research. Articles selected by an editor or editorial board with subject knowledge.	Relevance and usefulness varies considerably. Beware of possible bias.
Professional and trade journal articles	Articles written for members of professional or trade organisations, so related to their needs. Consist of a mix of news items and more detailed accounts of a practical nature. Articles rarely based on research, although some provide summaries of research.	Can provide useful insights into practice, although may be biased. Need to be used with considerable caution.
Newspaper articles	Articles written for members of public, most newspapers addressing a particular market segment. News presented is filtered dependent on events, priority being given to headline-grabbing stories that are likely to appeal to that newspaper's readers.	Good source of topical events and developments. May contain bias in reporting and coverage.
Conference proceedings	Articles consist of selected papers presented at a conference, often published as a book or special edition of a journal. Usually peer-reviewed. Increasingly available online.	Sometimes difficult to find. Very useful if the theme of the conference matches your research.
Reports	Reports on specific topics written by academics and various organisations, including market research organisations and government departments. Beware of possible bias. May not have gone through same review process as peer-reviewed academic journal articles, but those from established organisations often of high quality.	Often difficult to access or expensive to purchase. Can be a useful source of information when the topic matches your research.

2.5   Searching for and obtaining literature

Although your skills in using general search engines such as Google and Bing are likely to be excellent, we have found that many of our students are unaware of at least some of the search features of online databases of academic articles such as *Business Source Complete* and *Emerald*. While you will have already used these or similar online databases of academic journal articles for assignments, there are relatively simple things you can do to make your searches as fruitful as possible.

The process of searching for and obtaining the literature consists of five stages:

1 Decide on your literature search topic.

2 Identify the keywords and phrases you will use.

3 Choose your online databases.

4 Undertake your search.

5 Obtain the articles.

We will now look at each stage in more detail.

Decide on your literature search topic

You have probably already got a reasonably clear idea of your research topic. However, if you haven't, don't worry. Just turn back to Chapter 1 and look at sections 1.4 and 1.5 which talk about generating ideas for your research topic and refining these ideas. This process of refining these ideas is important because, unless you have a reasonably clear and specific idea of the topic you wish to search for in the literature, most of the items you find are not going to be of use for your research project!

Let's say you've defined your research topic as 'financial management' and decide to search for items on this topic in one of the online databases to which your university subscribes. Because the topic of financial management is so broad, your initial search for 'financial management' will probably find more than 50,000 items: far too many for you to ever download, let alone read! However, if you had defined your topic as 'the impact of the recession on financial management', you could have been more precise in your choice of keywords with which to search the literature. By using keywords and phrases such as 'financial management' and 'recession' as search terms, you would be likely to find about 500 items, a more manageable number for you to begin to look at. You might have been even more specific, defining your topic as 'the impact of the recession on financial management budgeting'. Searching for this topic in the online database using keywords and phrases such as 'financial management', 'recession' and 'budget' as search terms would find fewer than 100 items. Not only is this a far more manageable number to look at, but it is also likely that a greater proportion will be directly relevant to your research topic.

Identify the search terms and phrases you will use

Online databases find relevant items by matching specific words and phrases with either all or part of the item such as the abstract (summary) or title. You will have found when searching with Google or Bing that the more specific the word or phrase you type in, the more likely you are to find relevant web pages. You will have also found that if the word or phrase you type in is too specific, you don't find the web pages you need! The same principle applies to searching online databases, including those of academic journal articles. You therefore need to think carefully about the **search terms** you will use while searching and, when searching using Google or Bing, you need to be prepared to try a variety of keywords and phrases.

Definition

Search term: a word or phrase that describes your research topic, question(s) or objectives and can be used either on its own or in combination with other phrases in online databases.

Your ideas for possible search terms and phrases, such as 'financial management' and 'recession', are likely to be based upon what you already know about your research topic and any reading you have already done. In addition, you will probably find some of the techniques to generate research topics outlined in section 1.4 helpful. Techniques such as looking at past project titles, brainstorming, concept mapping and discussing your ideas can all help you clarify your thoughts and come up with possible search terms and phrases. You will also find that dictionaries and encyclopaedias (including Wikipedia) are often helpful for suggesting alternative words and phrases. We have listed six things to think about when identifying your search terms in Table 2.3. They are in no particular order.

Table 2.3 Six things to think about when identifying your search terms

Using:	Example
1 Terms appearing regularly in literature you've read	Downsizing and Redundancy
2 Both broad and narrow terms	Services and Restaurant
3 Different words with the same meaning (synonyms)	Motorcycle and Motorbike
4 Alternative spellings of the same word	Organisation and Organization
5 Abbreviations and the full term	EU and European Union
6 Old and new place names where these have changed	Peking and Beijing

Choose your online databases

Your choice of online databases will, not surprisingly, be dictated primarily by those available through subscriptions paid by your university. We have listed those most frequently available in Table 2.4, along with a brief description of what they cover and therefore what you can search for using your search terms and phrases. Of these, the most widely used by business and management students such as you are

Business Source Complete and Emerald. We would recommend that you start your literature search using these. However, these databases do not have a good coverage of older items, particularly those published over two to three decades ago. You will find the online database JSTOR a useful source for journal articles, particularly when you need to obtain a copy of that seminal article recommended by your supervisor!

Table 2.4 Frequently used online databases of academic articles in business and management

Database	Description
Business Source Complete (sometimes called EBSCO)	Full text articles for over 2,900 English language journals published worldwide. Covers all areas of business and management. Most journals are included only from the 1990s onwards. Embargo of up to a year for full text of articles from the most recent issues of some journals. Also includes Datamonitor company profiles for the world's 10,000 largest companies, Datamonitor industry profiles for various industries, and Economist Intelligence Unit country reports.
Emerald (sometimes called Emerald Management eJournals)	Full text articles for c.150 English language journals published in the UK by Emerald. Covers all areas of business and management.
JSTOR	Full text articles for science, social science, arts and humanities journals. Coverage usually extends back to volume 1, issue 1 of journals and more of the current issues of journals are also becoming available. Often the best place to find 'old articles'.
Blackwell Reference Online	Latest edition of the 12-volume Blackwell Encyclopaedia of Management, 22 Blackwell 'Handbooks' and 'Companions' covering business and management.
Wiley Online	Coverage includes over 1,100 full text journals covering the sciences, business, law, humanities, psychology and social sciences.
Google Scholar	Ranks scholarly literature consisting of articles, theses, books, abstracts or court opinions from many disciplines and sources. Usually provides a web link, but access can depend on subscription. Literature ranked according to the full text of each document, where published, author(s), how often and how recently cited in other scholarly literature.
Nexis	Full text of articles in UK national and regional newspapers as well as international news providers.

You will notice that we have included Google Scholar in Table 2.4. This is because it has a number of useful features to support your search of the literature and is readily available. In particular, once you know the names of recognised experts researching your topic, you can find out who has referred to (cited) their work by simply searching for their names. Google Scholar will rank all the recognised experts' publications, and for each list the full references of other documents that have cited the publication. This means you can see which of your experts' publications have been cited most and you can find these other documents that have cited these publications subsequently.

You will have also noticed that in contrast we have not included Wikipedia in our table. There is no doubt in our minds that Wikipedia is useful if you want to find out something quickly. However, the level of detail provided is unlikely to be sufficient for your research project. As you know, Wikipedia articles can be edited by anyone and are allowed to be imperfect. Despite Wikipedia's clear editing policy and their request that contributors show the information they add is verifiable, errors and mis-information can and do occur. While these errors are usually put right quickly, an article may be wrong at the time you read it. Finally, although Wikipedia expects articles to be phrased to reflect the present consensus on a subject, people with rival opinions do compete to change what is written, resulting in the information you find changing overnight. We therefore recommend that you do not use Wikipedia as a source for your literature review.

Undertake your search

Now you have identified the search terms and phrases you are going to use and chosen your online databases, all you need to do is click on the links on your university library's web page and you are ready to start searching.

Most online databases allow you to undertake a variety of searches ranging from 'basic' or 'quick' to 'advanced' in their complexity. Basic searches, as their name suggests, are relatively simple, often limiting the number of search terms you can type in. More advanced searches, as we will see shortly, allow you to specify your search more precisely. In addition, many databases have a browse facility allowing you to look through electronic copies of journals by title or by subject.

The first thing you need to do for a basic search is to type in the search term. If you look at the basic search screen for the online database Emerald, you will see that you can type in one term or phrase as a search term (Figure 2.2, point 1) and only have one option, selecting the content you want to search, in this case 'journals' (Figure 2.2, point 2). When you click on 'Go' this will retrieve all relevant items in the database containing the search term, in this example 'journal' articles about 'service quality'. For this example this is likely to be a great many, as the search term is very broad!

For more advance searches, again the first thing you need to do is to type in your search terms (Figure 2.3, point 1) using Boolean operators to link two or more search terms (Figure 2.3, point 2). Boolean operators are the words you use to join together your keywords and phrases for your search. If you look at the advanced search screen for the online database Business Source Complete (Figure 2.3), you will see that the search terms 'change' and 'psychological contract' are joined by the Boolean operator 'AND'. This means that when you undertake this search, you will only retrieve items that contain both these search terms. In other words the word 'AND' is narrowing your search to retrieve items that contains both search terms. Other Boolean operators that you may find useful are 'OR' and 'NOT'. The word 'OR' broadens your search by retrieving items that, in this example, contain either the search term 'change' or the search term 'psychological contract' or both scarch

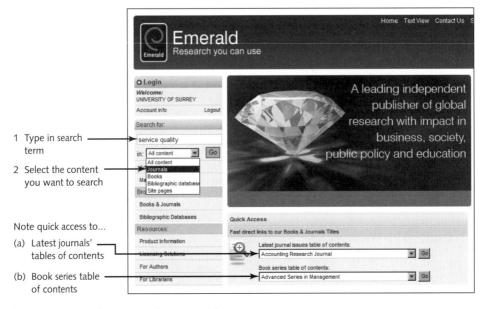

1 Type in search term

2 Select the content you want to search

Note quick access to...

(a) Latest journals' tables of contents

(b) Book series table of contents

Figure 2.2 Quick search using Emerald
Source: Emerald, reproduced with permission.

terms. The word 'NOT' narrows your search by excluding items. This means that if you searched for 'change' NOT 'psychological contract', you would only retrieve items that included the search term 'change' that did not also include the term 'psychological contract'.

You can also amend your search by truncating your search terms or using wild cards. For most databases the truncation character is *. If you truncate the keyword 'learning' to 'learn' by typing in the search term 'learn*', the database will retrieve all items that include the word 'learn', including 'learn', 'learning' and 'learner'. Wildcards are useful if you have to deal with spelling variations, particularly between US and UK English. The wild-card character differs between databases, but is often '?'. So, if you type in 'organi?ation' as a search term, you will retrieve items with both the US spelling organization and the UK spelling organisation.

You will find it is best to start most searches by looking for your search terms only in the abstract field (Figure 2.3, point 3). **Abstracts** are summaries of articles, books or reports that normally provide sufficient detail for you to decide whether or not they are likely to be useful for your research. By only searching for your search terms in the abstract, you will exclude literature which does not focus on your topic, even if your keywords appear elsewhere in the main text.

Definition

abstract: a summary of an article, book or report, providing an overview of what it contains and sufficient information for the original to be located.

1 Type in search term

2 Use Boolean operators to link search terms

3 Select where you will search

4 Select if you want full text only

5 Select if you want scholarly journals only

6 Select dates to time-constrain your search

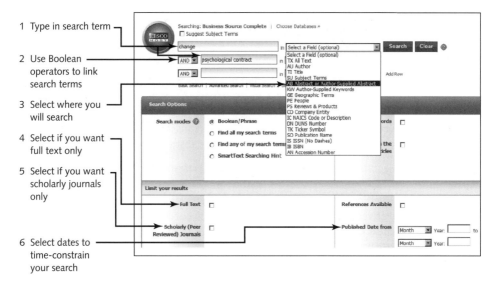

Figure 2.3 Advanced search using Business Source Complete
Source: EBSCO Information Services.

Most online databases, including Business Source Complete and Emerald, allow you to check ✓ whether you want to retrieve all items or only those where the full text is available (Figure 2.3, point 4) and you have access to it. Similarly you can often check whether you want to retrieve all items, or only those that have been peer-reviewed (Figure 2.3, point 5). Finally, you can specify the dates for which you want to retrieve publications (Figure 2.3, point 6). This can be useful if, say, you only want to retrieve items that have been published in the last five years.

Obtain the articles

Before you obtain a copy of an article, it is worth making a quick assessment of its likely usefulness to your research project. You can usually do this by downloading the abstract and reading it on the screen (Research in practice 2.2).

Obtaining your articles is very easy if you have checked the box for only retrieving articles where full text is available (Figure 2.3). For most of these articles you will only have to click on an icon to download an electronic 'PDF Full Text' copy which you can read using an Adobe Reader (if you have not already downloaded this, you can do so for free from *www.adobe.com/downloads*). For articles where an electronic copy is not stored in the database, you will often be able to click on a different icon and download the 'Linked Full Text'. Again, you will usually be able to be read this using an Adobe Reader. For those articles not available electronically, your library may well have a print copy. If not, you will have to order it from another library as an inter-library loan. You will probably be charged for this service, so use it very sparingly!

Research in practice 2.2

Using an abstract to assess likely use of an article

Spinder's research project was about changing employment practices in the UK's National Health Service and the impact this was having on employees' commitment. In a search using the Emerald online database she had found an article in the peer-reviewed academic journal *Employee Relations* by Wang and colleagues (2010) that she thought would be useful. She decided to read the abstract online to check.

Abstract

Purpose: To investigate the effect of the 'transfer' process on relationships between employees' perceived organizational support and affective and continuance commitment within the context of the move to a new employment relationship as part of a Public Private Partnership.

Design/methodology/approach: Eight semi-structured interviews informed the design of a questionnaire which was distributed to facilities management employees of a United Kingdom NHS hospital who had been seconded to a private-sector management company. This resulted in 101 effective responses (33 percent).

Findings: In new forms of employment relationship, employees' perceptions of the 'transfer' process significantly influence their perceptions of the management company and their commitment to it. Positively perceived organizational support from the management company significantly increases affective and continuance commitment to the management company, particularly amongst those who feel positive about the transfer process.

Research limitations: This research focuses upon employee commitment to the management company. Further research is proposed to investigate different foci of commitment as well as the influence of the psychological contract.

Practical implications: The effect of fairness in the 'transfer' process is far reaching, lasting beyond the initial transfer. Both parties should work together to enable a smooth employee 'transfer' process, supervisors particularly having a strong influence on employees' attitudes and behaviour.

Originality/value: There is a lack of research regarding the antecedents and consequences of commitment of employees who are managed by one but employed by a different organization. This study begins to address this gap.

The abstract confirmed that the **Purpose** of the article was to look at a change in employment practice, where employees had been moved to a new employment relationship as part of a public private practice and the impact of this on their commitment. More detail was given in the **Findings** and **Research limitations/implications** sections of the abstract. The **Design/methodology/approach** indicated that the research had been undertaken in a UK National Health Service (NHS) hospital.

Based on this information, Spinder decided that the article was likely to be useful to her research project, so she downloaded and saved an electronic copy.

2.6   Evaluating the usefulness of literature to your research

You have already started evaluating the usefulness of the literature to your research through reading the abstract (Research in practice 2.2). Inevitably, the usefulness of any item will depend on your research question and your aim and objectives. This means that an article which may be very useful for your friend's research project could be of little or no use for your research project. As you review the literature, you will need to read as much of the literature that is closely related and of value to your research question as time permits. Let's say your topic is one where research has been going on for some years. If this is the case, you should find plenty of literature of value that relates directly to your research question. However, if your research question is about a new topic, you may find that not much of value that is closely related has been published. You will therefore have to review the literature more widely and set your own research in a broader context of what is already known.

Each time you evaluate the usefulness of an article, book, report or other item for your research project, you are asking yourself questions about two interrelated aspects: its relevance and its value. Any item's relevance to your research project depends on the appropriateness of the research reported and the connections you can make with your own research project. In contrast, its value to you depends on the quality of the research that is reported. This includes things such as how well methods and theory have been used, as well as the quality of the argument.

Our students have found the questions in Table 2.5 helpful when they have been evaluating the relevance of an article to their research and we hope that you will also find them helpful for your own research.

Table 2.5 Questions to help evaluate the relevance and value of literature

Question	Comment
Relevance	
1 Is the item recent?	Although more recently published items are often more relevant, do not discount items just because they are old!
2 Is the topic of the research similar to your own?	If it is, you may be able to compare and contrast your findings.
3 Is the context of the research similar to your own?	Beware: do not discount items just because the context is different, you can often still get useful insights.
4 Is this item cited (referred to) in other items that you have also found useful?	If it is often referred to in other items, it is probably important.
5 Is the author cited (referred to) in other items you have found useful?	If yes, then the author is probably a recognised expert.
6 Does the author contradict or support the arguments you will make?	In either case it is likely to be useful!

$\rightarrow$

Table 2.5 Continued

Question	Comment
Value	
7 Does the author use emotional words, illogical argument or seem to only choose examples that support the points being made?	If the author does, the item is probably biased and needs to be used with caution. If you do use it, you should comment on the possible bias and give reasons why you think this is so.
8 Does the author describe theory clearly and in sufficient detail?	Even if there are gaps in the description of theory, the item may be useful for the references to the original theory.
9 Is the method used described clearly and in sufficient detail?	Even if there are gaps in the method, the item may still be of use. If you do use it, you may need to comment on those aspects of the method that are less clear.
10 Does the author highlight gaps in current research or offer suggestions for future research?	If the gaps or suggestions relate to your research topic, they could provide a useful justification for what you are doing.
11 Is there an extensive list of references at the end?	A long list of references will often include relevant articles that you have not yet discovered – a great help!

Source: Developed from Saunders et al. (2009).

Our students often ask us how many items they should read. This is really a question about whether they have read enough! The short answer to this is you need to have read enough to put your own research in the context of research already undertaken, referencing the main experts in that topic area. One way of knowing that you have read enough is when your additional searches of the online databases give you mainly references to items you have already read.

2.7 Reading, noting and correctly referencing useful literature

Reading and noting

You may be one of those people who, as they read an article or book, only uses a highlighter pen to mark those pieces they think are useful. If you are, beware! Just highlighting sentences and paragraphs that are likely to be useful will not help you concentrate nearly as well as making notes in the margin or on a separate piece of paper. Your notes can remind you why you thought the passage in the article was important, how an idea fits with your own research topic or even why you disagree with what you have just read. Making notes will help keep your mind focused on what you are reading and to remember what you have read.

Harvard College Library (2006) suggests that as you read, your note taking should focus on:

1 summarising;

2 comparing and contrasting.

When you write a summary of what you have just read in your own words, you probably find the process quite difficult. This is not surprising as, by summarising in your own words, you have to understand fully what you have read. In contrast, copying sentences just shows that you can copy! Copying sentences can also be a problem if you later forget they were copied and include them in your project report as your own words. Most **plagiarism** detection software will highlight your copied sentences as actual direct quotes and suggest their original source. If you have not put the copied sentences in quotation marks and also stated their source as a reference, you will, quite rightly, be accused of plagiarism. You can minimise this problem by making notes in your own words that summarise what you have read and always acknowledging the source of the ideas. If you decide you must copy a sentence exactly, enclose it in quotation marks and note the full reference and page number next to it.

> Definition
>
> **plagiarism**: presenting the work and ideas of other people and passing it off as your own, without acknowledging and referencing the original source.

As you make your notes, ask yourself how the item you are reading compares or contrasts with other articles and books you have read and your own thoughts upon reading it. Within this you need to think carefully about the clarity of the arguments and whether they are justified by the evidence presented. Let's say you have already read Hofstede's (2002) book *Culture's Consequences* about national cultures. The article you are now reading by McSweeny (2002) is very critical of Hofstede's research and in particular the assumptions on which he bases his conclusions. You are not sure who to believe, but no longer feel so positive about Hofstede's theories! You therefore emphasise in your notes that McSweeny believes Hofstede's arguments are flawed, the reasons why and that you don't feel so positive towards Hofstede's theories about national cultures. You also find your notes on Hofstede's book and add a brief comment 'See McSweeny (2002) for critique' to help ensure you do not forget to include this information in your literature review.

Five questions that can help you to read critically and make useful notes are listed in Table 2.6 (on page 48), along with a brief comment on each.

⬤ Referencing

As you write your project report, you will need to record the sources of all the information, research findings, theories and other ideas to which you refer in your text.

Table 2.6 Five questions to help critical reading and noting

Question	Comment
1 Why am I reading this?	This question will help you focus on the reason or reasons you are reading the item, rather being sidetracked by the author's agenda.
2 What is the author (or are the authors) trying to do in writing this?	Your answer to this question will help you to decide how useful the material that you are reading may be for your research project.
3 What is the author (or are the authors) saying that is relevant to my research topic?	Your answer to this question will give you the focus of your summarising notes.
4 To what extent am I convinced by what is being said and why?	Your answer to this question will help you make notes that compare and contrast what you are reading with the other items you have already read.
5 What use can I make of what I have read in my research project?	This question forces you to think about how you will write about what you have read in your literature review.

Source: Developed from Wallace and Wray (2011).

This process is known as referencing and allows you to acknowledge and give credit to the work of others, helping ensure you are not accused of plagiarism. It also allows you and anyone else who reads your project report to find the original source of this work. You reference work by identifying the source of the ideas briefly in your main text and then provide full details as a **list of references** or **bibliography** at the end of your project report. As a general rule, it is better to avoid quoting directly. However, if you do use a quotation, you must enclose this in quotation marks and state the number of the page from which it was copied. So, if you were quoting directly from a book Mark and Phil wrote with their colleague Adrian Thornhill, you would write:

'For some project reports you will be required to include a bibliography. Convention dictates that this should include all the relevant items you have consulted for your project, including those not referred to directly in the text. For others you will be asked to include only a list of references for those items referred to directly in the text' (Saunders et al., 2009, p. 95).

You would then provide the full reference at the end of your project report in the format preferred by your university.

Definitions

list of references: list of those items you have consulted, used and referred to directly in the text. Your university will specify the precise style.

bibliography: list of all relevant items you have consulted and used, including those you do not refer to directly in the text. Usually in alphabetical order. Your university will specify the precise style.

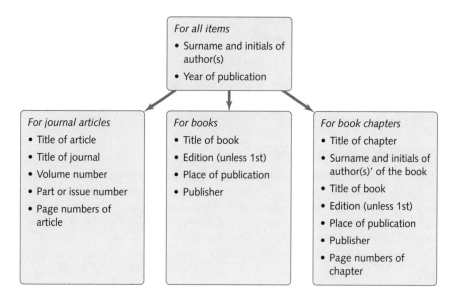

For all items
- Surname and initials of author(s)
- Year of publication

For journal articles
- Title of article
- Title of journal
- Volume number
- Part or issue number
- Page numbers of article

For books
- Title of book
- Edition (unless 1st)
- Place of publication
- Publisher

For book chapters
- Title of chapter
- Surname and initials of author(s)' of the book
- Title of book
- Edition (unless 1st)
- Place of publication
- Publisher
- Page numbers of chapter

Figure 2.4 Information you need to reference items

Your own university or faculty will have a preferred referencing style for recording articles, books and chapters in books as well as other items you have referred to in your literature review and elsewhere in your project report. It is essential that you obtain a copy of this and follow it exactly. Sloppy referencing suggests you do not care about your work and is likely to lose you marks. Whatever your university's precise style, the information you will need to record for the most common items you reference is listed in Figure 2.4.

The two most common referencing styles are author–date systems and footnotes systems. If you are using an author–date system (such as Harvard referencing), you usually use the author's (or authors') surname(s) and the year of publication to identify documents in the main text as you refer to them. All these references are then recorded in full in one alphabetical list by author's surname at the end of your project report under the heading 'References' (Research in practice 2.3). If you are using a footnotes system (such as Vancouver referencing), references in the main text are identified by a number that is usually in superscript. All these references are recorded in full in the order to which they were first referred, usually in one sequential list at the end of your project report under the heading 'References'. This means that, if you use the footnotes system, your list is unlikely to be in alphabetical order (Research in practice 2.3).

Research in practice 2.3

Footnotes and Author–date (Harvard) systems

Amina had used the footnotes system to reference the books and journal articles she referred to in the first draft of her literature review on strategic change. This is shown in the following two extracts from her literature review and list of references:

2.3 Barriers to strategic change

...The cultural web[22] offers a way of auditing an organisation's culture and the barriers to change that culture can present. It has been argued that the web can be used to help build a vision for the new organisation, which managers can then compare with the web for their existing organisation.[23] Despite the numerous obstacles to strategic change, summarised by Franken and colleagues[24] as ...

Refernces

22. Johnson, G., Whittington, R. and Scholes, K. (2011) *Exploring Corporate Strategy* (9th edn), Harlow: FT Prentice Hall.
23. Balogun, J. and Hope Hailey, V. (2008) *Exploring Strategic Change* (3rd edn), Harlow: FT Prentice Hall.
24. Franken, A., Edwards, C. and Lambert, R. (2009) Executing strategic change, *California Management Review*, Vol. 51, No. 3, pp. 49–73.

In his feedback her supervisor commented that, although she had used the footnotes system correctly, the university's assessment criteria asked for the Harvard author–date system. Amina checked the guidance notes on referencing provided by her university and amended her draft so that the references were in Harvard format. This is shown in the following two extracts:

2.3 Barriers to strategic change

...The cultural web (Johnson et al., 2011) offers a way of auditing an organisation's culture and the barriers to change that culture can present. It has been argued that the web can be used to help build a vision for the new organisation, which managers can then compare with the web for their existing organisation (Balogun and Hope Hailey, 2008). Despite the numerous obstacles to strategic change, summarised by Franken et al. (2009) as ...

Refernces

Balogun, J. and Hope Hailey, V. (2008) *Exploring Strategic Change* (3rd edn), Harlow: FT Prentice Hall.

Franken, A., Edwards, C. and Lambert, R. (2009) Executing strategic change, *California Management Review*, Vol. 51, No. 3, pp. 49–73.

Johnson, G., Whittington, R. and Scholes, K. (2011) *Exploring Corporate Strategy* (9th edn), Harlow: FT Prentice Hall.

2.8   Writing your literature review

● Deciding on the structure

Your literature review is likely to form either one chapter or a series of chapters in your project report. Within it you will need to discuss different themes and compare and contrast what different authors say about them. Your own opinions will also need to be justified by what you are writing.

Many students' early drafts of their literature reviews are simply listings of everything they have read, in which each author's ideas are described one after another for those themes they have discussed (vertical arrows in Figure 2.5). If you do this, your literature review will be boring and uncritical. You, and your readers, will find it much more interesting if you take a thematic approach and write about one theme at a time. As you compare and, where necessary, contrast those authors who have said something about each theme, you will be writing critically (horizontal arrows in Figure 2.5).

In our book *Research Methods for Business Students* (2009) we suggest that you should think of your literature review as a thematic funnel. This means you should take the following steps:

1   Begin by providing a more general overview of your research topic before narrowing down to your research question or research aim and objectives.

2   Start by providing a brief overview of the key themes and ideas in the literature reviewed.

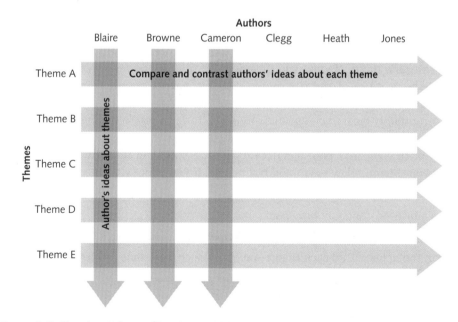

Figure 2.5 Structure of your literature review

3 For each theme, summarise, compare and contrast the research of recognised experts.

4 Within each theme highlight previous research you have found that is most relevant to your own research, including work that may not be by recognised experts.

5 Provide a detailed account of the findings of this previous research and show how they are related to the theme.

6 Use your review to highlight those aspects where your own research will provide fresh insights, linking these explicitly to your research questions or objectives.

7 Tell your reader that these aspects will be explored in subsequent sections of your project report.

8 Finish with a summary that links to your next chapter.

The key to you writing an interesting and critical literature review is therefore to link the different ideas you find within each theme in the literature, and then link the themes to form a clear, well-justified argument. You need to ensure that this places your research in the context of what is already known and justifies why your research is worth doing.

Getting on with writing

Although you will not be able to start writing until you have done some reading, it is important you begin to draft your literature review before you have completed reading all the literature. The process of drafting your literature review will help you get your ideas about your research clear in your own mind. As you read more, you can update and revise your draft as necessary.

You, like everyone we know, will find writing your literature review difficult! As you write, you have to get your ideas clear in your own mind and put them into words on your laptop screen such that anyone who reads them can understand. Phil refers to this writing process as the 'rewriting process', emphasising the need to improve early drafts of what you have written. Your literature review writing process will be no different and you should expect to have to rewrite your critical review more than once. Indeed, what you write at the start of your literature review will almost certainly have to be updated and revised as you read more over the course of your research project.

We often compare a poor literature review to a shopping catalogue. This describes what your literature review should not be like. If you wrote your literature review as a shopping catalogue, you would:

● Include every item you have read.

● Group each of the items you have read by themes.

● Sort the items within each theme some way, such as by date or author.

● Describe each item using a similar number of words.

Obviously your literature review will be far more than just a shopping catalogue, as you need to be critical! Your writing therefore needs to show that you have:

- Reflected on the value of the findings of each item you have read.
- Reflected on the value of the ideas of each item you have read.
- Made reasoned judgements about the value of each item you have read.
- Only included those items that are relevant.
- Organised the ideas and findings into a coherent logical argument by theme.

Look at the project report extracts in Research in practice 2.4. You will notice that in the first extract, Ben simply lists the ideas from the literature one after the other like in a shopping catalogue. The order in which he has written about each of the items does not appear to be logical, the more general ideas of Rousseau and of Schoorman et al. being described after his summary of more specific and focused arguments by

---

Research in practice 2.4

Writing – a shopping catalogue or critical review?

Ben was feeling pleased. He had spent a great deal of time reading the literature and felt he had described clearly everything he had read. He emailed the first draft of his literature review to his project supervisor in advance of his supervision meeting. At the meeting his supervisor was obviously not impressed by Ben's writing. She commented that his draft was 'more like a shopping catalogue than a critical literature review' and needed to be 'completely rewritten'. Ben listened carefully to his supervisor's comments and went back to his room to redraft his work as a critical literature review.

This extract is taken from Ben's first draft:

> ... Möllering (2001) argues that trust develops from favourable expectations based upon interpretations of the reality to which trust relates, enabled by a suspension of disbelief and a corresponding leap of faith. Rousseau et al. (1998) argue that the development of trust theory has, to date, been disparate, focusing on a range of levels of analysis from the interpersonal to the inter-organisational. Schoorman et al. (2007) recognise that there is a need for a context specific understanding of trust. Wikipedia (2011) states that trust is the willingness of one party to be vulnerable to the actions of another party, with the reasonable expectation that they will behave in a beneficial way...

This is the same passage after Ben had redrafted it as a critical review:

> ... Development of trust theory has, to date, been more disparate, focusing on a range of levels of analysis from the interpersonal to the inter-organisational (e.g. Rousseau et al., 1998) and recognising the importance of context (Schoorman et al., 2007). Although this has resulted in a variety of definitions of trust, these exhibit a number of common elements, including notions of 'favourable expectations' and a 'willingness to become vulnerable'. Möllering (2001) has sought to use and develop these common elements in his research, arguing that trust develops from favourable expectations that are based upon interpretations of the reality to which the trust relates, enabled by a suspension of disbelief and a corresponding leap of faith. This suggests that ...

Möllering. In addition, Ben has only listed the items and has not linked the authors' ideas together to form an argument. At the end of this extract, he quotes a Wikipedia definition rather than discussing the definitions used by academic researchers, something which is unlikely to please his supervisor!

Now reread the second extract in Research in practice 2.4. You will notice that, unlike in the first extract, the order in which Ben writes about the ideas from the literature appears more logical, going from more general to more specific ideas. He starts with a general summary statement, referring to two sources as examples (Rousseau et al., 1998; Schoorman et al., 2007). In the next sentence he provides a more detailed evaluation, highlighting similarities between authors. Ben uses the phrase 'although this has…' to link these two sentences. He then introduces Möllering's more specific and focused arguments, repeating the term 'common elements' from the previous sentence to help emphasise a clear link. This time Ben does not refer to Wikipedia. His final phrase 'This suggests that…' provides a link between his summary of Möllering's ideas and what he is going to write next.

Finally, a quick reminder. Don't forget to look at section 8.5, where we talk about the process of writing in much more detail.

Summary

- Your literature review should offer an overview of significant literature available in your chosen topic, including relevant peer-reviewed academic journal articles, textbooks and other sources. It should provide a discussion and critical evaluation covering each of these, the level of detail reflecting the significance of each item. It should develop a clear argument to contextualise and justify your research.

- Critically reviewing the literature is important because it will provide the base on which your research project is built, helping you to decide on your precise topic and place it in the context of other research findings. It will also provide insights into secondary data that are likely to be available, as well as possible ways of collecting and analysing your own data.

- The amount of literature available to you is expanding rapidly as more sources are made available via the Internet. In addition to the library catalogue, your university library web pages will provide a comprehensive list of the other sources you can access as a student and the types of literature they contain. The most useful sources will be the online databases of academic journal articles.

- Your literature review will consist predominantly of peer-reviewed academic journal articles, although you are likely to find textbooks helpful, particularly in the early stages of your reviewing.

- The process of searching for and obtaining the literature consists of five stages: (1) decide on your literature search topic; (2) identify the keywords and phrases you will use; (3) choose your online databases; (4) undertake your search; (5) obtain the articles.

- The usefulness of any item will depend on your research question and your aim and objectives. When you review the literature, you will need to read as much of the literature that is closely related and of value to your research question as time permits.

- As you read, you should make notes in your own words of ideas that are useful to your research. Your notes should provide a summary of the item and remind you why you thought the particular idea was important, how an idea fits with your own research topic or even why you disagree with what you have just read. Making notes will help keep your mind focused on what you are reading and to remember what you have read.

- As you write your project report, you will need to record the sources of all the information, research findings, theories and other ideas to which you refer in your text. This process is known as referencing and allows you to acknowledge and give credit to the work of others, helping ensure you are not accused of plagiarism.

- The two most common styles are author–date systems (e.g. Harvard) and foot-notes (e.g. Vancouver) systems. Your university will have a preferred referencing style and it is essential that you obtain a copy of this and follow it exactly.

- Think of your literature review as a thematic funnel in which you link the different ideas you find within each theme in the literature and then link these themes using a clear, well-justified argument.

Thinking about your critical literature review

→ If you have not yet begun to think about critically reviewing the literature, start now!

→ Write your research question or aims and objectives on a piece of paper and refer to them frequently to keep focused. (If you are still unsure what to do for your research project, turn back to sections 1.4 and 1.5.)

→ Based on what you already know about your research topic, identify the terms and phrases you will use as search terms. Be prepared to use a variety of different terms and phrases.

→ Use the online databases available through your university and your university library catalogue to search the literature for useful items. Although you will find textbooks listed in the library catalogue useful in the early stages of your review, you should focus mainly upon finding peer-reviewed academic journal articles, using online databases of journal articles.

→ Obtain the articles and other items that seem likely to be useful and assess their relevance and value (usefulness) to your own research.

→ Use Google Scholar to find more recent items written by others that refer to those items you have already found that you feel are most useful to your own research.

→ Make your own notes about these useful items and include a summary in your own words. As you make notes, write about how the item compares with other items you have read.

→ Note the full reference of each item, using your university's preferred style of referencing.

→ Begin to draft your critical literature review, using a thematic structure, comparing and contrasting what each author has to say about a theme. Be mindful that you will have to redraft your review more than once.

References

Harvard College Library (2006) *Interrogating texts: 6 reading habits to develop in your first year at Harvard*. Available at: *http://hcl.harvard.edu/research/guides/lamont_handouts/ interrogatingtexts.html* [Accessed 27 Nov. 2010].

Hofstede, G. (2002) *Culture's Consequences*, 2nd edn, Thousand Oaks, CA: Sage.

McSweeny, B. (2002) Hofstede's model of national cultural differences and their consequences: a triumph of faith – a failure of analysis, *Human Relations*, 55(1): 89–118.

Saunders M.N.K. (2012) Web versus mail: the influence of survey distribution mode on employees' response, *Field Methods*, 24(1).

Saunders, M., Lewis, P. and Thornhill, A. (2009) *Research Methods for Business Students*, 5th edn, Harlow: FT Prentice Hall.

Wallace, M. and Wray, A. (2011) *Critical Reading and Writing for Postgraduates*, 2nd edn, London: Sage.

Wang, C.L., Indridason, T. and Saunders, M.N.K. (2010) Affective and continuance commitment in public private partnership, *Employee Relations*, 32(4): 396–417.

Chapter 3

Managing the research process

3.1 Why you should read this chapter

In the first chapter of this book we noted that doing a research project gave you the chance to develop a number of skills. Much of this chapter focuses in part upon the development of your personal organisational skills. In Chapter 1 we talked of the importance of managing your own learning through choosing a research topic that will develop your skills and knowledge, as well as, possibly, your employment opportunities. We also noted the importance of choosing a topic which matched the resources available to you: in particular, time and data. All of this suggests the importance of you taking control of the research process. It is a process which you should lead, not one where you allow yourself to be led. In fact, we would go as far as to say that self-organisation is a crucial factor in determining a successful outcome to your research project.

So what are these components of the research process that need to be managed by you? Well, assuming that you are doing primary research in an organisation, the organisation itself in the form of its key personnel, or its customers, are obvious starting points. You will need to get access to the organisation in the first place. Then there are the respondents from whom you wish to get the data. Obviously, paying attention to these key resources is vital. Then there is the management of the components over which you have more control. First, we concentrate on the key component of managing oneself, where attention needs to be paid to wider topics than just managing your time. Then there is the relationship you have with your supervisor. Managing this does not mean that you 'take charge' of your supervisor. It's rather more subtle than that. Many students (and lecturers, for that matter) talk of unsuccessful student/supervisor relationships. We help you to ensure that your situation is successful. We then cover the relationship you have with the university through, for example, the importance of paying attention to the standards that are demanded of you.

Figure 3.1 Managing the research process

The final part of this chapter is about the ethics of doing research. This is becoming a much more central consideration in the conduct of research. It's essential that you consider the ethical implications of your research in order not to fall foul of the expectations of your host organisation, respondents, university and project supervisor.

3.2   Getting access to your research organisation and your respondents

So, your research questions and objectives mean that it's necessary to gain access to an external organisation, or a number of organisations, to do some research. Much of this section assumes that you will not be doing research using your employing or placement organisation as the main context, so it's one with which you are unfamiliar. (However, we do deal with issues that arise from being the 'insider' later in the section.) It's possible, of course, that you have some introduction to the organisation, from a friend or a previous connection. But even if that is so, there are still key issues that you need to consider. These issues are divided into two main parts in this section. First, we consider some of the main problems that you are likely to face when attempting to gain access to your chosen organisation. Second, armed with an awareness of some of these problems, we talk about how you may overcome them to achieve your goal of organisational access.

It would be good to think that the organisation in which you wish to do research will be keen to help you. You may be lucky: it may. But the reality is that most will not be keen. So what are some of the reasons for this possible lack of keenness to help?

What's in it for us?

The reaction of the manager who receives the request is likely to be, 'What's in it for the organisation?' Managers are busy people who are paid by the organisation to help achieve the organisation's goals, not *your* goals! This seems a most obvious point, but how often when we plan for a job interview, for example, do we concentrate on what we want and what we can offer and not think about the needs of the employer.

Oh no! Not another request!

Be aware of the fact that your request may be one of many. You will be aware that there has been huge growth in the amount of degree students in recent years, including business and management students. This means that research access requests are much more commonplace, particularly in a large national organisation.

Oh no! Not another student! Yet another demand on our time!

You must accept the fact that you may be a source of concern. This is probably the first time you have done something like this, so the manager has to balance the wish to help you (and many managers do genuinely want to help) and the risk that you may waste valuable organisational time.

The manager receiving your request is going to be mindful of the resources that will need to be devoted to you. That manager will need time to consider who may be responsible for dealing with your needs. In turn, the likelihood is that you will need to demand the time of other people, for example, more junior employees. This will impact upon the ability of people to do the jobs for which they are paid.

Who is going to get hold of this information?

There is also likely to be a worry about what you going to do with the information you get from the organisation. We are not just talking about commercial secrecy here, but organisational politics. Many managers are very sensitive about who knows what in their own organisation, so they are going to be even more concerned about the public availability of that knowledge outside the organisation. This may not necessarily be particularly rational – the information may not on the face of it seem sensitive. But we are talking about human behaviour here, which isn't always as rational as we may think!

Clearly, you will need to give assurances about treating such information that you collect with strict confidentiality, assuming that this is what is required. You may also need to promise that your respondents will be anonymous so that their identity cannot be traced.

Well maybe, but not right now...

Organisations will often cite reasons why they are not able to grant research access at the time when you approach them. Of course, there may be an element of putting you off here, in the hope that you will go somewhere else and leave them alone! But sometimes the reason may be perfectly valid. It may coincide with a particularly

busy period, such as new product launch, or a sensitive time such as the announce-
ment of a redundancy programme.

The discussion above refers to what may be called the 'gatekeeper' level of organisational access. But you will usually need to get through the 'gate' to see other
people. Although 'gatekeeper' access is essential, it may also be necessary for you to
gain acceptance and consent from intended participants within the organisation in
order to gain access to the data that they are able to provide. These participants may
be other managers, or their employees, whom you may need to see as individuals or
in groups. So, let's face it, the problems you may face when dealing with the **gatekeeper** are equally relevant at other levels!

> **Definition**
>
> **gatekeeper**: the person, often in an organisation, who controls research access.

3.3   What about access to information?

So far we have dealt with the question of access to the organisation in order to get
into a position where you can get the information you want. Now let's deal with
access to that information itself. Here you need to be clear about precisely what data
you wish to collect and the method or methods you intend to use to collect those
data. This raises two key questions:

1 Have you thought through fully the extent of the access that you will require in
   order to be able to answer your research question(s) and meet your objectives?

2 Are you able to gain sufficient access to answer these research question(s) and
   meet your objectives?

Both these questions point to the need for thorough preparation on your part – a
topic we will deal with in the next part of this chapter when we deal with strategies
to gain access.

Should organisational access be seen as a single event?

It may be that your research question(s) and objectives mean that you need to gain
information from people at different levels of the organisation, and from different
parts of the organisation, say different divisions or departments or geographical locations. Or it may be that you need to gather data in fragments, separated by time. All
of this suggests that access is a continuing process and not just an initial or single
event. So access negotiation becomes an even more important part of the management of the research process. Indeed, it may be continuous.

Getting access to the organisation as an 'insider'

We mentioned at the start of this chapter that you may be an employee of the organisation in which you wish to do research, or you may be, or have recently been, a placement student in the organisation. This is great because people in the organisation will know you and, hopefully, have positive views about you. But you are still likely to face problems in getting the data you need. However, they may be rather different to those faced by the 'outsider'.

The likelihood is that as the 'insider' you may still need to get formal approval to conduct the research. The larger or more geographically diverse the organisation, the more likely this is. All you may have is an introduction, so you may only be one step in front of the 'outsider'.

As the insider, you may come across the same issue of status. And it may not be just because you are seen as quite a junior member of the organisation (indeed, you may be rather senior). It will be an issue if, say, you belong to a part of the organisation which is seen to be more powerful than the one in which you wish to do the research. Feelings of suspicion may be even greater if you have been asked by your manager to take part in the research project ('What are *they* up to now?'). You may not feel much like a management pawn, but that's the way you could be seen.

There is another disadvantage as the 'insider' researcher. You may feel reluctant to ask very basic questions (e.g. What job does Mrs X actually do? Who is our biggest client?) because you feel you should know the answer. As the outsider, you would not be expected to know the answers to these questions, so you can go ahead and find out information that you really need to know to set your research information in context.

3.4	Six strategies for making sure that you get the organisational access you want

It sounds as if we are being totally negative in this chapter so far! Well, getting access to your research organisation certainly does pose challenges. But this chapter is all about managing the research process, so you need to manage the challenges!

You will have to plan your approach carefully. How do you do this? Well, we explain below six strategies you can adopt to manage the process.

Strategy 1: Try to use your existing contacts

It's undoubtedly easier to use any existing contacts you have to get access to an organisation to do your research. These contacts may come from friends, family, student colleagues, lecturer suggestions or contacts that you may make at meetings of the professional association related to your specialism. Having an introduction at least avoids that difficult stage where you approach the organisation as a complete unknown. Although using a contact who has mentioned you may not put the manager who receives your request under any obligation to give you the access you want, you are more likely to have the chance to make your request than in the case of the 'cold' approach.

We have already mentioned the possibility of using your work placement organisation as your research organisation. If your placement has been a success, you will have made useful contacts that may be able to help you. Potentially, this is much better than using contacts given to you by someone else. You are known and trusted, and the organisation's managers will know that you are familiar with the context of the organisation's work. So the demand on resources may not be as great. It may be even better to build on the work you did on the placement by doing a research project that relates to this work. This may lead to the ideal situation: access to an organisation in which you are welcomed to conduct some research that is valued by the organisation!

Strategy 2: Put yourself in the shoes of the manager receiving your request

If the organisation is likely to be resistant to your approach, you have to think about why it is that that organisation is likely to be resistant. Put yourself in the shoes of the manager receiving your request and think about how to overcome some of that resistance. Strategies 3–6 below offer specific guidance on practical steps you take to

---

Research in practice 3.1

Using contacts to assist organisational access

Stefan wanted to do his undergraduate research project on the topic of Internet shopping versus traditional high-street store shopping. What interested him in particular was the situation where well-known stores sold the same products on their websites at the same price as the retail store. This seemed to Stefan to contradict business logic since Internet trading was much less costly than store operation. It occurred to Stefan that there were a number of possible explanations, such as the principle of 'complementarity' where the website complemented the store offering. It was also useful where retailers offered the 'click and collect' service that had become more popular, where customers ordered through the website and nominated local stores at which they could collect the item. But Stefan wanted to find some authoritative answers.

Stefan's supervisor also taught a part-time MBA class and was friendly with one of the MBA students who was in a senior position in a national department store chain. Stefan's supervisor introduced Stefan to the MBA student who put Stefan in touch with her commercial director at Head Office. Stefan subsequently interviewed the commercial director who was so impressed with the background reading and thinking that Stefan had done, and the questions he asked, that he then introduced him to three contacts in different organisations whom he thought would be able to help.

When Stefan finally completed his project report, he was able to draw some well-argued conclusions based on eight interviews at senior level in six separate organisations.

overcome resistance. All these need you to think through how your request is likely to be seen by the manager receiving your request.

We noted above that the reaction of the manager who receives the request is likely to be, 'What's in it for the organisation?' which seems a reasonable reaction. So it's important to think about any possible benefits to the organisation. And there may be some. Experienced interviewees have sometimes confessed to us after an interview that they viewed the prospect of being interviewed as a bit of a chore. Yet we have been delighted to hear from them that they found the interview helpful. Rarely do they have the opportunity to talk through issues with an interested out-sider. The more probing your questioning, based on thoughtful listening, the more value the interviewee is likely to get from listening to the responses.

Interviewee(s) may also appreciate a summary report of the interview, although it is not normally appropriate to send them a copy of your project report. The report is for a different purpose. An interview summary helps in three ways. First, it enables the interviewee to check the accuracy of your summary; second, it allows the addi-tion of material which may have been overlooked during the interview and, lastly, it shows that you have actually done something as an end product of the interview.

Let's go back to the worry that the manager may have that you will take too much valuable organisational time. Your request for access is more likely to be accepted if the amount of time you ask for is kept to a minimum. And it's important to be realistic about the time you ask for. Be honest. For example, falsely stating that each interview will last for only thirty minutes, and then deliberately exceeding this, is very likely to upset your interviewee and may prevent your gaining further access.

Strategy 3: Make sure you give yourself sufficient time to set up the arrangement

We hope that one of the messages that comes across clearly in this book is that of giving yourself plenty of time to complete your research project. To summarise this message: start early!

Nowhere is this message more significant than the issue of allowing sufficient time to set up access to your research organisation. It can take weeks of delay between your original request and the final approval to go ahead (or, regrettably, the refusal). Even where the go-ahead is granted, there will be further delay before you gain access to the people from whom you wish to get information.

Assuming that you are not using an existing contact (and even where you may be), the likelihood is that you will not receive a direct reply to your first approach. There will be delay while you wait for this, and then for a response to your follow-up. This raises the question of the amount of time you should wait, and the 'tone' you adopt when sending your 'reminder'. You must ensure that you keep to the right side of the line between persistence and pestering. Whether you use email, tel-ephone or letter (or a combination of the three) is dependent on the situation. We have found that a telephone approach with a written follow-up can be very effective.

The larger the organisation, the more time-consuming the access negotiation process may be. Where you have no existing contact, it may be necessary to make several telephone calls simply to identify the best person to ensure that your request for access will be considered. If you use a contact given to you, you will still experience delay while your request is considered and an interview meeting arranged at a convenient time. This may take a number of weeks.

More time will be needed for those access requests that are more complex. You may wish to get data in a variety of ways from across the organisation which, of course, has the potential for more delays. The official go-ahead from the organisational gatekeeper may mean that you are 'in', but you still have to gain the consent, support and trust of those participants you will depend on for your research data.

One final note to emphasise is that the worst may happen and you receive a refusal. It is essential not only to have a plan B (or even C and D!), but also to make sure that the necessity to enact plan B does not seriously jeopardise your overall timescale. Following experimentation, psychologists recently have concluded that time passes quickest when we are busy. Many of our students have told us that this is not true: it passes like lightning during the time allocated to a research project!

Strategy 4: Make that written request professional!

Putting your request for research access into writing is highly advisable. Unless you read from script, it is unlikely that you could achieve the same level of precision in a spoken telephone request.

There are several reasons why it is advantageous to put your request in writing in a clearly written manner. Among these are the following:

1 It allows your intended participants to be aware precisely of what will be required from them. This is important because asking them for their help without being clear about your needs will probably lead them to be wary since the amount of time you require from them may be more than they may reasonably expect to give.

2 It gives you the opportunity to set your request in context. You can explain the overall purpose of the research, the reason you are doing it, the university and department in which you are studying and the course you are completing.

3 It gives you the opportunity to enhance your credibility by presenting a professional image through a well-written and carefully considered request.

Your written request should outline briefly:

- the purpose of your research;
- how the person being contacted might be able to help;
- the demands being made of the participant or participants;
- a guarantee of anonymity (where appropriate);
- what you will do with the information you get from the each participant, including any intention you may have of sharing the information during or after the data-collection stage;
- your contact details so that your participant can reply to you.

Should your written request be an email or a traditional letter? The advantages of an email are clear, but don't discount the value of a letter. The impact of the letter may be greater as it is more unusual these days; it is much less easy to delete or mislay; and it gives you greater opportunity to personalise and, therefore, impress. Whichever method you choose, it is essential that your communication achieves the highest standard of which you are capable! This warning is especially appropriate in the case of emails. We all know how easy it is for normal writing standards to drop when we send emails and how tempting it is to hit 'Send' without double and triple checking in the same way that we may do with traditional written forms of communication. Don't be tempted! The person reading your email may (like us!) be a stickler for correct written English, and may reject your request on these grounds alone!

Research in practice 3.2

Writing your research request

Mary Field was a final-year undergraduate pursuing research into staff recruitment and selection. Here is one of the emails that she wrote to prospective HR specialist managerial interviewees with a request that they allow her to conduct an interview.

Dear Mrs Darrow

Further to my telephone call to your secretary, Meena Patel, last Thursday March 11th, I would like to introduce myself and explain the reason for my contacting you.

My name is Mary Field and I am a final year undergraduate at the University of .... where I am studying Business and Management. I have to complete successfully a research project to pass my course. I plan a career in HR and I am particularly interested in recruitment and selection. I hope you are able to help me by allowing me to interview you.

The details of my research plan are attached in a Word document called 'Mary Field Recruitment Proposal'. Briefly, the purpose is to identify the operational differences between in-house and external staff recruitment, and to establish the implications for HR practice of these differences.

I am conducting a number of interviews with senior HR professionals in the .... region and would find your views extremely valuable. At the foot of the attached document is a suggested set of topics/questions for the interviews I will conduct, which I hope would be valuable for you in thinking about this prior to my visit. I assure you that I would take no more than 45 minutes of your time and that the information that you may give me would not be credited to you in any report that I subsequently write.

If, as I hope, you are able to help, please reply to this email. I will then contact Meena Patel to fix an interview at a time and place suitable for you. If you prefer to talk to me, my number is 07123 456789.

Yours sincerely
Mary Field

Strategy 5: Work hard to ensure there are no concerns about the way in which you will use the information

You will have noticed that one thing that virtually all organisations have in common is that they like to present a positive front to the world! Even if the news is bad, they work hard to put a less negative aspect on that news than perhaps is justified. Why else would large organisations spend millions on public relations specialists? There is a message here for those of us who want to pursue organisational research. You are unlikely to gain research access if the subject of your research can be perceived as negative. So an inquiry into the reasons for an organisation's market failure in a particular product area is to be avoided. However, you may learn from the public relations experts and lend a positive emphasis to this by, for example, using the organisation of your choice as a context for an inquiry into the changing nature of the demand for a particular product area and what may be learned. Your choice of language in the written request will have to be very carefully considered to ensure that no hint of negativity is suggested.

A more predictable area of concern is that of anonymity. This relates to that information which is given to you and what you do with it once it is given. Some organisations and some respondents will be extremely sensitive about anonymity. While this occasionally may be hard to understand, the point remains that it is their information and you must respect their wishes.

The introductory email or letter offers you the opportunity to give a guarantee of confidentiality in writing at the time of making the request for access. This is a good time to make the initial guarantee, as confidentiality may be uppermost in the minds of the managers who will consider your approach. But do not think of this initial guarantee as the only one you will make. As you meet more participants, you will need to repeat any assurances about confidentiality. This can be done, for example, with an assurance that any information given to you will not be attributed to any individual. It is essential that you honour this assurance, not only for your credibility, but also for those researchers who may follow you.

It is quite common for the organisation to ask you to not place your written report in the university library, although you may not have identified the organisation or any individual participants. You must check the course requirements here with your supervisor, but whatever the regulations, the confidentiality wishes of your research organisation come first.

Strategy 6: Underline your credibility!

Perhaps this sixth strategy is a result of the efforts you have put in making your request as professional as possible. The more credible you seem, the more likely you are to receive a favourable response to your request for research access. But there is one point we haven't mentioned so far which we think will really underline your credibility: find out as much as possible about the organisation before requesting access. The more you know about the organisation's context, such as their products and services, markets, competitors, trading position, current challenges and development plans, the better. This will really impress the person you're approaching, particularly if that knowledge blends thoughtfully with the information you are seeking, and your research question(s) and objectives.

In the end, do what's possible

Like many research considerations, getting access to your research organisation is a balance between what is ideal and what is possible. OK, so you want to make sure that you get a representative sample, conduct your interviews in a uniform way and collect sufficient data to ensure the answers to your research questions(s) and objectives are valid and reliable. But life isn't perfect. Your respondents will deny you access to information, limit your interview time, lose your questionnaire, go on holiday, and leave the organisation in the middle of your research. You are at the mercy of events. You can manage much of the process, but you can't control the uncontrollable!

Table 3.1 Checklist of points to follow to increase your chances of getting access to your chosen research organisation

- Be clear about the overall purpose of your research project.
- Write your research question(s) and objectives.
- Use existing contacts where possible.
- Consider using your work placement organisation (if appropriate) as a setting for your research project.
- Approach relevant appropriate local and/or national employer, or employee, professional or trade bodies to see if they can suggest contacts.
- Make a direct approach to an organisation to identify the most appropriate manager.
- Think about the possible benefits for the organisation, should access be granted to you.
- Offer a report summarising your findings.
- Allow yourself plenty of time for the entire process.
- Allow sufficient time to contact intended participants and gain their consent, once access has been granted.
- If you make your initial request for access by telephone, follow this with an email or letter to confirm your request.
- Make sure the construction, tone, language, spelling, grammar and presentation of an introductory email or letter are all likely to persuade the person to help you.
- Consider how you will address concerns about the amount of organisational time you would take up.
- Ensure you have considered any sensitivities concerning your research topic.
- Assure participants you have recognised any needs for confidentiality and/or anonymity.
- Think about a range of contact methods for potential participants to use to reply.

We now move on to consider the management of those components of the research process over which you have more control: managing yourself, your supervisor and your university.

3.5   Managing yourself

Managing your time

We have already mentioned in this chapter elements of time management, particu-larly those that refer to the process of gaining access to your research organisation. Here we consider time management more widely, both in terms of your research project schedule and the allocation of time to your research.

It is important that you complete a research project plan at the beginning of your research. Indeed, this may be a university requirement, as it helps your lecturers assess the viability of your research proposal. It's useful if you divide your research plan into stages. This will give you a clear idea as to what is possible in the given timescale. But don't forget that however well your time is organised, the whole proc-ess seems to take longer than you planned. An example of the sort of schedule you may develop is shown in Table. 3.2.

Table 3.2 Research project schedule

Task	To be completed by
Generate list of research ideas	10.10.2011
Choose research topic	1.11.2011
Undertake preliminary literature review	1.11.2011
Define research questions and objectives and submit research proposal	10.11.2011
Main literature reading	10.12.2011
Literature review written	31.12.2011
Methods chosen and draft method chapter written	10.01.2012
Fieldwork commenced	20.01.2012
All data collected and fieldwork notes completed	01.03.2012
All data analysed ready for draft findings and conclusions chapters to be written	20.03.2012
Final draft submitted	15.04.2012
Final submission	30.05.2012

Even if the inevitable happens and you find that you have some slippage in your schedule, at least you know what you are slipping from! Not having a schedule is simply unthinkable.

Just as important as the project schedule is your personal timetable which shows the amount of time you are going to devote to your research. Here you will have to be realistic. You have other demands. Other modules require lecture preparation and assessment completion. But it is all too easy to fall into the trap of allocating time by 'what's the next most important deadline'. Of course, there is always another deadline looming, but the trouble is that with your research project the big dead-line of final project submission is months away for most of the year and it's forever being left until later. It's best to schedule some time regularly, say each week, to do something towards your research. Do this at the start of the year and get into the habit of it. The beauty of personal timetables is that they become part of a 'self con- tract'. If you meet your contractual obligation, you can feel pleased with yourself; if you don't meet it, make sure you feel suitably guilty! There is no substitute for getting into a routine. You will probably have heard this before when you started university, but it's the same for doing research, or for us writing this book. Get into the habit of doing something towards your research right from the start on, for example, Monday afternoons in the library. It's always easy to find other things to do when the deadline is not pressing. Just try not to be like Oscar Wilde who could resist everything except temptation!

One final point about time management. We have known students who have been either perfectionists or 'just do enough to pass' types. Our advice is to be nei- ther. The perfectionist runs into time management problems because of the need to polish everything until it dazzles. This is great if there's time, but there never is. 'Just doing enough', on the other hand, can often lead to not doing enough and the necessity to re-submit the report.

⬤ Keeping up your motivation

You are likely to be doing your research project for an extended period, so expect your motivation to vary over that period. You may start and end on a high, but there will be times in between when you can't see your way forward. There are ways in which you can overcome this. Let's look at three of these.

First, set yourself short-term goals. Sports coaches are renowned for using this technique to improve participant performance. You can distinguish between long- term goals – for example, breaking the world record or successfully completing your degree; intermediate goals – such as lowering the 100m sprint time by 1 second or getting all your fieldwork done on time – and short-term goals. Short-term goals may concentrate on each training session, or, in research project terms, the completion of a set of notes at the end of a two-hour reading session of a particular article. Do remember that it's important that your short-term goals are SMART (specific, meas- urable, achievable, realistic and timely – see section 1.6).

Second, while we are on the subject of goals, think about setting some fresh learn- ing goals: Learn how to conduct group interviews effectively, use a new statistical analysis package or how to sort, label and categorise qualitative data in a systematic way. These goals will not only add to your repertoire of business skills but also give you a sense of achievement.

Third, do keep focused. You can do this by keeping in touch with your supervisor and talking through your progress. This can be quite motivational, either because you are further on than you thought, or in giving you a refreshed sense of direction if you have lost your way. Another important way of keeping focused is to review regularly your research question(s) and objectives. It's so easy to wander away from the main point of your research into all sorts of interesting diversions. A regular review of progress against your research question(s) and objectives is a vital way to keep focused. OK, so this may involve some revision of your question(s) and objectives, but at least this will mean that you're on track.

Keep in touch with individuals who can help

We have already mentioned the need to keep in touch with your supervisor. Don't forget there are other people who can help. It is useful to talk to these people regularly. Among these are those student colleagues who helped you think about your research topic in the first place and family and friends. It may also be useful to talk to the specialist librarian in your research topic area. This expert may be able to point you in the direction of new resources, and suggest different perspectives on your research.

3.6   Managing your supervisor

When you look back on your time at university and remember your research project, it's certain you will remember your research supervisor. Usually this is for the right reasons, because the relationship has been a fruitful one where both you and your supervisor have had your expectations met. But, of course, it can all go horribly wrong! Fortunately this happens rarely. But it can happen, so in this section we look at the expectations that you should have of your supervisor, and those that your supervisor should have of you. Being aware of these, and acting according to them should mean that your eventual memories of your supervisor are as favourable as those that we hope our students have of us!

What should you expect of your supervisor?

Your supervisor is there to advise you at every stage of your research project, from formulation of the project through to completion of the final report. However, do remember that it is *your* research project, and your supervisor is not there to write it for you!

What expectations should you have of your supervisor? Here are some of them.

You receive assistance with the selection and planning of a suitable and manageable research topic

You should not expect your supervisor to impose a topic upon you; it has to be your choice. But you should be prepared to have your ideas both praised and criticised. You want encouragement, but if your supervisor thinks an idea is a non-starter, you should be told this.

Your supervisor is sufficiently familiar with the field of research to provide guidance

This can be quite a problematic area. With the increasing amount of students who require supervision comes the need of the university to resource this requirement.

This sometimes means that there is not an ideal match between your research topic and your supervisor. However, do bear in mind that your supervisor will concentrate on the research process rather than simply the topic. In our view the more effective supervisors are those who are familiar with guiding their students on how to conduct the project rather than those who are subject only specialists. However, talk to the supervisors who are specialists about your research plans. Getting them interested may mean that you end up with both a subject specialist and someone who can guide you successfully through the project.

Your supervisor should be available for consultation and discussion about the progress of your research

How often you see your supervisor will depend upon several factors, not least of which will be the norm as it applies in your department. Usually, you will meet during the early stages of the project as things get going. As you become more confident, and you immerse yourself in reading or data collection, you would expect less frequent meetings. We usually find that our students value contact with their supervisor in the early and late stages of their project, when they are setting up and writing up. But do bear in mind that in most university departments the onus is on you to initiate meetings, although your supervisor may contact you to arrange the first meeting. You should check with your supervisor what the procedure is here.

At the end of each meeting with your supervisor, it is good practice to arrange the time of the next meeting and to agree what you should have done by that meeting. You then have the basis of an agenda for the next meeting. There may also be a procedure where a record is kept of the content of the meeting.

Your supervisor should respond to the work that you have completed

If you have sent your supervisor written work, as agreed between you, it is reasonable to expect that your supervisor will respond to this. You should expect to have helpful suggestions about how the work may be improved.

Your supervisor should point you in the direction of facilities or research materials

Again, the onus is on you to make arrangements to negotiate access to organisations, or libraries where you need secondary data. But it's reasonable to expect that your supervisor will have some ideas as to the sort of data that may be of help to you and where this may be available. As you make progress in your research, you will probably find that you know more than your supervisor about your research topic. However, in the early stages you are hungry for ideas and it's to be expected that your supervisor will provide some of these.

⬤ What your supervisor should expect from you

You should, in conjunction with your supervisor, develop a plan and timetable for completion of the stages of your research project, and meet all deadlines

Meet all deadlines, you say! Well, yes. But, for all sorts of reasons which we touched on earlier in this chapter, some delays may not be in your control. However, your supervisor will expect you to pay attention to the set deadlines and make your best attempt to meet them. Treating deadlines in a trivial way is a sure path to a hurried and ineffective conclusion to the project. The more you have to rush at the end, the less value you can expect from your supervisor's comments at that vital late stage when you are drafting your report.

You should meet with your supervisor when arranged and report fully and regularly on progress and results

It would be good to say that it's rare that students don't turn up for an arranged meeting, or show up and have not done the work that was agreed at the last meeting. But, unfortunately, it's not that rare. You will want to get the best out of your supervisor, so make sure that you demonstrate that you are businesslike and do what you have agreed to do. That way, your supervisor will respond in a similar way and a fruitful relationship will develop.

You should give due consideration to the advice and criticisms received from your supervisor

It would be foolish to ignore criticism from your supervisor. But that's not the same as saying that you should follow slavishly every word. Indeed, when your confidence grows as your work progresses, you may choose to listen to criticism but decide, after careful thought, to stick to your guns. After all, it's your project and you will have to live or die by the final outcome. But do bear in mind that your supervisor has probably seen many similar projects in the past and is likely to be one of the people assessing your project report, so do consider carefully any critical comments you receive.

You should keep yourself up to date on the subject of your research topic

The likelihood is that you will write your literature review early in your project's life cycle. Try to avoid the temptation of then closing your mind to this aspect of your work. There may be important developments in your topic area during the course of your work, so don't miss out on these. Ignoring recent news in some highly topical subject areas, such as new technological developments, will damage the credibility of your work and threaten the success of your final submission.

You should keep in touch with your supervisor and make yourself available for regular meetings at mutually convenient times

Most lecturers will tell you that the students who keep in touch with their supervisor are the ones who usually complete the research project successfully while those they rarely see are on course for failure! This may be because the more diligent students usually are successful. But we like to think that research supervisors can pass on a wealth of experience and know-how which you would be foolish to ignore.

3.7 Managing your university

At the beginning of your course, or research project, you should receive from your department a guide which will specify such items as aims, objectives and learning outcomes of the research project. The guide should also list the relevant regulations for the completion of the project. These regulations will cover such topics as any requirements to attend seminars, meet specific deadlines, submit the written report in a specified style and, of course, the academic standards you should meet in order to be awarded a pass for your project. It is this last aspect of the university's requirements that we concentrate on here.

The learning outcomes of any research project summarise much of what we cover in this book, as they emphasise the process of doing research. Table 3.3 is a good example of a statement of such learning outcomes.

Table 3.3 Example of a statement of learning outcomes for research project module

Upon completion of this module, students will be able to:

(a) demonstrate initiative and discrimination in the sourcing and selection of material;

(b) undertake critical reading skills and critical analysis of material;

(c) integrate data and knowledge and synthesise complex information;

(d) organise and structure a substantial piece of work;

(e) produce a clearly defined and usable outcome within a specified timescale;

(f) demonstrate a level of expert knowledge in a particular subject or issue;

(g) manage their own efforts effectively.

At the end of the successful completion of the module the student will have completed a submission in accordance with the course and thus fulfilled the aims outlined above.

Source: University of Greenwich 2010.

You should also pay particular attention to the assessment criteria which should be contained in your research project guide. Table 3.4 is a good example of clearly defined criteria which you can use as a checklist as you work through the research process and, in particular, write your final report.

Table 3.4 **Example of marking scheme guide for research project final report**

Strong	Weak
Clear and informative definition of the aims and objectives of the research or study topic/problem to be investigated.	Weak and cursory description of research topic/problem to be investigated.
Clear and coherent identification of how the study is to be undertaken and the intended research techniques.	Poorly developed description of intended techniques to achieve stated aims and objectives.
Extensive, appropriate and in-depth selection of materials, properly referenced. Ability to synthesise complex information, to identify relevant issues and to provide an in-depth discussion and summary of such materials.	Narrow, limited and/or inappropriate selection of materials, showing little evidence of ability to draw out and analyse the relevant issues, and/or an inability to deal with complex information.
Good analysis and presentation of the information gathered in the study, demonstrating comprehensive scope of the subject and in-depth insight and mastery of the subject.	Limited scope and depth of information. Misused analysis and unstructured presentation. Superficial understanding and mastery of the subject.
Effective and comprehensive achievement of the objectives and/or hypothesis.	Little/no achievement of the objectives and/or hypothesis.
Clear, logical and succinct writing style with good use of English. Good structure and organisation of work. Good quality of figures/tables, etc. and adherence to required word length.	Clumsy expression, repetitive, under/over length paragraphs/sentences. Ungrammatical sentences, much incorrect spelling, untidy, difficult to read. Poor quality figures/tables, etc.

Source: Developed from University of Greenwich 2010.

The criteria specified in Table 3.4. should come as no surprise to you as they may well be similar to criteria you have come across earlier in other modules. But do use these for your research project. We even urge you to have a session with your supervisor as you approach the writing-up stage to discuss the precise meaning of these criteria in relation to your written project report.

3.8   The ethics of doing research

In recent years there has been much more interest in the subject of **research ethics**, so much so that your university has probably made you aware of the ethical responsibilities you have while conducting your research.

Let's be clear about what we mean by ethics. Generally, ethics means 'standards of behaviour that guide the moral choices we make which govern our behaviour and

---

Definition

research ethics: the appropriateness of the researcher's behaviour in relation to the rights of those who become the subject of a research project, or who are affected by it.

our relationships with others'. Since virtually all research using primary data, that is data which we collect specifically for the purposes of our research, involves our relationships with others, this is clearly something we shouldn't ignore. Or can we? Well, even if you wanted to act in an amoral way towards your research participants, the rules of your university will stress the need for you to behave in an ethical way in the conduct of your research (see Table 3.5).

Table 3.5 Example of code of practice for ethical standards involving human participants

- No research should cause harm, and preferably it should benefit participants.
- Potential participants normally have the right to receive clearly communicated information from the researcher in advance.
- Participants should be free from coercion of any kind and should not be pressured to participate in a study.
- Participants in a research study have the right to give their informed consent before participating.
- Where third parties are affected by the research, informal consent should be obtained.
- The consent of vulnerable participants (e.g. children) or their representatives' assent should be actively sought by researchers.
- Honesty should be central to the relationship between researcher, participant and institutional representatives.
- Participants' confidentiality and anonymity should be maintained.
- The collection and storage of research data by researchers must comply with the Data Protection Act 1998.
- Researchers have a duty to disseminate their research findings to all appropriate parties.

Source: Oxford Brookes University (2010). Full version available at: www.brookes.ac.uk/res/ethics/ethics_codeofpractice.pdf

In this section we explore some of the ethical issues you may encounter through the different stages of your research. Ethical considerations impact on how you decide upon your research topic; design your research and gain organisational and respondent access; collect your data; process and store your data, analyse your data and write up your research findings. At all these stages you will need to ensure that the way you design your research is both methodologically sound and morally defensible to all those who are involved.

Here we consider the ethical issues at three main stages of the research process: research design, data collection and reporting. Of course, these issues don't fit neatly into each of the main stages. Nonetheless, we cover some of the main ethical points which we then summarise at the end of the section in Table 3.6.

What are the ethical questions you should consider at the research design stage?

Getting respondents' consent

The main issue to consider at the design and access stage of your research is that of respondent consent. Look again at Table 3.5. Following the principles here means that your participants should be free from coercion of any kind and should not be pressured to participate in a study. This is unlikely to be the case when you are approaching a senior manager who is the organisational gatekeeper, but it may be relevant when the senior manager arranges for you to see respondents more junior than themselves. You should be particularly sensitive to this situation. It is extremely unlikely that your respondents will refuse to cooperate, even if a feeling of being coerced by a senior manager exists. However, you will need full support from your respondents rather than grudging acceptance. Full support is more likely if you give assurances of confidentiality before the interview in a bid to secure informal consent.

The ethical situation relating to data collected by questionnaire is rather more straightforward. The return of a completed questionnaire by a respondent is such that completion by itself implies consent. However, this is not the same as giving you consent to use the data collected in any way you think fit. You should bear in mind that when respondents agree to participate, this does not necessarily imply consent about the way in which the data provided are subsequently used. You should tell them how you will use the data. Don't ignore another of the principles in Table 3.5: that honesty should be central to the relationship between you and your respondents. Consider the example of the phone caller who calls you at the most inconvenient time posing as a researcher but who, in reality, is a salesperson. This is infuriating, and quite the opposite of the standards you should be aiming at!

Consent – not coercion!

Conducting research in your own employing organisation presents different concerns. You may be tempted to apply pressure to others (colleagues or subordinates) to cooperate. They may cooperate from a feeling of social obligation to you. But the same effort to obtain informal consent applies as with other respondents. And like all respondents, you should emphasise their right to withdraw from your study at any time.

If you are being asked by the organisation to conduct your research project, you have a right not to be forced to choose a research project in which you are uninterested. This prejudices a valuable learning opportunity for you. It also threatens one of the most ethical obligations you have to all concerned – to produce research of the highest possible quality.

Your ethical obligation to use the time you have been granted by the organisation in a way that is of benefit to the organisation

If you are using an organisation as your research context, you will have an ethical obligation to use the time you have been granted by the organisation in a way that is useful to the organisation. That is not to say that you will necessarily tell the managers what they want to hear. But even if your conclusions are unfavourable, then the organisation has a right to expect that you frame your conclusions in a positive and constructive way. At the same time, you have a right not to be coerced by the organisation's managers to misrepresent the data which you have uncovered so as to portray the organisation positively.

Respondent vulnerability

Clearly, some topics carry a greater risk of a breach of ethical standards than others. A brief look at Table 3.5 shows that the standard of seeking the consent of vulnerable participants or their representatives is one that is potentially sensitive. On the face of it, this may relate more closely to education, health or social services. Yet, vulnerability may apply to employees whose jobs are changing or being made redundant; or it may relate to sensitive areas such as poor employee performance. If your research topic has obviously sensitive implications, you will need to pay attention to the ethical dimension in your research proposal.

What are the ethical questions you should consider at the data collection stage?

The importance of confidentiality

Often confidentiality is an important condition that your research organisation makes when granting you research access. Organisational gatekeepers often insist that you do not disclose the organisation's identity in any way. We deal with how to cope with this in your report in the subsection on 'confidentiality and anonymity at the reporting stage' later in this section.

It is often more important to guarantee confidentiality to individual respondents. This is particularly important in relation to names, addresses and personal data which may allow them to be identified. Not only is the issue of confidentiality important, but also harm may be done to individual respondents by information that you have obtained being attributed to them. You may, for example, have gained the trust of a respondent to the extent where you are told the individual's career plans, something that may be better kept from management. Again, as with the organisation, do make sure that your respondents' identities are not revealed accidentally in anything you write. You can use the same 'respondent A' method, or adopt a style such as 'one respondent told me...' The key point here is not to break your promise of confidentiality.

It's not just in reporting your data that you may reveal the identity of your respondents; this can happen in interviews. As you collect more data you may develop themes which have emerged during the process. Developing these themes may mean that your respondents can guess what previous respondents have said from the questions you are asking. This can lead to respondents indirectly identifying the person responsible for raising the earlier point that you now wish to discuss with them.

The confidentiality points above relate mainly to the collection and reporting of qualitative data. Such issues are equally important when it comes to the collection and reporting of quantitative data. Here your main concern is to report aggregated data, in order to establish the patterns that emerge. So making quantitative data anonymous is less problematic.

Causing harm through the collection of primary data through interviewing

In addition to confidentiality, conducting interviews raises other ethical considerations. The potential to harm your respondents can arise in many ways. We deal with three here.

First, it is important to be sensitive to any reluctance that your participant may have to answer your questions. As your confidence in interviewing builds, it may be easy to start pressing participants for answers without realising that what they are experiencing may be quite stressful for them. It's important to make clear to participants that they have a right to refuse to answer any question, for any reason. It doesn't happen often, particularly when you have built rapport with the interviewee, but it can.

Secondly, do be careful that the questions you ask are not likely to be harmful to your participant. These may relate to personal circumstances or be of such a nature that they humiliate your interviewee. Such questions may be quite unintentional. They may not form part of your planned interview schedule. But it's easy for a follow-up question to come out in a way that had not been planned.

Thirdly, do be mindful of the circumstances of your participant. Simple things such as setting a time, location and interview duration that is convenient to your participant is important. If the participants are quite junior in the organisation, it's important that you stick to agreed arrangements as they are likely to have less time flexibility. Be on guard for signs of discomfort because, for example, you're running over the agreed time. Not only is this discourteous, but also, once again, you may be causing stress and inconvenience to your participants.

Causing harm through the collection of primary data by observation

Should you wish to collect some or all of your data by observation, you will face particular ethical problems. Let's say, for example, that you want to observe the behaviour of airline cabin crew members as they deal with customers, in order to establish the extent of the engagement that they demonstrate. Central to this is the choice you have over whether you should disclose your purpose to those crew members you intend to observe. Given everything that has been said so far in this section, this seems a clear-cut decision: you should disclose your research purpose.

However, you then face the problem of '**reactivity**' (or 'observer effect'), which is a particular problem with observation. This happens when those you are observing adapt their behaviour as a consequence of your observation. Obviously, this threatens the reliability and validity of your data. So you have a choice: you disclose your purpose and seek approval of the organisation and the crew members in the normal way, or you go ahead and do your observation covertly.

> Definition
>
> **reactivity**: reaction by research participants to any research intervention that affects data reliability.

Let's say that you seek approval of the organisation and the crew members and then you are refused access. You could carry on covertly, in your role as a customer, or abandon the plan. If you decide to carry on covertly, then those being observed may discover your actions, with the consequence that you must explain what they would see as your deceit. It is our view that researchers should not practise deceit at any time as this is a clear violation of the principles of ethical research.

Causing harm through unauthorised use of secondary data

It's not just through the collection of primary data that you can cause harm. The collection of secondary data also raises ethical issues. Say, for example, you want to establish a sample of customers from whom you want to collect data on service satisfaction levels. This may involve a study of customer databases to form the sample. From the databases you may have personal details of many individuals who have not consented to your having this information. It's important that you treat this information in the strictest confidence and don't use it in any way that might cause harm to these individuals.

It's also important that you are honest and stick to the declared purpose of your research and not use secondary data in any other way than that which you originally intended.

Data collection and honesty

Having raised the topic of honesty in the previous subsection, it's here that we touch on the most apparent dishonest behaviour in data collection, that of making up the data. This can be blatant, such as completing questionnaires for interviews not conducted. On the other hand it can be more subtle, where you decide to record contributions which suit you for some reason and ignore those that do not suit you. Not only do you have an ethical duty to report your findings honestly, but also your data will be unreliable and invalid if you have practised dishonesty in your data collection.

Ethical issues and data collection using the Internet

The emergence of the Internet has presented many new opportunities for conducting research, including some in the business arena. The main ethical consideration is likely to revolve around the issue of consent. The potential topics here are so varied that it is well to check with your university's research ethics guidelines if you think that your research topic may breach any ethical guidelines. An example of the sort of topic which may be involved is shown in Research in practice 3.3.

Compliance with the data protection legislation

The principles of data protection legislation such as the Data Protection Act 1998 have implications for all research projects that involve the processing and storage of personal data. It is as well to be aware of these before you reach this stage of your research project. The principles mean that anyone collecting personal information must:

Research in practice 3.3

Ethical issues in research

Magdalena was interested in the way in which the Internet had lessened the power of big organisations and put more power in the hands of individual citizens. However, she was not a politics student but an undergraduate business and management student specialising in marketing. So she had to think about how to apply her interest to her degree subject. Having talked to her friends about this, she hit upon the idea of examining customer product reviews on the website of the UK's biggest online retailer. She reasoned that this gave consumers the power to shape the marketing plans of those organisations selling their products through the online retailer. Her plan was to assess the extent to which the reviews presented either free advertising through positive reviews, or the need for action by suppliers to repair brand damage through poor reviews. Having made this assessment, she intended to approach the suppliers experiencing poor reviews to ask them what action they had taken to repair the situation created by the poor reviews.

She outlined her plan to her research supervisor who, while enthusiastic, raised the ethical question as to whether Magdalena should be using data freely supplied by individuals to the online retailer without the consent of those individuals. Magdalena had not anticipated this, so she did some thinking and library research. Her library search seemed to indicate that, in general, it was acceptable to use data that are officially, publicly archived; no password is required for archive access; the site policy does not prohibit its use and the topic is not highly sensitive. Magdalena then checked with the online retailer's website. This made clear that the individual reviewer forfeited all claim to the rights of the reviews once they had been posted online. Finally, Magdalena's supervisor checked with the university's research committee chair, who gave a favourable ethical opinion.

- fairly and lawfully process it;
- process it only for limited, specifically stated purposes;
- use the information in a way that is adequate, relevant and not excessive;
- use the information accurately;
- keep the information on file no longer than absolutely necessary;
- process the information in accordance with your legal rights;
- keep the information secure;
- never transfer the information outside the UK without adequate protection.

Source: DirectGov (2010).

What are the ethical questions you should consider at the reporting stage?

Confidentiality and anonymity at the reporting stage

Earlier in this section, we mentioned how organisational gatekeepers are often very reluctant to allow the organisation to be named in anything you write as a result of your research. You can overcome this by referring to the organisation as, for example, 'Organisation A', etc. But sometimes organisations are not so sensitive. If the research topic is not controversial in any way, then confidentiality may not be an issue, and the organisation can be named. If the organisation is particularly sensitive about being identified, you must ensure there are no 'clues' in anything you write, so you will need to conceal details such as the organisation's location, products and market if these details are likely to allow readers to guess the organisation's identity.

If the organisation is named in your report, then it is almost certain that you will need to let them read your work to understand the context within which they will be named. Indeed, even if the organisation is made anonymous, managers may still want to see the report to ensure that you have honoured your promise of confidentiality.

As well as the organisation, you have an ethical responsibility to protect individual respondents' right to anonymity in your project report, unless, of course, you have their explicit permission to do otherwise.

Your ethical obligation not to report conclusions which would be harmful to your participants

Earlier in this section, we commented on the ethical obligation you have to use the time you have been granted by the organisation's managers in a way that is of benefit to the organisation.

Another ethical consideration is the use that may be made of the conclusions you draw in your project report. Clearly, you face a dilemma if information you have been given freely by cooperative respondents is reported by you in such a way that it can be used to harm them. This is particularly the case if you have their permission to name them in your report. It may be less problematic if your respondents are made anonymous. If you feel at the beginning of the data collection stage that your results may point to conclusions that could result in actions which disadvantage your respondents, then it will be more honest to tell them this. It may mean that you are not given access to all the data you wish for, but at least you will be behaving honestly.

It may be wiser to write your research question(s) and objectives in such a way that conclusions which would be harmful to your participants are not possible.

Table 3.6 Possible ethical issues and how you may deal with them

- Use your university's, or professional body's, research ethics code of practice as a guide at all stages of your research.
- Anticipate potential ethical issues that will affect your proposed research and plan to overcome problems.
- Always get informed consent from your participants through the use of openness and honesty at all times.
- Don't make dishonest promises about the likely benefits of your research to your participants.
- Respect your participants' rights to privacy at all stages of your research project.
- Be honest and objective about your data, both in the way you collect them and their analysis.
- Consider how you will use secondary data in order to protect the identities of those who contributed to their collection or who are named within them.
- Don't forget that interviews mean that there is greater scope for ethical issues to arise.
- Don't refer to information gained from a particular participant when talking to other participants as this may allow identification of the individual with possibly harmful consequences to that individual.
- Be very careful about the conduct of covert research and consider its ethical implications.
- Make sure that you honour the promises you give to all participants regarding the confidentiality of the data obtained and their anonymity.
- Ensure you comply with all of the data protection legal requirements.
- Be aware of the complex ethical considerations in using the Internet and email to ensure high ethical standards are maintained.
- Make sure you preserve the anonymity of your participants in your project report unless you have their permission to do otherwise.

Summary

- Organisations are less likely to grant you research access if you are from outside the organisation.
- If you are from inside the organisation and wish to do research in that organisation, you will face other problems such as those concerned with status.
- There are strategies you can adopt to ease the process of gaining access to organisations to do research. These include using existing contacts; anticipating the responses of the organisation's gatekeeper; ensuring you have sufficient time to accommodate the inevitable delays; presenting a professional written request and boosting your credibility through reducing concerns of the organisation.
- Strategies for managing yourself through the research process include managing your time; maintaining your motivation and keeping in touch with individuals who can help.
- Strategies for managing your supervisor through the research process include being clear about your expectations from your supervisor and what your supervisor should expect from you.

- Managing your relationship with your university involves being clear about the standards expected from you, particularly the academic standards in the final written report.

- You must be very conscious of your ethical responsibilities while conducting your research.

- The key ethical principles you should adopt are: not causing harm to research participants; ensuring people are not coerced into participating in your research; seeking the consent of participants; maintaining high standards of honesty and preserving confidentiality.

- Awareness of your ethical responsibilities applies to all stages of the research process.

Thinking about your research process

→ Think about the data you will need to answer your research question(s) and meet your objectives. Assuming you need access to an organisation to get some or all of these data, make a list of possible obstacles to gaining access. Then, using the checklist of points to follow to increase your chances of getting access in Table 3.1, plan how these obstacles might be overcome.

→ Draft a request for research access to be sent to your research organisation's gatekeeper. Your request should focus on the purpose of your research; the demands being made of the participant and what you will do with the information you obtain.

→ Draw up a 'contract' to discuss with your supervisor, which should include the expectations you have of your supervisor and the expectations you think your supervisor should have of you.

→ Get hold of a copy of your university's code of research ethics. Note those aspects of the code that you feel are relevant to your research and list the implications for action you need to take to ensure the code is followed.

References

DirectGov (2010) *Data protection*. Available at: *www.direct.gov.uk/en/ Governmentcitizensandrights/Yourrightsandresponsibilities/DG_10031451* [Accessed 20 January 2011].

Oxford Brookes University (2010) *Ethical standards for research involving human participants: code of practice*. Available at: *www.brookes.ac.uk/res/ethics/ethics_codeofpractice.pdf* [Accessed 20 January 2011].

University of Greenwich (2009) *Dissertation Handbook*. Available at: *www.gre.ac.uk/__data/ assets/pdf_file/0006/342951/UG-Dissertation-Handbook-for-BUIL-0015-09-10.pdf* [Accessed 20 January 2011].

Chapter 4

Using secondary data

4.1 Why you should read this chapter

When you started to think about how you would obtain the data to answer your research question, you probably began by considering how to design your own questionnaire or the people you were going to interview. While this is not unusual, it is a great shame as it meant you implicitly ignored the vast amount of data that have already been collected by other people for other purposes, which could also be useful in answering your research question. In this chapter we look at using data that were originally collected for some other purpose, termed **secondary data**, for your own research. Such secondary data can be contrasted with **primary data**, which are data you collect specifically for your research project. We talk about this in Chapter 6.

Over the past decade, the number of sources of potential secondary data and the ease of getting access to them has expanded rapidly alongside the growth of the Internet. Increasingly, national governments, non-governmental agencies and other organisations have allowed open access to the data they have collected, making it available for anyone to use on the Internet. These data include the results from large-scale surveys such as national censuses as well as more specific organisational surveys and research reports. They include numeric data such as official statistics (often in the form of downloadable tables) and non-numeric data such as government reports, interviews, documents, photographs and conversations. You can also find such data in printed media such as quality newspapers as well as on associated websites. Quality newspapers contain a wealth of data on organisations and business and management issues in both numeric and non-numeric forms. You can easily obtain up-to-date statistics such as share prices. They also

---

| Definitions |

secondary data: data used for a research project that were originally collected for some other purpose.

primary data: data collected specifically for the research project being undertaken.

often report interviews with business leaders and politicians along with commentaries on the content of the actual interview.

We believe that such secondary data can provide you with fantastic research opportunities which would otherwise be outside your reach. For example, it is extremely unlikely that you will have either the time or the financial resources to design and distribute a large questionnaire survey to thousands of potential respondents to collect data for your research project. Similarly, you're unlikely to be granted access to interview the chief executive of a large multinational company. However, through using secondary data such as that already collected through an existing large-scale survey or in the form of a published interview with a chief executive, you will still be able to gain insights for your own research.

In this chapter we begin by exploring the questions, 'What forms does secondary data take?' and 'Why should you use secondary data?' We then discuss the pitfalls of using secondary data and offer advice on how to assess the suitability of secondary data for your research project. We finish with suggestions of where and how to find secondary data. However, before you decide to use secondary data for a research project, we would urge you to check your research project assessment regulations very carefully. For some research projects your university may expect you to only use secondary data. For other projects you may be required to collect primary data or use a combination of both primary and secondary data.

4.2 What forms does secondary data take?

Secondary data comes in many forms. As we hinted in the introduction, these include both **quantitative data** consisting of numbers such as tables of figures and **qualitative (non-numerical) data** types. The latter include text materials such as organisations' policies or minutes of meetings, and non-text materials such as video and voice recordings, and images such as photographs. Secondary data can include **raw data** that have not been processed, such as actual responses to questionnaires or the transcript of a television interview, as well as **compiled data** where the data presented have either been selected or summarised from the raw data. However, we've found it more useful to group the forms of secondary data using the actual source or sources of the data, in other words from where it was originally obtained. These we've divided into three groups: survey, documentary (in some form) and multiple source (Saunders et al., 2009) which are summarised along with examples in Figure 4.1.

Definitions

quantitative data: data consisting of numbers or data that have been quantified, such as tables of figures.

qualitative data: non-numerical data or data that have not been quantified, such as text materials, and non-text materials such as videos, voice recordings and images.

raw data: data for which no processing has taken place.

compiled data: data that have been processed, such as through some form of summarising or selection.

Figure 4.1 Forms of secondary data
Source: Developed from Saunders et al. (2009).

Survey secondary data

Our first form of secondary data are those which were originally obtained using some form of survey, usually a questionnaire. In recent years these data have increasingly been made freely available (particularly by public authorities) either as compiled data tables or, more frequently, as downloadable data sets which can be downloaded and opened in a spreadsheet. Not surprisingly such data sets are predominantly quantitative and so you will need to analyse them using statistics and graphs (section 7.3). These data will have already been obtained using one of three types of survey strategy:

- *Censuses* are official counts conducted by a government or on behalf of a government to meet the needs of government departments, with the aim of collecting data from every household in a country. Many governments have collected data about their entire populations for more than a hundred years through a census: for example, the UK's decennial *Census of Population*, the most recent of which took place in 2011. Because they are official, participation in censuses is usually obligatory and so the level of response is usually high. Census data are usually collected using some form of questionnaire, the precise method and questions used being clearly documented. You will find such data are widely available and easy to obtain using the Internet and in printed reports.

- *Continuous or regular surveys* are those, other than censuses, that are repeated over time but do not collect data from an entire population. They include surveys where data have been collected both on behalf of governments and by non-governmental bodies such as private organisations throughout the year, often using a questionnaire or structured interview. You will find that data collected by some of these surveys, particularly those undertaken by or for government organisations are available both using the Internet and as printed reports. However, where data have been collected for a commercial purpose, or is of a sensitive nature, they are unlikely to be so easy to obtain. For example, although many organisations conduct ongoing surveys of their customers' satisfaction as well as employee attitude surveys, it is unlikely you will find, or be allowed access to, more than a brief summary of the associated findings to support your research project.

- *Ad hoc or 'one off' surveys,* as their name suggests, are one-off surveys. Like continuous or regular surveys, these surveys do not collect data from an entire population. Ad hoc surveys are likely to be far more specific than the other forms of survey in their subject matter. They include questionnaires and structured interviews undertaken by organisations and by independent researchers such as your lecturers for a specific purpose. However, invariably because of their ad hoc nature, it is much more difficult for you to locate such surveys, let alone gain access to the associated data. At best, you're likely to be reliant on an associated summary report (Research in practice 4.1).

Research in practice 4.1

Private organisations' survey data

Jemma's research objective was to explore differences in the level of trust employees have in line managers and chief executive officers (CEOs) and possible reasons for such levels. As part of this, she needed to establish whether there was a significant difference in the extent employees trusted their immediate line managers when compared with their organisations' CEOs. When reviewing the literature, she had discovered the summary report *Index of Leadership Trust 2010*, jointly authored by the Institute of Leadership and Management and the magazine *Management Today* (2010). This research measured employees' ratings of trustworthiness of line managers and CEOs →

across UK private, public and third sector organisations. It contained the results of a survey of 5,000 UK employees. The method section explained that each of these employees had been asked to assess the relative importance of six dimensions of trust-worthiness and, subsequently, to rate their line managers and their CEOs against these six dimensions on a scale of 1 to 10. The relative importance assessments and ratings for the CEOs and line managers were then used to calculate a trust index score whose values could lie between 0 and 100. These scores were presented in the report and formed part of the secondary data for Jemma's research project:

	Chief Executive Officer	Line Manager
Integrity	68	70
Ability	69	71
Fairness	61	62
Consistency	59	65
Openness	58	66
Understanding	54	72
Overall	63	69

Source: Institute of Leadership and Management and Management Today (2010).

Jemma combined these ad hoc survey data with reports from quality newspapers about the changing levels of trust in CEOs. Using these data and research findings reported in the academic literature, she was able to argue that there were significant differences between employees' trust in their line managers and their trust in their chief executive officers, particularly with regard to understanding, openness and consistency.

Documentary secondary data

Documentary secondary data consist of both text and non-text materials that were originally collected for some other purpose. As with survey secondary data, the rapid development of the Internet means it is now relatively easy for you to access these data. You can now obtain these data easily from public bodies such as government departments and media corporations such as the BBC and Sky as well as from video sharing websites like YouTube. Indeed, although most of the video content on YouTube is uploaded by individuals, media corporations including the BBC and CBS also upload some of their material on this site. Whether or not such materials are considered secondary data is dependent upon how you use them.

When you analyse such 'documents' directly as part of your research, you're using them as secondary data However, you're more likely to be simply using them as a place to find secondary data. Let's take an example of a BBC news report uploaded on YouTube. If you want to use this to explore the media's attitude to the government and in particular how they have reported government policies, then the BBC news report on YouTube is secondary data. This is because the video clip itself is the subject of your analysis. However, if you're using this YouTube video clip as a place to find secondary data, say, a record of government figures for the number of people who are unemployed and seeking work, the video clip is only the source of your secondary data. Your secondary data are the number of people who are unemployed and seeking work. This is because you are treating the data which have been reported in the video clip as the subject of your analysis, rather that the video clip itself. In other words, the YouTube news report is simply where you found these data. It is a source in which the secondary data on government figures for the number of people who are unemployed and seeking work you're using have been recorded subsequent to their being collected. Once obtained, you can analyse these secondary data using either or both quantitative and qualitative techniques (Chapter 7).

Documentary secondary data will have originally been collected in one of two forms:

- *Text materials*. This form of secondary data consists of a wide range of textual secondary data, including those documents held as administrative and public records such as reports and minutes of meetings. Text materials also include books, journal articles and newspaper reports, as well as diaries and transcripts of interviews (including those originally broadcast on the radio and television).

- *Non-text materials*. Non-text documentary secondary data include video and voice recordings, podcasts, films, radio and television programmes, images such as photographs and drawings as well as organisations' databases.

Multiple source secondary data

Our final form of secondary data, multiple source, consists of different data sets which have been combined to form a new data set prior to your accessing the data. Such secondary data can be based entirely on documentary or on survey secondary data or a combination of the two. You almost certainly come across such data on a daily basis as tables and listings in quality newspapers such as the *Financial Times* (and associated websites). These are compiled from a variety of sources, an example that appears in the *Financial Times* and on its associated website *www.ft.com* being the FT Global 500. This provides a snapshot of the world's top 500 companies for that year, bringing together data from different sources, to record their market capitalisation, sector, turnover, net income, total assets and number of employees. These data can provide you with extremely useful background material for your project when, for example, researching a particular market sector.

Data are combined into a multiple source secondary data sets in one of two forms: either as a snapshot or longitudinally as a time-series.

Snapshot

Snapshot multiple source secondary data consist of data drawn from more than one source which relates to a single time. You will find that these data are often combined geographically in country or region reports such as the European Union's *Eurostat Yearbook 2010* (Pirto, 2010) and country profiles for member states. They include both quantitative and qualitative data. As with much European Union data these can be accessed using the Internet. Data may also be combined for a particular industry or sector to create a snapshot. The online database and analysis services company Datamonitor, for example, has produced numerous industry research reports for a range of sectors, including healthcare, automotive and technology sectors, some of which you can download using the Internet free of charge. For others, you may well find the price prohibitive, although occasionally a reference copy may be held in your university library.

Time-series

Time-series multiple source secondary data are created by combining comparable variables (we defined these in section 1.6) collected through different surveys at different times, or through the same survey that has been repeated over time. These include series of data such as number of people out of work, manufacturing output and, as illustrated in Research in practice 4.2, changes in retail prices. You can also combine different secondary data sets to create time-series data, such as changing attitudes to gender discrimination. For many research projects, this will be the only way in which you will be able to obtain longitudinal data because of the time constraints set by the research process.

4.3 Why you should use secondary data – the potential?

We've already mentioned the potential of secondary data in terms of saving you time and money by allowing you access to larger data sets than you could ever hope to collect yourself. This huge variety of large, often high-quality, data sets that are readily available at no cost is one of the major opportunities offered by secondary data; as Mark says to his students, 'If someone else has already collected suitable high-quality data which you're allowed to use, why bother to collect the data yourself?' The use of such data also allows you to show that you can find and integrate valuable material into your arguments, giving your project an air of authority. However, in addition to access to larger data sets than you could collect yourself, the authority such data sets can provide, and time and money savings, there are a number of other reasons for using secondary data in your research project. These are listed in the following sections.

Data are often already in the public domain

For many researchers a key advantage of using secondary data is that much of these data are already in the public domain. This means you do not need to negotiate access to research participants (Chapter 3) or obtain permission to use the data. Indeed,

> **Definition**
>
> **time-series**: a set of data recorded over time, usually at regular intervals.

Research in practice 4.2

UK government longitudinal data

As part of his research project examining trends in the retail industry over the past two decades, Philippe was interested in how UK retail sales had altered. Searching the UK Government's website *www.statistics.gov.uk*, he initially found a graph and commentary of retail sales for the period June 2009 to August 2010. This provided him with some useful background for his research project; he then explored the 'related links' listed on the right of the web page. One of these links 'Retail Sales Index – Statistical Bulletin' linked to another website 'Retail Sales Index Dataset' from which he was able to download an annual time-series of retail sales data for each year from 1988 onwards as a spreadsheet file. Philippe subsequently reanalysed these data.

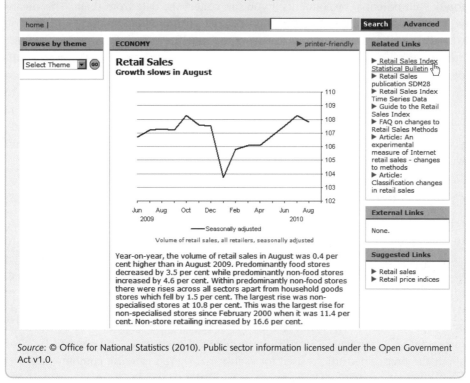

Source: © Office for National Statistics (2010). Public sector information licensed under the Open Government Act v1.0.

many public authorities include a statement explicitly granting all users permission in the form of a licence to use the data, usually providing that you acknowledge the source with an appropriate attribution statement such as 'Public sector information licensed under the Open Government Act v1.0' (Research in practice 4.2). However, for data that are not in the public domain, such as that contained in organisations' databases or administrative records, you will still need to obtain permission.

Data are often available in software compatible formats

While secondary data are available in many forms (section 4.2), they are increasingly available using the Internet in formats that can be read directly into spreadsheets and other analysis software such as SPSS (Research in practice 4.2). Some public authority data sets also allow you to select and download the precise data you require rather than downloading a large data set, much of which you will not need. This means you can focus on what data you actually need while also saving considerable time by not having to type your data into, for example, spreadsheets.

It is an unobtrusive method

Not surprisingly, as secondary data have already been collected, you will not need to ask your potential respondents if you can collect the data from them! This means you will be respecting their privacy and rights as individuals to be left alone. You will also not be taking up any of their time in either seeking permission (where data are in the public domain) or actually collecting data. Issues relating to confidentiality of participants are also reduced or avoided as the data have already been anonymised as part of the original collection process. This means you're unlikely to risk breaching your university's code of ethical practice (Chapter 3). However, if you intend to use data held by a particular organisation, such as one for which you work, you will need to ensure the anonymity of that organisation is preserved and obtain written permission to use their data for your research project.

Data sets can be readily combined

Data from a range of secondary sources, such as different surveys, can be combined to create one new data set. You will find this particularly helpful if you wish to undertake a longitudinal study. For such studies you can combine data from a series of surveys where the same questions have been asked into one data set. Indeed, for many public authority data sets, aggregation of variables or the combining of data from different surveys has already been undertaken before the data are made available (Research in practice 4.2 and 4.3). However, as you can see in Research in practice 4.3 (see page 93), to fully understand such data, you need to be clear about the precise definitions used for each variable. You can also combine data sets from different geographical areas such as countries or regions to make comparisons between countries or regions. This can be useful if, for example, you're comparing changes in manufacturing output between two countries.

Data are more open to public scrutiny

Choosing to use secondary data can provide you with access to data of very high quality. For example, the surveys conducted by professional researchers working in government departments or private survey organisations have to meet exacting scrutiny standards in terms of rigour of the research method used. These data sets are therefore likely to be larger and of better quality than any survey you can design and

Research in practice 4.3

European Union report containing clearly defined data tables

As a keen skier Jason had decided to pursue a research project on winter tourism and in particular why some resorts were more popular than others. The European Union's Eurostat website included a link to the report *Winter Tourism Trends 2009/2010* (Dimitrakopoulou, 2010) which contained two tables of data he felt could be most useful:

- Table 1: Nights spent in hotels and similar establishments
- Table 2: Net occupancy rates of bed places in hotels and similar establishments.

These tables presented data collected for the 2008–9 and 2009–10 winter seasons, highlighting massive differences in the number of nights spent in hotels and similar establishments between member states, the highest number of nights being recorded for Germany, Spain, France and Italy. The data also indicated that for some months for some member states, net occupancy rates of bed places in hotels and similar establishments were far higher than others. For example, net occupancy rates in Austria were over four times higher than those in Bulgaria in 2010.

However, before using these data, Jason needed to be sure he understood precisely what the data meant. He therefore turned to the 'concepts and definitions' section of the report. This defined hotels and similar establishments as 'Hotels, apartment hotels, motels, roadside inns, beach hotels and other similar establishments which provide hotel services including more than bed-making and cleaning of the room and sanitary facilities' (Dimitrakopoulou, 2010: 4). It also explained that the net occupancy rate of bed places was calculated for one month 'by dividing total overnight stays by the product of the bed places on offer and the number of days when the bed places are actually available for use (net of seasonal closures and other temporary closures for decoration, by police order, etc.) for the same group of establishments, multiplying the quotient by 100 to express the result as a percentage' (Dimitrakopoulou, 2010: 4).

deliver yourself. The majority of them, in addition to the data collected, provide you with information about precisely how the data were collected, including sample size and selection, response rates, a copy of the data collection instrument used (such as a questionnaire) and an assessment of how representative the data are. This information can be used by you and other users to judge the quality of the data and can, as we outline in section 4.4, also help you to assess the suitability of the secondary data for your research.

Data can provide contextual background

If you're collecting your own data, it is often useful to set the findings from your own data within a broader context. For example, if you have collected data for your research project through interviews with a particular service organisation's potential customers, you can use secondary data such as a market research report for that service to locate your findings in the broader context of that particular industry. Alternatively, you might wish to use recent government population estimates to assess the generalisability of your findings by assessing whether your participants were representative, being present in the same proportions for each age group as in that population.

4.4   What are the pitfalls of using secondary data?

As you will have gathered from reading this chapter so far, we are fans of using secondary data in research. However, our enthusiasm, and hopefully yours, needs to be tempered with realism. While secondary data offers considerable potential for many research projects, its very nature means that it is open to a variety of often valid criticisms. As our definition of secondary data indicates, it was collected for a different purpose. This means the data may not meet your research needs fully, and it may have been manipulated in some way. Data collection will not have been undertaken by you. You're therefore very unlikely to know precisely how the data were collected or the impact this will have on the actual data you are now going to use. Finally, despite public authorities making their data available free of charge, the cost of actually obtaining such data means that other organisations (such as market research companies) may ask you to pay for it. In addition, the commercial sensitivity of some data means organisations may refuse to allow you to use their data even if you're employed by them. These criticisms represent potential pitfalls about which you need to be aware and which we will now discuss in more detail.

Only meets the research needs partially

Unlike data you collect yourself to answer your research question, secondary data are unlikely to have been collected for that same purpose. This means the data may be inappropriate for your research question or, as is more likely, only partially relevant. Reasons for this are varied, but include the data not being current, problems with definitions used for particular secondary data variables, the way in which data have been aggregated not matching your needs, and because the data contain clear errors.

Most secondary data are still only available from published reports in tables (Research in practice 4.1 and 4.3). Where the tables into which data have been aggregated do not meet your needs, perhaps due to the categories used being too broad, this may cause problems. Similarly, where definitions used for the data variables (Research in practice 4.3) in these tables are different from those in other tables or are unclear, this is also likely to be problematic. Invariably, the solution here depends upon the extent to which you judge the secondary data to be inappropriate for your own research. Where the data do not meet your needs at all, your only solution is to find alternative data. However, where the data meet your needs partially, you will need to adapt and compromise. The extent to which you compromise will depend upon what other secondary data are available and whether you're able to collect appropriate data yourself. If you do decide to compromise, you will need to explain in your project report your concerns and the compromises you have made, and why you still feel able to use these secondary data. For example, if you're comparing data on satellite TV subscribers between countries in Europe, the most recent data you will be able to obtain is likely to be only available for some countries and at least a few years out of date. In your project report therefore, you need to make clear these omissions and when the data were collected, explaining it is the most recent data available.

Data are not always value-neutral

The original purpose for which secondary data were collected is invariably reflected in the way they are presented and the interpretations of those who produced them. Data are often used to support an argument or make a particular point and so may be presented in the way that best supports that argument. This is often apparent if you compare the data presented about the same topic by two newspapers with different political affiliations. When you do, you will probably see that although some of the data used are the same, different data from the same original data set will also have been quoted selectively by each newspaper to support their different interpretations.

Definitions used can also change within a single data set over time, impacting on the meanings attributed to the data. For example, between 1979 and 1994 there were nine significant changes in the calculation method used for the UK's monthly count of unemployment claimants, resulting in the overall number of claimants being reduced by 481,000 (Fenwick and Denman, 1995). Not surprisingly, the claimant count became widely criticised as a data source because it 'seriously underestimated' the number of people out of work, the definitional changes making any serious estimation of changes in the unemployment rate over time 'virtually useless' (Levitas, 1996: 46). It is therefore important that you remember secondary data may have been manipulated by people to serve their own purpose and thus assess the likely impact of this on actual data values. In particular, you should not accept any secondary data without first understanding the precise definitions used and, for longitudinal data, whether these have been altered over time.

Unlikely to know precisely how the data were collected

When using secondary data, you have no control over the quality of the data. You therefore have to infer the likely quality from other information provided. Researchers should always provide clear information about the method of data collection and the variables about which questions were asked. This should be in sufficient detail for you to infer the quality of the data in both reports and articles as well as for actual data sets. Despite this, it is unlikely as a user of secondary data that you will ever know the precise context in which each of a series of interviews took place or the nuances of the relationship between an interviewer and the participant. Whatever the level of detail provided about the method, you will obviously know less than if you had collected the data yourself. For some secondary data sets, no information will be provided about how they were collected. It is best to treat these data with caution, as often this information is not provided because it would indicate that there are problems with these data. However, this is not always the case. A number of excellent market research companies provide very limited information about their data collection methods as they consider such details commercially sensitive.

Can be costly to obtain

Where data have been collected for commercial reasons, you're likely to find access both difficult and costly. Market research reports such as those produced by the Mintel International Group, although easy to identify and locate using the Internet, are expensive to purchase. This means, if they are not available in your university library or at another library you can visit, you will be unable to access the data such reports contain.

4.5   Assessing the suitability of secondary data

When deciding whether to use secondary data, there are a number of things you need to think about. Like many students, you may think that using secondary data is easy because you do not need to design a data collection method or collect the data yourself. This is not the case. The time you have saved will be used in ensuring you have access to the data and that the data will enable you to answer your research question. Fortunately, because the data already exist, you can assess their suitability before you begin your analysis. Inevitably the suitability is dependent upon the data being relevant to your own research. However, if the data are relevant, suitability will also depend on the purpose for which the data were originally collected and the method that was used. Let's now discuss these in more detail.

The relevance of the data

The most important criterion regarding the suitability to you of any data set is that it provides you with the information you need to answer your research question. This means that the data collected, and the definitions used for the variables in which you're interested, must be a close match to the data you ideally require. Often you will find that the data available and the definitions that were used are not exactly as you would wish for in an ideal world. For example, you may ideally require data on the purchasing power of children, defined as the under-18 demographic group. If the secondary data defines this group as less than 17 years of age, these data will not match your requirements exactly. However, the world of secondary data is not perfect. You may therefore decide to use these data and state in your project report that they do not include 17-year-olds, offering an indication of the likely impact of this on your subsequent analysis. In doing this, you're offering both an assessment of the suitability of these data to answering your research question and ensuring that those who read your project report are aware of possible limitations and their likely implications.

When using secondary data, you will need to exclude those data that are not relevant to your research question. Data on the UK will need to be excluded if your research is only concerned with mainland Europe. However, in doing this you need to beware that this may result in your having insufficient data to undertake quantitative analysis, if the assumptions of statistical tests you intend to use are no longer satisfied (section 7.3). Alternatively, some secondary data sources, in particular those collected by government surveys, may not include all the data variables you would ideally require for your analysis. You will need to make an assessment as to whether these missing variables are essential to answering your research question. If they are, then the data are not suitable and you need to look elsewhere.

The original purpose of the research

Assuming that a data set contains suitable secondary data, you need to look in more detail regarding the reasons why the data were originally collected. A good place to start when trying to establish the original purpose is to look for the objectives or research questions. These are often stated in the introductory section of the research report or article containing the data (Research in practice 4.1) or, for data accessed using the Internet, in the accompanying documentation or notes. Alternatively you can look at who commissioned the research. For example: was it commissioned by a public authority such as a government department, or by a private organisation that employed a market research company or perhaps an academic to collect the data? The answers to such questions will give you an idea of the original motivations behind collecting these data and, as a consequence, your analysis and interpretation. If, for example, the research was undertaken for a trades union, it is likely that the focus of the data collected and the associated report will be different than if it was undertaken for an employer or employers' organisation. You may consider the original focus of the research too narrow in relation to your own research question, highlighting the need to either find additional secondary data or to collect your own primary data. Alternatively you may feel that the data, although useful, needs to be treated with caution because of the potential for bias caused by the original purpose of the research. Whatever you decide, it is important you explain the reasons for your decision clearly in your project report.

The method used

Assessment of the method used is concerned with how the data were collected, including the actual questions used to obtain the data. When assessing the method, you need to establish precisely how data were collected, including any personal interaction between participants and the person collecting the data. Data collected using a web-based questionnaire will inevitably constrain those who participate (and therefore the data collected) to people who have Internet access and, in most cases, an email address. Similarly, data collected using a telephone interview will restrict those who participate to people who have access to a telephone. In both examples, the people who respond may not be representative of the population as a whole or those you wish to research. You therefore need to treat the data with care. Data collected using structured interviews conducted by a professional interviewer either by telephone or face to face are likely to have followed a set and detailed script, meaning that all participants are likely to have been asked exactly the same questions in the same way. In contrast, questions asked by amateur interviewers might unwittingly have been reworded for some participants, prompting a different response indicating that perhaps the data quality is more variable. You therefore need to pay particularly careful attention to who conducted the interview.

The questions used

For data collected using interviews or questionnaires, question design is crucial. For large-scale questionnaire surveys, organisations spend a vast amount of resource in trying to ensure that the questions asked will not be misinterpreted and are neither biased nor leading. Despite this, it is still worthwhile examining carefully the questions asked to ensure that the data collected is relevant to your own research and, of equal importance, that you do not misinterpret responses in these data.

4.6   Where and how to find secondary data

The breadth of forms of secondary data we've discussed in this chapter serve also to emphasise the variety of places that you may find secondary data. Despite the Internet and availability of general search engines such as Google and Bing, finding suitable data still depends in part on your awareness of **information gateways** and potentially useful secondary data sites. It is also important to recognise that not all secondary data will be in electronic form or accessible using the Internet. Some will be paper-based and listed in your own university library's catalogue. Other paper-based secondary data will be in reports that are held only in specialist libraries or organisations. The latter of these will be the most difficult to locate and may involve you visiting a specialist library or, if permission is granted, an organisation to browse through publications or reports. Remember, even if you intend to use data you know is held by an organisation for which you work, you will still need to seek written permission to reuse these data for your research project.

For secondary data published by governments, finding the data on the Internet is relatively easy compared to other sources. Precise references to particular government sources are often given in journal articles and books, although often the associated web addresses will have changed. Some governments and government

---

Definition

information gateway: website that provides access to specific websites and pages, each site having been evaluated prior to being added to the gateway.

departments provide guides or lists of statistics they make available. However, like the majority of other secondary providers, most governments expect you to use either a combination of menus and web links or the search engines within their own information gateway to find data that are available. It is therefore important that you have a reasonable idea of the sort of data you're looking for and the search terms and phrases that are likely to have been used to describe it. Providing you then know the web address of an appropriate information gateway (Table 4.1), it is relatively straightforward to search for specific secondary data published by governments.

You will find data held by non-governmental organisations more difficult to locate. For data that are available on the Internet, there are a number of other information gateways that are of use (Table 4.1). If you find that these do not eventually produce useful data, general search engines such as Google, Bing and Yahoo can help you locate potential data sources. In some cases, these data will be held in reports that can be downloaded from sites hosted by professional and trade associations. In others, there will only be a reference to an internal report for a private company, and it will be necessary for you to request the document and seek written permission before the data can be used.

Table 4.1 Selected information gateways to secondary data sources

Name	Internet address	Content
Office for National Statistics	www.statistics.gov.uk/	UK national statistics
Direct.gov	www.direct.gov.uk/	UK government information service
Eurostat	http://epp.eurostat.ec.europa.eu/	European Union and member states statistics
Europa	http://europa.eu/	European Union information service
USA.gov	www.usa.gov/	USA government information service
University of Michigan Documents Center	www.lib.umich.edu/government-documents-center/	International agencies, government websites, statistical agencies
RBA Business information on the Internet	www.rba.co.uk/sources/	Business, statistical, company and country information

Summary

● Secondary data are data that were originally collected for some other purpose. They can be contrasted with primary data, which are collected for the specified purpose.

- Secondary data comes in many forms including both quantitative (numerical) data and qualitative (non-numerical) data. These can be grouped using the actual source or sources of the data into survey, documentary and multiple-source secondary data.

- Secondary data can provide you with fantastic research opportunities which would otherwise be outside your reach, by allowing you access to larger data sets than you could ever hope to collect yourself and by saving you time and money.

- Other reasons for you using secondary data include:
  - the data are already in the public domain, thereby often avoiding concerns about access and permission to use the data;
  - the data are often available in software-compatible formats, allowing easy analysis;
  - the data provide an unobtrusive method, respecting individuals' rights to privacy and being left alone;
  - the data can be readily combined with other data sets, allowing, for example, longitudinal studies;
  - the data can provide contextual background to a research project.

- However, using secondary data has a number of possible pitfalls, including:
  - the data may only meet your research needs partially;
  - the data may have been manipulated in some way and so not be value-neutral;
  - the definitions used within the data may have changed over time;
  - the data can be costly to obtain.

- The suitability of secondary data to your research project is dependent upon:
  - the relevance of the actual data to your research question;
  - the purpose of the original research;
  - the methods used to collect the data and the actual questions asked.

- The growth of the Internet alongside the increasing provision of open-access data by governments has increased the availability of secondary data considerably.

- Not all secondary data will be in electronic form or accessible using the Internet. Some will be paper-based and available in your own university's library. Other secondary data will be in reports that are held only in specialist libraries or organisations.

Thinking about using secondary data

→ Think about how you might use secondary data to answer you research question(s) and meet your objectives. If you consider secondary data would be helpful, or its use is a criterion for your assessment, make a list of the data variables you think you're likely to require, being as precise as possible in the terms you use.

→ Initially, use the information gateways listed in Table 4.1 to search the Internet for secondary data information sources that contain these variables. If these result in no suitable data, try using general search engines such as Google or Bing or other sources.

→ Evaluate the relevance of the data variables in each of these sources against the data variables you require (section 4.5). Remember it is unlikely that you will find secondary data that matches your requirements exactly.

→ Evaluate the suitability of each secondary data source by considering the original purpose of the research, the methods used and the questions used as outlined in section 4.5.

→ If the data are suitable, where appropriate seek and gain permission to use the data before obtaining a copy.

References

Dimitrakopoulou, C. (2010) Winter season tourism trends 2009/2010 *Eurostat Data in Focus 41/2010*. Available at: http://epp.eurostat.ec.europa.eu/cache/ITY_OFFPUB/KS-QA-10-041/EN/KS-QA-10-041-EN.PDF [Accessed 12 October 2010].

Fenwick, D. and Denman, J. (1995) The monthly unemployment count: change and consistency, *Labour Market Trends*. November 397–400.

Institute of Leadership and Management and Management Today (2010) *Index of Leadership Trust 2010*. Available at: http://www.i-l-m.com/downloads/ILM_Index_Leadership_Trust_2010_Report.pdf [Accessed 12 October 2010].

Levitas, R. (1996) *Interpreting Official Statistics*. London: Routledge.

Office for National Statistics (2010) *Economy: retail sales – growth slows in August*. Available at: http://www.statistics.gov.uk/CCI/nugget.asp?ID=256&Pos=1&ColRank=1&Rank=374 [Accessed 12 October 2010].

Pirto, J. (ed.) (2010) *Europe in Figures: Eurostat Yearbook 2010*, Luxemburg: European Union.

Saunders, M., Lewis, P. and Thornhill, A. (2009) *Research Methods for Business Students*, 5th edn, Harlow: FT Prentice Hall.

Chapter 5

Choosing your research design

5.1 Why you should read this chapter

Perhaps when you first started thinking about your research project you thought about collecting the data, maybe through a questionnaire. This is perfectly normal as it is an exciting part of any research project. But as on any journey, the research journey may take a number of routes and be accomplished by a variety of methods. The most obvious option is not always the best, whether deciding which route to use when travelling from one city to another or the method for researching the reasons why consumers prefer recording television programmes rather than watching them live. So it will not surprise you to learn that there are many options which face you when designing your research project. What will be a major factor in determining the quality of your research proposal is the extent to which you have considered these various options, and the clarity of thought which you have displayed in coming to a decision as to which design to adopt. The main part of this chapter is concerned with the different options you face when designing your research. We examine the differing purposes of projects which we call exploratory, descriptive and explanatory research. These project purposes may be thought of as the overall umbrella under which more detailed research strategies shelter. We then go on to detail these research strategies: the general ways in which to set about answering the research questions, the setting of which we examined in Chapter 1. Such strategies may be combined in a research design. Consequently we consider the research design which encompasses more than one of the research strategies: so called mixed-method designs. Our practical examination of research design and strategies ends with a consideration of the time-frame applying to the research. It may be that the research questions you have set dictate that the research be carried out over an extended period of time. Alternatively a snapshot may be perfectly acceptable.

The chapter begins and ends with two other issues which impart quality to your research design. The first of these is the subject of research philosophy. A consideration of research philosophy helps you to examine your fundamental ideas about research: those ideas that will underpin your research and which you may not have even thought about!

In other words, it starts you thinking about your thinking. The second research issue is that of research credibility. Here we address the question of whether you have taken the steps in your research design to ensure that your findings and conclusions are believable. Obviously this is crucially important. If the reader has doubts about the credibility of your research, then you may have wasted your time and that of others. In addition, you may suffer practical consequences such as failing the research module!

The research onion

At this point let us introduce our research onion. We introduced this in the first edition of our book in 1997 and it has survived the journey to the fifth edition (Saunders et al., 2009)! This serves as a route map to chart our way through this chapter. In addition, the onion is a metaphor for describing the layers of the research process. The outer layers of the onion contain thinking about research philosophies and approaches. The central layers reflect the need to consider research strategies and choices, while at the centre of the onion data collection and analysis are the central concern.

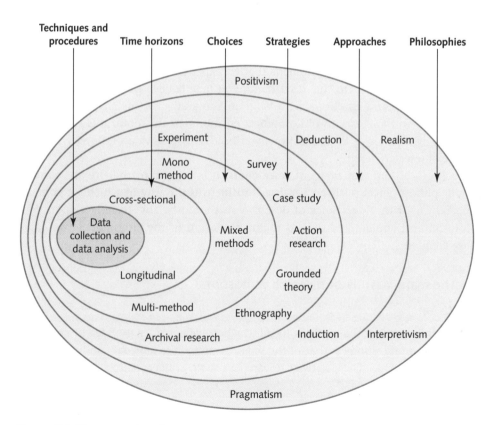

Figure 5.1 The research onion

Source: © Mark Saunders, Philip Lewis and Adrian Thornhill (2008), reproduced with permission.

5.2   The importance of research philosophy

What is meant by the term 'research philosophy'?

We all think we can explain what we mean by terms such as 'philosophy' but when we set about doing so we realise that there are many different ways of defining the term. It isn't that some are right and some wrong – it's just that the emphasis given leads to differing definitions. In the case of philosophy, it may be that we are thinking of the outlook individual human beings have on life – we refer to a system of values by which one lives. We may say that an individual has an unusual philosophy of life. Alternatively, we may think of philosophy as addressing such profound questions as 'what is the meaning of life?' raising philosophical questions concerning the reasons why we as humans exist. Neither of these strands of philosophy underpin this section. What we mean by philosophy is the critical analysis of the fundamental assumptions or beliefs held by an individual, such as yourself.

You may not realise it, but the **research philosophy** you adopt contains important assumptions about the way in which you view the world around you. These assumptions will underpin your research strategy and the data collection methods you choose as part of that strategy. For example, you may believe that the purpose of research is to describe the phenomena that we experience – to focus on what we can observe and measure. On the other hand, you may believe that individual values, beliefs, feelings and emotions are a valid area to study. In this chapter we attach some labels to these various philosophical positions. At this point it is sufficient to say that, whichever of these positions you hold, it will have an influence on your choice of research design.

As business and management researchers, it is important that we are mindful of our philosophical position because it influences the way in which we conduct research. As with your choice of design, you should be able to reflect upon your philosophical choices and defend them in relation to the alternatives you could have adopted.

The main strands of research philosophy

Positivism

A convenient image that springs to mind when we consider the idea of **positivism** as a research philosophy is that of the scientist in a white lab coat conducting a scientific experiment. The positivist researcher's main concern is to study observable

---

Definitions

research philosophy: overall term that relates to the development of knowledge and the nature of that knowledge in relation to research.

positivism: a research philosophy similar to those used in the physical and natural sciences. Highly structured methods are employed to facilitate replication, resulting in law-like generalisations.

and measurable variables in certain controllable conditions and to describe the reaction of these variables to treatment applied by the researcher. The emphasis is on predicting the outcomes of the research in order that these variables may be controlled in the future. At the root of the positivist research philosophy is the law of cause and effect. Applying treatment A to variable B will lead to result C, with A being the cause and C the effect. Scientific method suggests that the principle of cause and effect means that we can propose theories which we can test. As a result of our inquiry, we may find that the proposed theory is not confirmed by the findings. Consequently we need to revise our theory to better predict reality. In this sense the positivist researcher pursues a cycle of attempts at establishing cause and effect until future events may be accurately predicted.

You may have come across the study of Pavlov's dogs. Pavlov (1927) conducted research on the digestive system of dogs. He noticed that, rather than simply salivating in the presence of meat powder, the dogs began to salivate in the presence of the lab technician who usually gave them their food. Following this observation, Pavlov predicted that if a particular stimulus in the dog's environment was evident when the dog was given meat powder then this stimulus would become associated with food and cause salivation on its own. Subsequently Pavlov designed an experiment where he used a metronome to signal to the dogs the readiness of their food. Repetition of the signal prompted the dogs to salivate in response to the metronome.

You may think that this is a long way from business and management research. But this is not necessarily so. The commercial eBay seller may be interested in the levels of sales to consumers when the balance of shipping fee to product price is adjusted. Free shipping and a higher product price may generate more sales revenue than charged shipping and a lower product price. This balance can be manipulated and the results tracked, leading to a predictive theory of shipping cost/product price balance.

Realism

Like positivism, **realism** relates to scientific inquiry. The basis of realism is that what our senses show us as reality is the truth; therefore, objects have an existence independent of the human mind. Realism holds that there is a reality quite independent of the mind. The opposite of realism is idealism – the theory that only the mind and its contents exist. Let us make the nature of realism clearer by contrasting two forms of realism. The first type of realism is direct realism. Direct realism states that what you see is what you get: that what we experience through our senses is an accurate representation of the world. The second kind of realism is called critical realism. Critical realists argue that what we experience are sensations, the images of the things in the real world, not the things directly. Critical realism advocates

Definition
realism: a research philosophy which stresses that objects exist independently of our knowledge of their existence.

that experiencing the world is in two steps. First, there is the object itself and the sensations conveyed by the object. Second, there is the subjective processing that is present in our minds after that sensation meets our senses. The direct realism position is that the first step is sufficient.

Once again we can hear you saying 'What has all this to do with business and management research?' The answer is that the distinction between direct and critical realism is important for much business and management research. We are often concerned with first describing complex business situations in order to understand what is going on. So we need to study not only what is immediately apparent, but also what lies behind what is immediately apparent. We need to understand the deeper structures and relations that are not directly observable but lie beneath the surface of social reality. Let's say you had to study a major organisational problem such as that experienced by British Airways when Heathrow Terminal 5 opened in 2008. In order to arrive at a conclusion for the causes of organisational problems from which others may learn, you would need to understand a good deal about, for example, the relationships between managers, between employees and managers, the attitude of employees to change, the receptiveness of employees to training and the ability of managers to impart such training. All of this material would not be immediately apparent to the researcher but would necessitate understanding the structures and relationships that were beneath the surface.

Interpretivism

The concern with greater organisational complexity in the critical realist perspective points the way towards **interpretivism**. Interpretivism relates to the study of social phenomena in their natural environment. So a wish to understand what is going on in a work organisation, for example, would mean the necessity to conduct research in that organisation among its 'social actors'. The term 'social actors' suggests the metaphor of the theatre. As humans we play a part on the stage of social life. Movie actors play a part which they interpret in a particular way (it may be their own or that of the director) and play their parts in accordance with this interpretation. Similarly, as social actors we interpret our everyday social roles in accordance with the meaning we give to these roles. The way in which you quickly have to move from the role of student to that of employee means a process of social adaptation on your part, which reflects your interpretation of which behaviours are appropriate for this new role. If we interpret the roles which we play according to our definition of what is appropriate, then we also interpret the social roles of others in accordance with our definition. This suggests that, as researchers, our values play a part in the research process. This is inevitable. It would be naive to think that our own personal values play no part in our research. Even the choice of research topic, as well as the

> **Definition**
>
> **interpretivism**: a research philosophy which advocates the necessity to understand differences between humans in their role as social actors.

decision about the research methods to adopt, is a reflection of our values. Clearly, it is something of which the skilled researcher needs to be wary. Understanding the social world of our research subjects from their point of view is the key here.

For business and management research, the interpretivist perspective is very relevant, particularly in such fields as organisational behaviour, marketing and human resource management. Not only are business situations complex, but they are also unique. They represent a particular set of circumstances and individuals coming together at a specific time to create a unique social phenomenon.

Pragmatism

Although our choice of research methods may be a reflection of our values, it would be wrong to think that the differing philosophies we have outlined above should be thought of as a 'shopping list' from which to choose a philosophy. In practice, you are far more likely to be guided by what is possible. This is the **pragmatic** position. It suggests that the most important determinants of the research philosophy you adopt are your research question(s) and objectives.

The pragmatist would argue that it is quite possible to work with methods that indicate, for example, a positivist approach, say a quantitative questionnaire, alongside a more interpretivist stance, through studying the interaction between key participants at meetings. This echoes an argument which runs through this book: that mixing methods, both qualitative and quantitative, are possible, and may be highly appropriate, within one study.

> **Definition**
>
> **pragmatism**: a research philosophy which argues that the most important determinant of the research philosophy adopted are the research question(s) and objectives.

5.3 Differing approaches to research: deduction and induction

We now move to the next layer of the onion to examine two different approaches to the conduct of research: deduction and induction. Having thought about your philosophical position on research, it's now time to think again about the topic of theory which we mentioned in Chapter 1. You will remember that theory is broadly defined as an explanation of the relationship between two or more concepts or variables. The role of theory will loom large in your study, as all projects will need to link to theory in some way. The most likely link will be to an existing theory explained in the literature relevant to your research topic. For example, you may wish to explore the theory in a different context, say, in your own employing organisation. The purpose will be to explore the extent to which the theory applies, or suggest a modification to the theory based on your own findings and conclusions.

The distinction between deduction and induction takes us back a stage to the development of the theory which you may be using from the literature. Although, as we said, you may be using existing theory, it is useful to see how that theory may have been developed.

Deduction: clarifying theory at the beginning of the study

Deduction is a research approach which involves the testing of a theoretical proposition by using a research strategy designed to perform this test. There are five sequential stages in deductive research. These are:

1 defining research questions from the general theory that exists;

2 operationalising these questions (i.e. specifying the way in which the questions may be answered);

3 seeking answers to the questions defined in stage 1;

4 analysing the results of the inquiry to determine whether it supports the theory or suggests the need for its modification;

5 confirming the initial general theory or modifying it in the light of the findings. (In the event of step 5 resulting in a modified theory, the five sequential stages are repeated to test the new theory.)

The key characteristics of deduction are, first, to explain causal relationships between variables. For example, you may wish to establish the reasons for too many errors being made by call centre operatives in giving information to customers. Having studied the error patterns, it seems to you that there may be a relationship between the amount of errors and the length of the initial training programme received by operatives. You define your research questions (stage 1) which explore the proposition that those operatives receiving the shorter version of the initial training programme are more error-prone than those who undergo the longer version. Secondly, you need to operationalise the relevant concepts (stage 2). These concepts need to be expressed in a way that enables facts to be established. In the example above the two key concepts are error levels and training-programme length. The second concept may be more straightforward than the first. For example, you would need to be clear about what constitutes an error and distinguish between the seriousness of errors. The third characteristic of deduction is the need to collect and analyse data to answer the research questions (stages 3 and 4), and the fourth is the use of a clearly structured methodology to facilitate replication. This is important to achieve reliability, as we see later in this chapter.

| Definition |

deduction: a research approach which involves the testing of a theoretical proposition by using a research strategy specifically designed for the purpose of its testing.

Induction: conducting and developing theory from the explanations that arise

If deduction has a 'top down' flavour, then **induction** suggests a 'bottom up' approach to theory development. Inductive reasoning moves from specific observations to broader generalisations and theories. With inductive reasoning, we begin with specific observations and measures, begin to observe patterns and repeated occurrences of phenomena and formulate some speculative hypotheses which can be investigated. All this is with a view to developing some general conclusions or theories.

Using the inductive approach, you need to gain an understanding of the meanings humans attach to events. Let's consider again the example of the error-prone call centre operatives. An important impression you would want to gain is whether the operatives actually like their jobs. The literature on call centres you have reviewed suggests that it is possible to distinguish between those jobs that are intrinsically interesting and those that are simply dead boring! Some jobs may be more demanding and stressful than others. Some operatives may simply not be cut out for this type of work. Already you can see that alternative explanations are beginning to form for the differential levels of operative errors. It may be that the explanation is more complex than the amount of training that the operatives receive.

With induction, the emphasis is on a close understanding of the research context. We raised the point earlier about the necessity to conduct research in more than one call centre in the ability to generalise a theory across all call centres. Similarly, from an inductive stance we may want to get a clearer picture of the experience of working in different call centres that have different environmental characteristics.

Induction possesses a more flexible structure to permit changes of research emphasis as the research progresses. It may be that stress in the call centre operatives you are studying becomes a major issue in your data collection. This may present itself as an alternative explanation for high error levels to that suggested by insufficient training. In that case, it may be sensible to build much more attention to stress experience into your research questions.

Definition

induction: a research approach which involves the development of theory as a result of analysing data already collected.

Combining research approaches

It would be quite wrong to think that you have to make a choice between deduction and induction. We think that it is often a good idea to combine deduction and induction within the same piece of research. It would be quite usual, for example, to start with an exploratory study in order to arrive at a tentative theory inductively before testing that theory in a deductive piece of quantitative work. In our example of error-prone call centre operatives, a few focus groups may give some clear indications as to the reason for some staff making more errors than others. These indications may then form the basis for questionnaire design and administration. We cover mixed-methods research later in the chapter.

The world is rarely as simple as offering a straight choice between two research approaches. The example in Research in practice 5.1 (on page 112) below comes nearest to being described as a piece of inductive research which uses a quantitative, scientific method! We say inductive, because it may be used as a forerunner to some positivist work designed to test a theory emerging from the wealth of data generated by this study.

5.4   Differing types of studies: exploratory, descriptive and explanatory studies

Exploratory studies

Exploratory research is about discovering general information about a topic that is not understood clearly by the researcher. This lends itself particularly well to new phenomena where you may not be prepared to launch into a piece of full-scale research but want to gain some insights that will inform your research design. The marketeer, for example, may be aware that there is a change in the consumers' preference away from organic food after the initial enthusiasm for such food. But the marketeer may not fully appreciate what form that preference is taking and why the phenomenon is happening. An **exploratory study** may well provide tentative answers to these initial questions, which need to be followed up with more detailed research to provide more dependable answers.

The most usual ways of conducting exploratory research are:

● searching the academic literature;
● interviewing 'experts' in the subject;
● conducting interviews.

The Internet is now particularly useful for doing some basic literature search work in an exploratory study. This may be useful in pointing you towards relevant academic journal articles to be found on academic journal databases in your library. Examples of these are Emerald and Business Service Complete. Of course, non-academic articles from the Internet, such as those in newspapers or produced by commercial enterprises, should not be thought of as an alternative to academic articles.

As well as literature searching, exploratory studies are well suited to qualitative methods such as interviewing. For example, informal discussions with consumers,

---

Definition
exploratory study: research that aims to seek new insights, ask new questions and to assess topics in a new light.

organic food growers and supermarket executives may provide useful insights into changing preferences for organic food. Consumer focus groups are a well-known method of establishing consumer views which may be valuable as a piece of exploratory research. Case studies of families' food consumption may be helpful in an explanatory study, as may small-scale pilot studies.

Although the methods used in exploratory research indicate a good deal of flexibility, they do not mean absence of direction to the enquiry. It means that the focus is initially broad and becomes progressively narrower as the research progresses.

While exploratory research provides insights into, and a fuller understanding of, an issue or situation, definitive conclusions should only be drawn with extreme caution. But it is very valuable in helping you to decide the best research design, data collection method and selection of subjects. Of course, it may point to the fact that the issue which you thought was of great importance is in fact a non-issue! In that case, you will have saved yourself going up a blind alley and delivering a meaningless piece of research!

Descriptive studies

You may have received comments on your assessed assignments from lecturers which say something like, 'It's good as far as it goes but it tends to be too descriptive'. This means that they wanted you to analyse and explain what was going on with a given topic. The question 'Why did the situation occur?' is the question to which they wanted the answer, not the answer you supplied which was likely to have been a description of the situation. However good your description, the point remains that describing a phenomenon is much easier than explaining why it occurred. That said, descriptive research certainly has an important role to play, often as the forerunner of explanatory research.

Descriptive study or research seeks to describe accurately persons, events or situations. It is appropriate for asking such questions as:

- What is the employee absentee rate in particular departments?
- What is the level of employee turnover in those same departments?
- What is the average length of service for those employees who are most frequently absent?

Look again at the three questions above. You will note that they each require quantitative responses. They each involve the collection of measurable, quantifiable data. So, the methods typically used in descriptive research are:

| Definition |

descriptive study: research designed to produce an accurate representation of persons, events or situations.

- questionnaire surveys;
- sampling;
- interviews;
- reanalysis of secondary data.

Descriptive research should be thought of as a means to an end rather than an end in itself. This means that if your research project utilises description, it is likely to be a forerunner to explanation. However, descriptive research can tell us a lot about the world around us, which is very valuable in its own right, as the example in Research in practice 5.1 indicates.

Research in practice 5.1

A descriptive study of children's Internet usage

The usage of the Internet among children is often framed in terms of the threats that exist to their well-being. Yet this is a topic of great importance to marketeers interested in the shift of advertising from the traditional media to the Web, those directly concerned with the marketing of goods and services to children or, more generally, the adult consumers of tomorrow.

Ofcom, the UK communications regulator, published a report in October 2009 which charted Internet usage among the UK's 5–15 age group. It is a quantitative survey that involved 1,044 in-home interviews with parents and children aged 5–15 from April to May 2009. Among the findings are the following:

- There was an increase in the number of children aged 5–7 using the Internet at home.
- Internet take-up has increased in lower socio-economic group households since 2008, but it is still lower than for other socio-economic groups.
- One in six children aged 8–11, and one-third of 12–15-year-olds have Internet access in their bedrooms.
- One in twenty 5–7s, one in eight 8–11s and one-quarter of 12–15s watch TV or film content via UK TV broadcasters' websites.
- The majority of parents say they trust their child to use the Internet safely. Approximately one-half of parents whose child uses the Internet at home say they use Internet controls (e.g. filtering software).
- Approximately four out of ten homes have parental rules for TV, the Internet and games. This is particularly the case for 5–11s.
- Two-thirds of children aged 12–15 make some kind of check when visiting new websites. However one-quarter do not make any checks.
- One in three children think that search engines list the most truthful sites highest in the list shown.

● Two-thirds of 12–15s with Internet access at home say they have set up a social
networking site profile. One in five of 8–11s say they have set up such a profile.

Source: OFCOM (2009) *UK Children's Media Literacy*.

Although the Ofcom research in Research in Practice 5.1 tells us a lot about children's Internet usage, it does not tell us why children prefer using the Internet rather
than watching TV. Is it because it is an interactive medium rather than, as with TV, a
more passive one? What is the attraction of watching movies from TV broadcasters'
websites rather than on TV? The fact that we do not know the answers to these questions suggests the need for a follow-up explanatory study.

Explanatory studies

Explanatory studies takes descriptive research a stage further by looking for an explanation behind a particular occurrence through the discovery of causal relationships
between key variables. As we saw in Research in practice 5.1, the question moves
from 'how frequently do children use the Internet?' to 'why do they prefer the
Internet to TV?'

The methods typically used in explanatory research are:

● case studies;
● observation;
● historical analysis;
● attitude surveys;
● statistical surveys.

Explanatory research can be quantitative or qualitative. This depends to a large
extent on the focus of the research. The focus may be on exploring factors, such as
frequency of Internet usage. If this is the case, quantitative values can be attached
to the variables and they can be subjected to statistical tests such as correlation in
order to get a clearer view of the relationship. Alternatively, the focus may be on
exploring factors such as the reasons why Internet usage varies between the under-
30s and the over-60s. Much of the explanation may centre upon differing attitudes
or beliefs which may be difficult to quantify. Even if your feeling is that qualitative
research may be appropriate for your research questions and objectives, most qualitative research will benefit at some stage from an element of quantitative processing
of data.

Definition

explanatory study: research that focuses on studying a situation or a problem in order to explain
the relationships between variables.

5.5   Differing strategies

Now we concentrate on the research strategies you may use. Let's make it clear at the beginning of this section that the label that is attached to a particular strategy is relatively unimportant. What is important is that the strategy you choose will enable you to answer your particular research question(s) and meet your research objectives. Nonetheless the labels are a useful way of categorising the different strategies available to you.

Each of the strategies can be used for exploratory, descriptive and explanatory research. Some of these more clearly belong more closely to the deductive approach, others to the inductive approach. But, as with the attachment of labels, it is not helpful to allocate strategies to one approach or the other. We emphasise that your research strategy will be guided by your research question(s) and objectives as well as the extent of your existing knowledge, the amount of time and other resources you have available, as well as your own philosophical leanings. Finally, we must point out that these strategies are not mutually exclusive. So, for example, a case study may include a survey and archival research.

The order in which we explain the strategies below is simply that which they appear in the onion (Figure 5.1). It does not imply that those explained earlier are any more important than those below them in the list.

Experiment

The purpose of an **experiment** is to study causal links between variables; to establish whether a change in one independent variable (e.g. the running of a sales promotion) produces a change in another dependent variable (e.g. the level of sales). The essential components of an experiment are the following:

1 Manipulating the independent variable. To pursue our sales promotion example, the sales promotion may be manipulated by differentiating the offer, altering the time period over which it runs or changing the level of advertising.

2 Controlling the experiment by holding all other variables, except the dependent variable, constant. Therefore, the sales experiment would be held at the same time of year, in the same (or similar) location.

3 Observing the effect of the manipulation of the independent variable on the dependent variable.

4 Predicting the events that will occur in the experimental setting.

> **Definition**
>
> **experiment**: a research strategy that involves the definition of a theoretical hypothesis; the selection of samples of individuals from known populations; the allocation of samples to different experimental conditions; the introduction of planned change on one or more of the variables; and measurement on a small number of variables and control of other variables.

The steps in the experiment are the following:

1 Identify and define the issue that is to be studied (e.g. the effect upon sales of promotions).

2 Formulate research hypotheses (e.g. the sales revenue of yogurt will double when a 'Buy 2 get 1 free' offer is run).

3 Design the experiment (by:

    (a) selecting the relevant product and sales promotion;

    (b) identifying and controlling the factors which may affect the outcomes (e.g. time, location);

    (c) choosing the way in which the outcomes will be measured;

    (d) conducting a pilot study to test the effectiveness of the experiment and predict any problems which may be overcome by adjusting the experiment design.)

4 Run the experiment and collect the data.

5 Assemble the data and apply relevant tests to ensure statistical significance of the findings.

Although our sales promotion example is a situation where an experimental strategy may apply in business, the strategy is not applicable to many business and management research questions. This may be for a number of practical reasons. For example, it may be seen as unfair to apply certain disadvantageous working conditions to one group of employees and not the other. Moreover, it would be unethical if the disadvantaged employees were not told of the experiment and the way it would involve them. Seeking volunteers may be problematic, as some people are unwilling to participate in experiments and so those who volunteer may not be representative of the population you wish to study. This is why the experiment strategy is often used only on captive populations such as university students! In addition, if the results are to be valid, then an experiment that involves a large group of subjects may be necessary with all this implies in terms of cost and complexity.

Survey

When you mention the term 'research' to most people, it is often the **survey** method which springs most readily to mind. Few days pass without the news reporting the results of a new survey that indicates a snapshot of social and economic life. Indeed, the notion of the researcher selecting a sample of respondents from a population and administering a standardised questionnaire is the image with which you may be most familiar. The survey strategy is popular in business and management research. And because it is so widespread, people find it easy to understand and place a good

---

| Definition |

survey: a research strategy which involves the structured collection of data from a sizeable population. Data collection may take the form of questionnaires, structured observation and structured interviews.

deal of faith in the results which flow from surveys. Surveys are particularly suitable for asking questions such as: 'who?' 'what?' 'where?' 'how much?' and 'how many?' These types of question make them useful for exploratory and descriptive research. One of the reasons surveys are so popular is that they allow the collection of data about the same things from a large number of people in a cost-effective manner. This is because sampling (see Chapter 6) makes it possible to generate findings that are representative of the whole population at a lower cost than collecting the data for the whole population.

The questionnaire is usually a written document with a set of standardised questions. The questionnaire may be completed by the respondent or an interviewer in a face-to-face situation. Alternatively, it may be completed online or by telephone. Standardised questions make it possible to easily compare responses across different locations or time-frames.

It would be wrong to think that administering a questionnaire is quick and easy. Ensuring that your sample is representative, designing and piloting your data collection instrument and trying to ensure a good response rate are all very time-consuming. So is the analysis of the data, even though there are several software packages to help you. But from a practical viewpoint the survey strategy does offer you certain advantages. This comes largely from the feeling of being in control of the process. With more qualitative strategies, for example interviewing, you are often dependent upon others for their time. The fact that you will be more in control of your time schedule in the survey strategy makes it an attractive proposition for students who usually have a set period of time, often an academic year, to complete a piece of research.

One of the drawbacks of the survey is that the data collected are unlikely to be as detailed as those collected by other research strategies. Clearly, it is not advisable to ask too many questions, so comprehensiveness is bound to be limited. We have all switched off when faced with the fourth page of a questionnaire, not a reaction which will lead to credible research results! But perhaps the biggest disadvantage with the questionnaire method is the attraction that it seems an easy option. Be warned: designing a questionnaire is very easy; designing a good one is enormously difficult.

It would be misleading if we did not mention that the survey strategy is also associated with structured observation and structured interviews (see Chapter 6), both of which are based on the principle of standardisation.

Case study

We noted above that the survey method is suitable for asking questions such as 'who?' 'what?' 'where?' 'how much?' and 'how many?' In contrast, the **case study** strategy is more appropriate for asking the question 'why?' (although the questions

---

Definition

case study: a research strategy which involves the investigation of a particular contemporary topic within its real-life context, using multiple sources of evidence.

'what?' and 'how?' are also relevant). Consequently the case study strategy is most often used in exploratory and explanatory research.

Case studies are particularly good at enabling the researcher to get a detailed understanding of the context of the research and the activity taking place within that context. So, if you are concerned with understanding why managers make decisions in certain ways rather than an analysis of the decisions that are made, who makes them, the frequency of decisions and their perceived importance, the case study may be for you. The key word, of course, is 'context'. Often the key to explaining social phenomena is context. For example, managerial decisions taken in an environment where senior managers are highly supportive of their managers and reasonably tolerant of their failure are likely to be much more adventurous than in an unsupportive climate.

Data collection techniques used in a case study may be varied and include a combination of interviews, observation and documentary analysis as well as questionnaires. Case studies often use a variety of methods, so you are likely to need to triangulate multiple sources of data, a principle which we explain in the last section of this chapter.

The question arises as to whether a single case or a number of cases is most suitable for your research. As with many other decisions related to strategy, this is likely to be governed by what is ideal as a strategy for answering your research questions and what is possible in terms of practical considerations such as access and resources. Like many students, you may choose the organisation in which you work. This is often going to be a practical option. Yet there are likely to be limitations on the extent to which you can call your organisation typical of all similar organisations. For this reason, a case study strategy can also incorporate more than one case. You may choose to use more than one case if you need to generalise from your findings.

Some criticise the case study strategy because they feel that one case, or even a small number of cases, is no basis for placing faith in the findings. They also argue that close exposure to the study of the case biases the findings. For this reason they dismiss case study research as useful only as an exploratory tool. But a well-designed and skilfully executed study of real-life issues will yield insights not possible in more descriptive strategies.

Action research

In one application of the case study strategy, you may be working in one organisation in order to gain insights into an aspect of that organisation's life from which you may draw conclusions. Similarly, with **action research** you may be working in one organisation. But with the case study, the likelihood is that you are 'on the outside looking in' (although you may be a part of that organisation). With action research, the emphasis is on you taking an involved role as a participant in planning

---

| Definition |

action research: research strategy concerned with the management of a change and involving close collaboration between practitioners and researchers.

and implementing change; you are very much the insider. Here you are conducting experiments and acting upon them by making changes and observing the results. Your role is decidedly active rather than passive.

There are four common themes within action research which make its practical application, and value, much clearer. These are listed below.

1 As noted above, the purpose of the research is to be part of and study research in action rather than to conduct research about action. A typical emphasis for the research may be the change process in an organisation.

2 The joint working of organisational members, for example managers and other key workers, and researchers in the action research project. The researchers may be pursuing academic research or they may be consultants from within or outside the organisation. So the researcher is part of the organisation and the change process. This contrasts with more normal research or consultancy where participants are objects of study.

3 The cyclical nature of the process of action research which consists of diagnosing, planning, taking action and evaluating (see Figure 5.2). The diagnostic stage will begin with the establishment of a clear project purpose and continue with fact finding and analysis on the situation under study. The core of the cycle involves the planning, implementation and evaluation of the changes themselves.

4 The final stage in the cycle is the key one if you are using the action research strategy as an academic project. This is the evaluative stage where you will draw from the research the lessons which may be learned. These lessons may have a

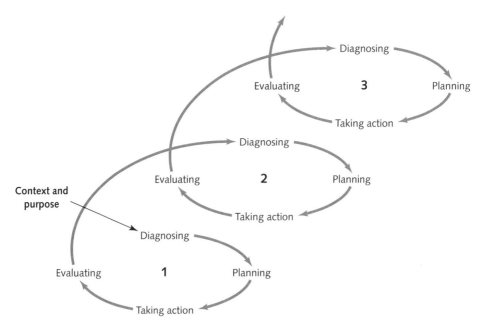

Figure 5.2 The action research spiral

Source: © Saunders et al. (2009), reproduced with permission.

practical dimension (for example, the pitfalls that managers should avoid when introducing a new pay system) or a more theoretical perspective (say, the development of a model of employee behaviours in the pay change process). It is clear here that action research should have implications beyond the immediate project. It must have a wider application.

You will see that action research differs from other research strategies because it is concerned with action, in particular the promotion of organisational change. So it is particularly useful for 'how' questions. A project using action research promises excellent insights into organisational change processes as well as an absorbing project report which, because few student projects use this strategy, will have a distinct novelty value! You may ask why few students pursue action research. The answer is that it is demanding both in terms of hours that need to be devoted to a project, and the length of time needed to progress the action research cycle. It also demands a high level of researcher skill and maturity.

Grounded theory

Grounded theory, usually associated with Corbin and Strauss (2008), belongs principally to the inductive approach to research because you develop theory from data generated by a series of observations or interviews. However, there is an element of deduction (remember – theory to data) in this strategy.

Unlike the deductive approach, data collection starts without the formation of your initial theory, as you would in a deductive approach. Theory is developed from data generated by a series of observations, discussions and interviews. The element of deduction is introduced when these data lead to the generation of predictions which are then tested in further observations. These further observations may confirm, or otherwise, the predictions. A continual process of testing leads to the development of theory.

This all becomes a bit clearer with a practical explanation of how grounded theory works, as you will see in the Research in practice 5.2 example (on page 120).

Definitions

grounded theory: a research strategy in which theory is developed from data generated by a series of observations or interviews principally involving an inductive approach.

ethnography: a research strategy that focuses on describing and interpreting the social world through first-hand field study.

Ethnography

Ethnography is concerned with understanding another way of life from the perspective of those pursuing that way of life. Its traditional roots are in the anthropological study of primitive societies. The key concern is learning from people rather than studying them.

Research in practice 5.2

The use of grounded theory in a study of teamwork

Richard was a part-time student. His research project was concerned with discovering the reasons why some teams in retail stores worked effectively and some did not. His job was with a major retail store chain where he was a store trainer; therefore he had access to a number of stores. His job meant that he worked in each store for a week at a time.

When in stores, Richard was very careful to keep notes of all the aspects of team behaviour he observed. This included the ways in which team members interacted with one another, the extent to which they helped each other and any negative indications of team behaviour, such as members criticising others behind their backs. He also held informal interviews with team members and had informal conversations about team performance. (He had briefed all store workers about the topic of his research.)

At the end of each day Richard noted any common themes which were emerging. A key theme seemed to be the degree to which team members trusted one another. This led Richard to the literature on trust in organisations, which enabled him to further develop his thinking about the project and ask what more he may look for in his data collection. In particular, Richard became aware that trust was enhanced when team members had a high regard for each others' job expertise.

Gradually the focus of Richard's observations, interviews and conversations were geared towards the topic of trust. This enabled him to gather a wealth of relevant data which, when related to the literature on trust in organisations, led him to an interesting set of theoretical conclusions, which were reinforced by relevant literature.

Such studies in business research are unusual. But one stands out as one of the most famous of the late twentieth century. It was published in a book called *Working for Ford* by Huw Beynon (1973). Beynon spent much of 1967 in Ford's Halewood plant on Merseyside talking to workers, trade union officials and management. The picture Beynon paints of life on the production line stems largely from the words of the workers themselves: an approach which really brings Beynon's writing to life. Beynon concluded that the work was dull and boring and the whole experience pretty bleak. In his view Ford was still then run on the principles established by its founder, Henry Ford – principles which emphasised that man is subservient to the machine.

Ethnography is obviously a research strategy that is very time-consuming since it takes place over an extended time period. So, it tends not to be used extensively in business research. Indeed, Beynon started his research in the pursuit of a PhD, but had to abandon the plan simply because he had so much data. He decided to write a book instead.

Although ethnography is time-consuming, the grounded theory example in Research in practice 5.2 has some similarities with ethnography. If you are conducting research similar to that in this example, you may wish to look at the ethnographic strategy in more detail.

Archival research

Archival research uses administrative records and documents as the principal source of data. These may, for example, be minutes of meetings, memos or emails containing information or instructions, accounts, contracts or letters. For example, you may wish to study the way in which key messages about company performance are communicated to staff.

Such research concentrates on past events and may allow changes over time to be charted. But the extent to which you use the archival strategy will depend on the availability of key documents. Of course, even if relevant documents exist, and you are allowed access to them, they may not meet your precise research needs.

Archival research may not be appropriate for many business research projects as the main research strategy. But it may play a useful supporting role at some stage in many projects if you wish to supplement other data collection methods.

> **Definition**
>
> **archival research**: a research strategy which analyses administrative records and documents as the principal source of data.

Combining research strategies

We made the point earlier that it is perfectly possible to combine research approaches and strategies within the same study. You may wish to do some preparatory work in an exploratory phase before you firm up your research questions and objectives. This may involve informal discussion or interviews with key personnel. This could be supplemented with an element of scanning of organisational documentation. The exploratory strategy could then be continued with survey work using both questionnaire and structured interviews. A final stage may utilise the explanatory strategy by attempting to get greater meaning to the exploratory work through, for example, a case study approach. The important point to bear in mind is that different strategies may work at different stages in the study, depending, of course, on their suitability to answer your research questions and objectives.

Mixed-methods designs

Mixing approaches and strategies in the pursuit of an answer to your research questions and objectives will usually involve the use of a mixture of research methods. The section immediately above on combining research strategies suggests that certain approaches and strategies are more suited to particular stages of the research than others. In the same way, using a variety of data collection methods may present advantages for the following four reasons.

Reason 1: Some data collection methods are more suited to particular tasks than others

If you wish to establish the extent to which children use the Internet, this can be done by a questionnaire survey to a sample of children; if you want to understand why some teams work better than others, it is better to use qualitative discussions and interviews. Those two examples are, of course, separate projects. But the same argument applies when you are thinking about one project. Your research objectives may be: 'To what extent do Internet-based suppliers use a multiplicity of carriers for shipping goods?' and 'What are the reasons for the use of multiple carriers?' The first question may collect data through an Internet-based scan by you of leading supplier websites, followed by a questionnaire of a sample of suppliers. You may follow this up with some interviews with the distribution managers of suppliers in order to get a grasp of the reasons for multiple-carrier usage. The different methods are then integrated into a single research design.

Reason 2: Focusing on different aspects of the study

It may well be that different data collection methods may be better at different research tasks within the study. So you may want to gain an overall view about the way in which companies outsource aspects of their business from studying secondary sources, or even from a quantitative survey. This will probably not give you a sufficient grasp of the reasons why some companies are more likely to be more enthusiastic about outsourcing than others. Nor will it tell you why some functions are greater candidates for outsourcing than others. This may need some interviews with key executives.

Reason 3: Corroborating your research findings within a study using two or more independent sources of data or data collection methods

When you have finished this chapter, we hope you will have a very clear understanding of the importance of establishing the credibility of your research findings. This topic is dealt with in the chapter's final section. One way you can do this is through the process of triangulation. Triangulation is the use of two or more independent sources of data or data collection methods within one study in order to help ensure that the data are telling you what you think they are telling you. In an ideal world, a questionnaire, say, will yield highly credible data, particularly if the guidelines to effective survey design and implementation are followed. But if you have triangulated your questionnaire findings with some interviews and find that the survey findings have been confirmed, then you will feel more content in the knowledge that you have done all you can to provide credible results. Of course, it may be that both sets of data are questionable, so even triangulation does not provide final confirmation.

As well as using two or more data collection methods to triangulate your findings, it is possible to vary aspects of the data collection while using the same method. These aspects may be the populations from which you are collecting the data, the time at which the data are collected and the location of the data collection. For example, if you are studying the behaviour of consumers in a supermarket, data collection through observation may differ from town to town, or in the mornings and afternoons. If they are broadly the same, this suggests that the findings are robust.

Differences may point to the need for more research. If, say, consumers spend more time making buying decisions in the afternoons, this may suggest less busy consumers. Alternatively, it may be that there are fewer customers in the afternoon which in itself prompts more time to be taken by consumers. So triangulation in this case may not only cause concern over initial findings; it may also indicate the need for a revision of initial conclusions.

It may also be fruitful to triangulate the research by using the same data collection methods and sources of data but changing the data gatherer. So if you are the research manager of a large market research company employing many interviewers and you notice that one set of data is seriously inconsistent with the others, this may tell you more about the interviewer than sources of the data! It is not unheard of for some data to be invented! But more usually, two individual researchers conducting semi-structured interviews with similar subjects may generate different data, at least in emphasis, because of, say, the stress put on certain questions, or the way in which answers have been followed up.

Reason 4: Using qualitative methods to explain relationships between quantitative variables

Think again about the sort of research findings you hear in the news every day. We often hear that people in Northern Europe are heavier consumers of alcohol than those in the South of Europe. This statistic may be of interest as far as it goes, but it doesn't go far enough. What is it about living in Northern Europe that leads to greater alcohol consumption? Is it colder? Is alcohol cheaper? We don't know from the broad statistics. We need to ask some searching questions to find out what is leading to this particular phenomenon.

◼ Differing time dimension: cross-sectional or longitudinal?

If you are like most of our readers, you will be time-constrained in the completion of your research project. For this reason you will probably opt for a piece of cross-sectional research. This is a 'snapshot' of a particular research setting at a particular time. On the other hand, a research design which tracks events over time is called a 'longitudinal' design. The main difference between the two designs is the ability of the longitudinal design to note change. Which you choose will probably depend on practical considerations. However, we will show below that an element of longitudinal design is perfectly possible within the constraints of one academic year.

Cross-sectional studies

In a **cross-sectional research** design you would collect data from participants at only one period in time in what is often termed a 'snapshot'. The data are typically collected from multiple groups or types of people in cross-sectional research. For

---

| Definition |

cross-sectional research: the study of a particular topic at a particular time, i.e. a 'snapshot'.

example, data in a cross-sectional study might be collected from male and female consumers, from those of different ages, from people in different socio-economic classes or from consumers with different levels of educational achievement. A classic example of the cross-sectional research design is the opinion poll. It is an excellent way of taking the 'snapshot' of current thinking.

In the opinion poll, the cross-sectional study would usually employ the survey strategy and produce quantitative data. As well as describing the incidence of a phenomenon, you can explain the relationship between certain variables: for example, the relationship between expenditure on sales promotions and sales revenue. But the cross-sectional study may also use qualitative methods. For example, interviews conducted over a short time period, either as the sole data collection method or as one of a mixture of methods, may be equally useful.

Longitudinal studies

As we mentioned above, the main advantage of a **longitudinal study** or research design is the capacity that it has to study change and development over time. This may conjure up images of annual visits to managers to track their progress as part of a coaching programme. It could also be that the manager keeps a diary of relevant thoughts and actions, much the same as the learning log idea that you may have come across. These may be powerful ways of collecting data to chart change. But they may be impractical for the student researcher, given time (and, possibly, access) constraints. However, what may be useful is to introduce a longitudinal element to your research by using one of the secondary data sources produced by longitudinal surveys that are available on the Internet, such as the Family Expenditure Survey (see Research in practice 5.3).

Definition

longitudinal study: the study of a particular topic over an extended period of time.

Research in practice 5.3

The UK Family Expenditure Survey

The UK Family Expenditure Survey is a continuous survey of household expenditure and income which has been in existence since 1957. Annual samples of around 10,000 households are selected each year. Approximately 60% of these households co-operate by providing information about the household income and expenditure. This includes household and personal incomes and certain payments that recur regularly (e.g. rent, gas and electricity bills, telephone accounts, insurances, season tickets and hire purchase payments). Households also maintain a detailed expenditure record for 14 consecutive days.

The main purpose of the survey is to provide the weights for the UK Retail Price Index (RPI). The survey is also a cost efficient way of collecting a variety of related data that the government departments require to correlate with income and expenditure at the household, tax unit and person levels. Data are held from 1961 onwards.

From 2001, the FES and the National Food Survey (NFS) have been combined and replaced by a new survey, the 'Expenditure and Food Survey' (EFS). There has previously been considerable overlap between the FES and NFS, with both surveys asking respondents to keep a diary of expenditure. The NFS, sponsored by the Department for Environment, Food & Rural Affairs (DEFRA) covers only food expenditure but in more detail than the FES.

Source, and more details from: www.esds.ac.uk/Government/fes/

5.6   Making sure your research conclusions are believable

When your supervisor or examiner sits back and fixes you with an inscrutable gaze and asks you, 'Why should I believe your theory and/or conclusions?' you should know that all the careful thought you have put into designing your research strategy is going to pay off! All the research design sophistication in the world is of no significance if you cannot say with calm authority, 'I have done all I can to ensure that my conclusions are valid'. Well, you cannot guarantee that your conclusions will be valid, but you can do all you can to limit their invalidity.

One way we have used to help people to think about the validity of their research conclusions is to perform the 'reverse test' in examining their validity. This starts with questioning the validity of the theory and/or conclusions in relation to the findings that gave rise to them and working backwards from there. So, the key questions are the following:

- Does the theory, or do the conclusions, flow logically from the findings?
- Are the summarised findings consistent with the data collected and presented?
- Is it plausible to assume that the data are such that it would have been collected by the methods stated?
- Are the methods employed those that you would expect to find in the research strategy that has been articulated?
- Is there coherence between the research strategy and the research questions and objectives?

Let's examine each of these questions in turn.

Does the theory, or do the conclusions, flow logically from the findings?

You may not end your research with an overall theory. This may not be required. Even if it is not, it may be implicit in what you have written. Let's say that your overall conclusion is that the quality of service in fast food restaurants is the result of effective staff supervision. This sounds reasonable enough. But one of your key conclusions may be that restaurants with high levels of consumer satisfaction reported in consumer surveys are those where there are the most experienced supervisory staff, as measured by length of service. Does it necessarily follow that service quality is the result of effective staff supervision? Here you are equating 'length of supervisor service' with 'effective staff supervision'. It may be a valid assumption if those ineffective supervisors have been weeded out and only effective supervisors remain. But you cannot assume it.

Are the summarised findings consistent with the data collected and presented?

Your presentation of data may lean heavily towards lots of tables and graphs depicting the quantitative data which you have collected. If this is so, the findings about data representing consumer satisfaction and length of supervisor service must be correlated by restaurant to support the findings which suggest a link between the two. This implies the need for appropriate statistical techniques, which are covered in Chapter 7 of this book. In the case of qualitative data, the need for a clear relationship between data and findings suggests the need for skilful and convincing presentation. This will ensure that the findings are supported by a narrative which persuades the reader that you have the data to substantiate the findings.

Is it plausible to assume that the data is such that it would have been collected by the methods stated?

Overstatement is a sin punishable by failure! This is particularly an issue with regard to qualitative data collection. For example, it is easy to fall into the trap of making extravagant claims about the data collected when it is based on a very small amount of interviews. Let's go back to the example of effective supervision in fast food restaurants. If you have made claims for this as one of your findings, it does raise questions such as 'What is effective supervision in this context?' 'What methods were used to assess the extent to which it is practised?' It is difficult to see how a small amount of interviews would enable you to collect data on effective supervision. Some first-hand observation may be required. But even if interviewees are used, it raises questions such as 'Who was interviewed?' 'What were the interviewees asked?' and 'Did the interviewees have sufficient knowledge to be able to answer the questions credibly?'

Are the methods employed those that you would expect to find in the research strategy that has been articulated?

So, you have said in the early part of your research methodology chapter that you are going to pursue a piece of qualitative research using the inductive approach. When your readers look at what you have done, or what you propose to do, they see quantitative questionnaire data or results based on tightly structured observation. This does not mean that what you have done in employing these methods is wrong. But it does suggest presentational incoherence and, worse, muddled thinking.

Is there coherence between the research strategy and the research questions and objectives?

This is the fundamental question and underpins all of this chapter's content. It is a question of 'fit for purpose'. In this case the purpose is 'credible research findings and conclusions'. If the consumer of your research cannot have faith in what you have said, then what you have done will be of poor quality and questionable utility. So, the question becomes 'Which research strategy will enable me to answer my research questions and meet my research objectives in a way which will yield results that can be depended upon?'

Validity and reliability: what is the difference between the two?

Above, we use the term 'validity' in relation to the credibility of research findings and conclusions. It is an important concept in designing a research strategy. So is reliability. In the last section of the chapter, we explain what we mean by these terms and what practical dangers exist in research strategy design which may threaten the credibility of your research.

Validity

Put at its simplest, **validity** is concerned with whether the findings are really about what they appear to be about. Obviously, it is a crucial factor in research strategy design. This is because any research can be affected by different kinds of factors which can render your findings invalid. The practical message here is that you must eliminate all factors that threaten the validity of the research. The principal factors are listed in Table 5.1.

Table 5.1 Principal factors which threaten the validity of research findings and conclusions

Factor	Refers to:
Subject selection	The biases which may result in selection of particular research subjects which may be unrepresentative of the research population.
History	Specific events which occur in the history of the project (for example, between first and second phases of the research) which have an important effect on findings.
Testing	Any effects that the data collection process itself may have on the subjects (e.g. respondents keen to impress the interviewer).
Mortality	The loss of subjects during the research: this is a particularly important issue for the conduct of longitudinal research.
Ambiguity about causal direction	Confusion over the direction in which the flow of cause and effect runs: for example, are poor call centre operator performance ratings caused by a negative attitude towards the way their performance was rated, or were the poor ratings causing the negative attitude?

> **Definition**
>
> **validity**: the extent to which (a) data collection method or methods accurately measure what they were intended to measure and (b) the research findings are really about what they profess to be about.

Table 5.1 refers to internal validity. Another type of validity is external validity. This refers to the extent to which your conclusions are generalisable to other research settings. So, for example, if your research is set in one organisation, there is obviously a question about the degree to which your conclusions are generalisable to other organisations. The simple response to this possible problem is to increase the number of organisations in which you are conducting your research. However, your concern may not be to produce a theory that is generalisable to all populations but to try and explain what is going on in your particular research setting. This is fine, providing that you do not claim that your results, conclusions or theory can be generalised.

Reliability

If your research is to be reliable, it must employ data collection methods and analysis procedures which produce consistent findings. Such consistency refers to the degree to which:

- the measures you use will produce the same results if used on other occasions;
- other researchers, when using the same methods and procedures in the same way, will produce similar results;
- those interpreting your research can see clearly how you came to your conclusions from the data you collected.

As with validity, there are factors which threaten the **reliability** of your research findings and conclusions. These are listed in Table 5.2.

Table 5.2 Principal factors which threaten the reliability of research findings and conclusions

Factor	Refers to:
Subject error	Measurement which may take place at different times: for example, a questionnaire administered to night-shift workers may produce significantly different results to day-shift workers.
Subject bias	Research subjects giving you unreliable information because they think that telling the truth may, for example, show them in a bad light.
Observer error	The way in which different researchers may, for example, ask the same questions in different ways, thus biasing the results.
Observer bias	The way in which different researchers may interpret the same data in different ways, thus biasing the findings and conclusions.

Definition
reliability: the extent to which data collection methods and analysis procedures will produce consistent findings.

Summary

- Research philosophy helps you to 'think about thinking'.
- The main research philosophies are positivism, realism, interpretivism and pragmatism.
- Two of the main approaches to research are deduction and induction.
- The three main purposes of research are exploratory, descriptive and explanatory.
- The main types of research strategy are experiment, survey, case study, action research, grounded theory, ethnography and archival.
- There are significant advantages in combining methods in research design.
- Research studies may be cross-sectional or longitudinal, or combine an element of both.
- Applying the 'reverse test' to the main theory and/or conclusions of the research report is a way of thinking about the research's credibility.
- There are a variety of threats to research validity and reliability which need to be controlled.

Thinking about your research design

→ Look again at the material on deduction and induction in this chapter. Which of these approaches do you feel (a) appeals to you most, and (b) fits your research question(s) and objectives?

→ Go back to your research question(s) and objectives and think about which of the research strategies is most appropriate. Look again at any studies which are similar to yours and see which strategies they have used and the reasons the authors have given for their choice.

→ In what way may you combine different research methods in your study? What advantages may there be in using mixed methods?

→ How may both longitudinal and cross-sectional time dimensions be used in your design?

→ Make a note of all the threats to reliability and validity contained in your research design.

References

Beynon, H. (1973) *Working for Ford*, London: Allen Lane.

Corbin, J. and Strauss, A. (2008) *Basics of Qualitative Research: Techniques and Procedures for Developing Grounded Theory*, 3rd edn, London: Sage.

Family Expenditure Survey (2009) ESDS Government. Available at: *www.esds.ac.uk/Government/ fes/* [Accessed 27 November 2010].

OFCOM (2009) *UK Children's Media Literacy (2009)* London: OFCOM.

Pavlov, I.P. (1927) *Conditioned Reflexes*, London: Oxford University Press.

Saunders, M., Lewis, P. and Thornhill, A. (2009) *Research Methods for Business Students*, 5th edn, Harlow: Pearson Education.

Chapter 6

Collecting data

6.1 Why you should read this chapter

You may be thinking, 'I don't need to read this chapter' or 'I can read this chapter later when I need to collect my data'. It might be, as we mentioned in Chapter 4, that your university expects you to use only secondary data for your project and so you feel there is little point in reading this chapter. Alternatively, your university may only require you to write an extended essay or literature review and so you believe reading a chapter on collecting data will be of limited, if any, use. Or, you might be thinking that, as you have only just started reviewing the literature for your project, it is too early to start learning about collecting data. However, if you are thinking that you don't need to read this chapter on collecting data now, this is not the case.

To assess the suitability of secondary data for your own research project you need to understand the methods that were used to collect it (section 4.5). Even if your project is an extended essay or literature review, you still need to read this chapter and learn about different methods of collecting data as early as possible. Without this knowledge, you will not be able to evaluate fully the journal articles, reports and book chapters you review (section 2.6). This will reduce your ability to assess the quality of the data used. It will also lessen your ability to evaluate the quality of the findings and conclusions. Even if you are not collecting your own data, you need to know about methods for collecting data. This will help you to infer the quality of potential secondary data for your project, the quality of research reported in the literature you read and the value of both to your own project.

The overall purpose of this chapter is to enable you to answer the question 'Do the data collected enable the research question to be answered?' By being able to answer this question, you will be able to do the following:

- Assess the value of secondary data to meeting your own research question and objectives.

- Assess the suitability of data used in research you read about in the literature, and form judgements about the quality of that research.
- Ensure that you use appropriate data collection methods to collect data to meet your own research question and objectives.

In this chapter, we start by talking about different ways of selecting samples from which data will be collected. We then go on to discuss how particular methods are suited to collecting different sorts of data, considering two frequently used methods of collecting primary data in more detail. In this we we look at how to design and distribute questionnaires, including the use of web questionnaires; and how to design and conduct face-to-face, telephone and web interviews.

6.2   Selecting samples

Throughout your life you have been selecting **samples**. Before you download a whole album of songs from iTunes or purchase a CD from Amazon, you will probably listen to one or two tracks from that album to see if you like them. When you were applying to your university for your course, you probably heard opinions from some students and lecturers about that course before making your application. You were basing your decision to purchase on feelings after listening to a few rather than all of the tracks on the album, and your decision to apply on the opinions of some rather than all students and lecturers for that course. Each of your decisions was based on a sample (subgroup) of the **population** (complete set) that was likely to be available to you. Yet it is unlikely that you spent much time considering your reasons for using these samples rather than different samples, or even the whole population. You also probably did not spend much time thinking about whether the sample you selected was the most appropriate to help you make your decision. These aspects are crucial for all research projects. You need to consider the appropriateness of the sample used in each research article or report you read in relation to the research question being answered. You also need to do this whether you are assessing the usefulness of secondary data, or planning how to collect your own data to answer your own research question. In this section we look briefly at reasons for selecting a sample rather than collecting data from the whole population, before talking about different ways of selecting samples and their use.

Definitions

sample: a subgroup of the whole population. The subgroup need not necessarily be a subset of people or employees: it can, for example, be a subset of organisations, places or some of the tracks listed for a music CD.

population: the complete set of group members. The population need not necessarily be people or employees: it can, for example, be organisations, places or the complete track listing for a music CD.

◉ Reasons for selecting samples

Researchers usually collect data from a sample rather than the whole population simply because it is not practicable to collect data from the whole population. This may be because you do not know what the whole population is; it is difficult to make contact with the whole population; or because time or financial constraints prevent you from collecting data from the whole population. However, you should not assume that collecting data from the whole population is always better than just collecting data from a sample.

You have a fixed amount of time to complete your research project because you will also need to complete other work for your course. Within the time you give to your research project, you may have to collect your own data. This means that, like other researchers, if you spend a long time collecting data from a large population, you will have less time to work on the other parts of your project report. Collecting data from a sample of this population will give you more time for the other parts of your project. Some of this time can even be used to test that the methods you use to collect the data will work, providing you with precisely the data you need to answer your research question and meet your objectives.

◉ Ways of selecting samples

As with all research the way you select your sample will depend upon whether or not you know what the total population is and can get a full list of all its members. This complete list of the population is called the **sampling frame**. Let's say an organisation you work for has asked you to collect data from a sample of all their employees. Your organisation is able to give you list of all these employees, using their payroll system. Not surprisingly, this list is up to date and complete as employees are keen to ensure they are paid! In contrast, it is unlikely to be so easy for you to get a full list of a supermarket's customers. While the supermarket will record names and contact details of those who have a loyalty card, this only includes some of their customers. In addition, even if you work for the supermarket, it is unlikely that you, as a student, will be given access to the list of loyalty card customers for both commercial and data protection reasons.

For populations where you are able to obtain a complete list, such as your organisation's employees, you can select your sample using one or more sampling techniques that are called 'probability sampling' (Table 6.1). Because you have a complete list, you can select employees at random from your list. You can also say statistically the chance or probability that each of these employees has of being

---

> ### Definitions
>
> **sampling frame**: the complete list of all members of the total population. You select the sample from this list when using probability sampling.
>
> **probability sampling**: a variety of sampling techniques for selecting a sample at random from a complete list of the population. Because you have a complete list and select at random, you know the chance or probability of each member of your population being selected.

selected for your sample from this list. If your complete list contains 200 employees and you select a sample of 100 employees using a probability sampling technique, then each employee has a 50 per cent chance of being selected. If you select 50 employees from your complete list of 200 employees using a probability sampling technique, then each employee has a 25 per cent chance of being selected. Providing you have selected your sample using a probability sampling technique, your sample will represent your population statistically. The level of certainty with which you can say it represents your population is dependent upon the size of your sample and of your population, details of this being given in Saunders et al. (2009). Not surprisingly, the larger the sample, the more certain you can be that it represents the population precisely. You therefore need to collect data from as large a sample as possible. Like all researchers, you will need a probability sample if you want to statistically estimate the characteristics of the population. As you read section 7.3, you will also discover that statistical tests require a sample of at least a certain size to minimise spurious results. In general, this means you will need to collect data from a probability sample of at least 30 respondents.

Often the data we and other researchers use has not been collected using a probability sample. Let's look at your supermarket customers again. As you cannot get a complete list of customers, you do not know how many there are and so will not be able to work out the chance of each customer being selected for your sample. You will therefore have to use one or more of a different group of sampling techniques that do not require a complete list of the population. These are called 'non-probability sampling' techniques (Table 6.1) and, if you select your sample using these, it will not represent your population statistically. Non-probability samples are often analysed using qualitative analysis techniques. As you read section 6.4 you will discover that, other than for quota samples, these often require smaller samples. The actual sample size from which you will need to collect data will depend on the nature of your population. In particular, for homogeneous (similar) populations such as male UK-born business studies students aged 21 at your university, the non-probability sample size is likely to be about 10. In contrast, for heterogeneous (more varied) populations, such as male and female students of all ages studying any programme at your university, the sample size will be larger, say between 15 and 25 (Saunders et al., 2009).

> **Definition**
>
> **non-probability sampling**: a variety of sampling techniques for selecting a sample when you do not have a complete list of the population. Because you do not have a complete list of the population, you cannot select your sample from this population at random. This also means you do not know the chance or probability of each member of your population being selected.

Probability sampling techniques

Having given you a general overview of the difference between probability and non-probability sampling techniques, let's look first at the probability sampling techniques listed in Table 6.1 in more detail.

Table 6.1 Probability and non-probability sampling techniques

Probability	Non-probability
Simple random sampling	Quota sampling
Systematic random sampling	Purposive sampling
Stratified random sampling	Snowball sampling
	Self-selection sampling
	Convenience sampling

Simple random sampling

If you have ever bought a lottery ticket, you will have experienced the results of **simple random sampling**! Simple random sampling uses a series of random numbers, such as those generated by the RAND formula in Microsoft Excel, to select a sample of members from a population. Like the lottery balls, each member of the population in your list (sampling frame) is given a unique number. Random numbers are then used to select the numbers of those members of your population from the sampling frame who will be in your sample.

Five sets of numbers drawn at random recently for the UK's National Lottery (selected from the numbers 1 through 49) are:

14	16	23	24	25	43
4	15	19	44	45	49
20	21	22	24	27	34
4	10	18	41	42	47
11	30	38	45	46	49

Although each draw of six numbers has been selected at random, you can see that these numbers are not spread evenly between 1 and 49. Rather, some numbers (such as 23, 24 and 25 in the first draw) are close together and then there are large gaps (for example, 25 and 49 in the first draw). This is a property of random numbers that often occurs when you use them to select a sample of less than a few hundred members. It means that researchers, including you, should not use simple random sampling to select a sample of less than a few hundred if your sampling frame has been sorted in some way. For example, if your sampling frame is sorted in order of employees' seniority, although your sample of employees will have been selected at random, the occurrence of random patterns, such as those illustrated by the five lottery draws may mean that certain levels of seniority in your population are underrepresented and others are overrepresented.

Definition

simple random sampling: a type of probability sampling in which each member of the population has an equal chance of being selected at random and included in the sample. Each member is usually selected using random numbers.

Systematic sampling

For a **systematic sample**, members of the sample are selected from the sampling frame at regular intervals. To ensure your sample is entirely random, your first sample member is selected using a random number before subsequent members of your sample are selected systematically. If we return to the example of your organisation's employees and the sampling frame which you got from payroll, we can see how this sampling technique works. The list you have been given by payroll is in descending order of salary, your organisation's chief executive being listed first, followed by the most senior managers. The last employee on your list is a newly appointed school leaver who earns the lowest salary. To select a sample of one-fifth of employees (20 per cent), you need to perform the following steps:

1 Select your first employee from the sampling frame at random using a random number, between one and five for a 20 per cent sample, in this example employee number two.

2 As your sample is a fifth (20 per cent) of employees, you then select the 7th, 12th, 17th, 22nd and 27th employee in your sampling frame, continuing to select every fifth employee until you reach the end of the list.

By selecting the first sample employee using a random number, the rest of your sample will also have been selected at random. This technique works well, providing there are no regular patterns in the sampling frame. Let's say your sampling frame consists of UK Premier League football club first team players who started the match for their team last Saturday. These players are listed in your sampling frame by team starting with the captain of each team, and ending with the goalkeeper. If you were to select a sample of 1 in 11 players (approximately 9 per cent) and the first player you selected at random was the 11th player, then you would subsequently select the 22nd, 33rd, 44th and 55th player until you reached the end of your list. However, your sample would consist entirely of goalkeepers! Providing there are no regular patterns in your sampling frame, this technique usually works well and also has the advantage of being relatively easy to explain!

> **Definitions**
>
> **systematic sampling**: a type of probability sampling in which the first sample member is selected from the sampling frame at random, using a random number. Remaining sample members are selected subsequently at regular intervals from the sampling frame.
>
> **stratified random sampling**: a type of probability sampling, in which the sampling frame is first divided into relevant strata. Sample members are then selected at random from within each stratum, using either simple random or systematic random sampling.

Stratified random sampling

Not surprisingly, given its name, **stratified random sampling** is a modified version of random sampling! When using this sampling technique, the sampling frame is divided into strata or layers that are relevant to your research question, your sample being selected separately from each stratum or layer using either simple random sampling or systematic sampling. Let's say you are selecting a sample of web-based customers for a small web-based retailer, using their complete list of customers as your sampling frame. This alphabetical list includes each customer's name and their postal region (UK, mainland Europe, North America, rest of the world). You therefore perform the following steps:

1 Split your sampling frame into relevant separate strata or groups (using the four separate postal regions as your strata).

2 Select a random sample from within each stratum or group using either:

   (a) simple random; or

   (b) systematic sampling.

By doing this, each postal region or stratum will be represented in the same proportion in your sample as they are in your complete population.

Non-probability sampling techniques

As you read at the start of this section, researchers, including you, are often unable to obtain a list of their total population. This means that probability sampling cannot be used as there is no sampling frame. Fortunately, there are a variety of non-probability sampling techniques that can be used. We will now look at those we listed in Table 6.1.

Quota sampling

You have probably been selected for a **quota sample** at some time in your life. Sometimes when you are shopping, a person with a clipboard asks you if you would mind answering a questionnaire. If you answer 'No', the next question you are asked is something like, 'Which one of the following age groups are you in?' after which a number of different age groups are read out to you. This is often followed by a question about your occupation or, perhaps, the newspaper you read (which may be used to indicate your social class). The person asking the questions (interviewer) has been given a number or quota of people to interview, such as '3 working class males aged 25–55' and '2 female students aged 24 or under', and so on. If the interviewer has already filled her or his quota for the group your answers place you in, you will not be asked any further questions. However, if the interviewer continues to ask you questions from the questionnaire, you will become part of their quota.

Quota samples are used as a substitute for a probability sample to select participants when a sampling frame is not available. This means the sample size is similar to those used for probability samples, and the data are likely to be analysed using

---

Definition

quota sampling: a type of non-probability sampling that ensures the sample selected represents certain characteristics in the population that the researcher has chosen.

statistical techniques (section 7.3). However, while data used to be collected from the sample by a team of interviewers each of whom has a quota to fill, this is becoming less common. Rather, as you will read in Research in practice 6.1, the quota samples used by large commercial polling organisations are increasingly selected from a panel of volunteers, who then agree to take part answering questions online.

Research in practice 6.1

Quota sampling

As a major UK polling organisation, YouGov conducts online polls about politics, brands and consumer trends. The sample for each poll it conducts is selected from a large panel of volunteers whom YouGov pays to take part in their polls. YouGov has selected their panel of volunteers to represent all groups in society, although not in the same proportions as in the population as a whole. For each poll, the sample YouGov uses is made up of a number of demographic groups. These groups are specified in much the same way as a quota sample group would be, using data such as volunteers' age, gender, social class and region where they live. The members of each demographic group are subsequently selected at random from YouGov's panel of volunteers. YouGov argues that this method of sampling is closer to quota sampling than random sampling, email invitations to take part being sent to random selections from each demographic group. Those who agree to take part become part of the quota for a particular demographic group, answering the questions via the Web.

Source: Developed from Wells and Twyman (2010).

Purposive sampling

Purposive sampling is the most frequently used form of non-probability sampling. It is used particularly to select a small sample when collecting qualitative data. When a researcher selects a purposive sample, she or he is using their judgement to actively choose those who will best be able to help answer the research question and meet the objectives. Some of the population will have a chance of being chosen by the researcher while others will not.

Let's say you have read a journal article where the researcher has selected two major banks to explore the impact on individual banks of the financial crisis that started in 2007 with the liquidity shortfall in the United States banking system. These two banks have been selected purposively because they represent the extremes of what happened to banks in one country. The bank at one extreme was nationalised by the government; the bank at the other extreme has received no support from the government. The author of the article argues that, when contrasting the findings

Definition

purposive sampling: a type of non-probability sampling in which the researcher's judgement is used to select the sample members based on a range of possible reasons and premises.

from these extreme cases, differences will be more obvious and that her findings are relevant in understanding or explaining the impact on other banks. On reading the article, you feel this is an appropriate reason for selecting the sample which allows her research question to be answered fully. You also feel the generalisations she has made about other banks on which the impact has been less extreme are logical.

You use purposive sampling when you need to understand what is happening so you can make logical generalisations. This means that you, like other researchers who select a purposive sample, need to explain clearly the criteria you have used to select your sample, the reasons for this and the underlying premise on which these are based. Your selection can involve a variety of different purposive sampling techniques, which we have summarised in Table 6.2, along with reasons why you might use them and the underlying premises on which your reasons are based.

Table 6.2 Varieties of purposive sampling

Purposive sampling variety	Reasons for use	Underlying premise
Typical case	Sample will be illustrative and considered representative, albeit not statistically.	Sample is typical of the population.
Critical case	Sample will either make a point dramatically or be crucial to addressing the research aim and objectives.	Topic of interest is most likely to occur in the sample selected, or sample selected is essential to the operation of the process.
Extreme case	Sample consisting of unusual or special participants will enable you to find out the most.	Findings from extreme cases will be relevant in understanding or explaining more typical cases.
Heterogeneous	Sample will have sufficiently diverse characteristics to provide the maximum variation possible in the data collected.	Any patterns that emerge are likely to be of particular interest and value, representing key themes.
Homogeneous	Sample consisting of one particular subgroup will provide minimum variation in possible data collected.	Will allow characteristics to be explored in greater depth and minor differences to be more apparent.

Snowball sampling

Snowball sampling is used when it is difficult to identify members of your population. Let's say that you wish to research people who are working in the informal economy while claiming unemployment benefit. As these people are difficult to reach, snowball sampling may provide the only possibility for finding potential participants.

> **Definition**
>
> **snowball sampling**: a type of non-probability sampling in which, after the first sample member, subsequent members are identified by earlier sample members.

Alternatively, your population may be like chief executives of Fortune 500 companies, easy to identify but difficult to access. Once again, by using snowball sampling, you may be able to reach such people. To obtain your snowball sample of chief executives of Fortune 500 companies you would need to do the following:

1 Make contact and collect data from an initial chief executive of a Fortune 500 company.

2 Use the initial chief executive to identify a number of other chief executives of Fortune 500 companies and to support your gaining access.

3 Use these chief executives to identify further chief executives of Fortune 500 companies and to support your gaining access, so the sample increases in size like a snowball that is rolled...

Remember, those selected for a snowball sample are most likely to identify others who are similar to themselves, resulting in a homogeneous sample.

Self-selection sampling

If you ask your sample members to identify themselves, say, by putting an advertisement in appropriate media inviting them to take part in your research, you are using **self-selection sampling**. Increasingly, researchers are inviting potential participants using a variety of electronic media such as intranets, blogs and bulletin boards alongside invitations through general letters or all user emails (Saunders, 2011). However, when using self-selection sampling, you need to be careful. Those who self-select to be members of your sample often do so because they have strong feelings or opinions about your research topic and consider it sufficiently important or interesting to give it some of their time. This means they are likely to be different from people who do not offer to be involved in some way and so are not representative of the population.

Definitions

self-selection sampling: a type of non-probability sampling in which possible sample members are asked to identify themselves as willing to take part in the research.

convenience sampling: a type of non-probability sampling in which the sample the researcher uses is those who are easy to obtain rather than because of their appropriateness.

Convenience sampling

The last variety of non-probability sampling which we talk about, **convenience sampling**, is one that is rarely used by researchers and one, we hope, you will not use for your own research! It simply involves 'using' ('selecting' is too positive a word!) those who are easiest to get hold of for your sample. Say you have to find out managers' views about something. We know you won't do this, but let's pretend that you decide to collect your data from part-time students in your class. These people are only in your sample because of the ease of getting hold of them and have little, if any, relevance to your research. Like most convenience samples, they are likely to be of limited use in answering your research question and meeting your objectives.

6.3 Collecting data using questionnaires

Questionnaires are used widely to collect data and we have no doubt that you have completed questionnaires and used data that were collected by questionnaires. Your lecturers will have asked you to complete module evaluation questionnaires so they can find out your, and your classmates', opinions about their modules. You will also have used the results of questionnaires in your assignments, discussing journal articles in which research findings were based on data collected by questionnaires.

The term 'questionnaire' refers to all methods of data collection in which each potential **respondent** is asked to answer the same set of questions in the same order. It therefore includes questionnaires that are used to collect data:

- by web, each respondent reading the questions and recording her or his own answers;
- by post, each respondent reading the questions and recording his or her own answers;
- by hand, each respondent reading the questions and recording her or his own answers;
- by telephone by an interviewer who also records each respondent's answers;
- face to face by an interviewer who also records each respondent's answers.

When a questionnaire is used by an interviewer to collect data, it is often called a **structured interview**.

Questionnaires are a good method for collecting data about the same things from large numbers of respondents. Questionnaires allow you to ask the same set of standardised questions to a large number of respondents. Because the questions are standardised, the data collected by questionnaires are often used either for descriptive research, such as students' opinions of a module they have just taken, or for explanatory research to test a theory. These data are usually analysed statistically (section 7.3). Let's say you have a theory that the more time students spend working on their projects, the more they will enjoy the work. In explanatory research, you use the data you collect to examine and explain such relationships statistically: in our example to see whether or not students' enjoyment of their work is statistically related to the amount of time they spend working on their projects.

Definitions

questionnaire: a general term that includes all methods of data collection in which each person is asked to answer the same set of questions in the same order. Questionnaires can be distributed face to face by an interviewer, by telephone, by hand, by post and by the Web.

respondent: the person who answers the questions in a questionnaire.

structured interview: a method of data collection using a questionnaire in which each person is asked the same set of questions in the same order by an interviewer who records the responses.

In this section we will look at how to perform the following:

1 design individual questions;

2 design the questionnaire;

3 write the covering letter or email;

4 pilot testing;

5 distribute the questionnaire to a sample of potential respondents using each of the distribution methods listed above.

How to design questions

A questionnaire is only useful if:

● it collects data that are needed to answer the research question and meet the objectives;

● it collects data from a large enough number of respondents to answer the research question and meet the objectives;

● the questions asked are understood and interpreted by the respondents in the way the researcher wanted them to be understood and interpreted.

This means you need to be very clear about the data you need to collect, and design your questions to collect these data, minimising the chances of questions being misinterpreted. In making sure that your questions (and so your questionnaire) will provide you with enough data to answer your research question and meet all your objectives, you are ensuring what researchers call 'content validity'. By designing your questions carefully and ensuring that they actually collect data about what you intend them to measure rather than something different, you are ensuring what researchers call 'construct validity'. When you are reading about other researchers' research that has used questionnaires, you will need to look at the actual questions that were asked to see if they are valid. This will allow you to better understand and assess the conclusions these researchers reached, based on the answers their respondents gave to these questions.

When you design your questionnaire, your first stage will be to design individual questions to collect the data you need to answer your research question and meet your objectives. When you do this you can:

● use questions from other researchers' questionnaires (providing you reference the source and obtain permission where necessary);

● adapt questions from other researchers' questionnaires (providing you explain how you adapted them, reference the source and obtain permission where necessary);

● design your own questions.

| Definitions |

content validity: the extent a data collection tool, such as a questionnaire, provides enough data to answer the research question and meet all the objectives.

construct validity: the extent the questions asked actually collect data about what they are intended to measure.

However, before you decide to use someone else's questions, beware. There are a lot of poor questions and badly designed questionnaires available! You also need to be certain the wording of each question will be suitable for your sample and the context in which they will complete the questionnaire. If your questions are going to be answered only by accountants, you will be able to use far more specialist language than if they are going to be answered by people in general.

Saunders et al. (2009) highlight seven types of question that can be used in questionnaires. These are listed in Table 6.3, along with a brief description of when to use them and examples.

Table 6.3 Types of question for use in questionnaires

Type	Use when...	Examples
Open	...unsure of the response, require a detailed answer, or want to find out what is uppermost in respondent's mind.	If there are any other areas or issues that concern you, please feel free to comment below.* What do you like most about visiting this theme park?
List	...you need to be sure the respondent has considered all possible answers.	Which of the following fruit juices have you purchased in the past week? [please tick ✓ all appropriate boxes] Apple ☐ Orange ☐ Cranberry ☐ Pineapple ☐ Tomato ☐ Other (please say) ....
Category	...you need to ensure the respondent's answer will only fit into one category.	Are you? (*Interviewer, listen to the respondent's answer and tick the correct box*). Male ☐₁ Female ☐₂
Ranking	...you want the respondent to place a list in rank order.	Number each of the holiday destinations listed below in order of their attractiveness to you for your next holiday. Number the most attractive holiday destination 1, the next 2 and so on. If a destination is not attractive, leave blank. *Destination* *Attractiveness* England [ ] Scotland [ ] Wales [ ] Ireland [ ] France [ ] Germany [ ] Spain [ ] Holland [ ]

Table 6.3 Continued

Type	Use when...	Examples
Rating	...you want a respondent's opinion or belief.	For the following statement please tick ✓ the box that matches your opinion most closely.

<table>
<tr><td></td><td>Agree</td><td>Tend to agree</td><td>Tend to disagree</td><td>Disagree</td></tr>
<tr><td>I generally believe what my manager tells me</td><td>☐</td><td>☐</td><td>☐</td><td>☐</td></tr>
</table>

How likely do you believe it is that you will pay off your overdraft within a year of graduation?

Very likely	Quite likely	Not sure	Quite unlikely	Very unlikely
☐	☐	☐	☐	☐

Type	Use when...	Examples
Quantity	...you want the respondent to tell you a number or amount.	How many dependent children do you have living with you? [ ] [ ] *(For example for 2 write:* [ ] [2])
Matrix	...the responses to two or more questions are selected from the same set of possible answers.	The following statements ask about your feelings regarding the future of the Happy Toy Manufacturing Company.

	Strongly agree	Agree	Disagree	Strongly disagree
I feel the future for the company is getting brighter	☐	☐	☐	☐
I would be happy to spend the rest of my career at the company	☐	☐	☐	☐

*Some researchers would term this a 'request' rather than a 'question'.

The example questions in Table 6.3 show how the answer you get depends on the way your question is worded. Looking at the first open question, this could result in some respondents writing hundreds of words commenting about the issues that concern them, and others writing only a few words or even nothing! In contrast, the second open question asks the respondent to only answer what they like most. For all your questions, you will need to decide the data you need to answer your research question and meet your objectives and, therefore, in how much detail you want your respondents to answer. However, beware of including too many open questions; they are extremely time-consuming to analyse.

Next, compare the list question and the ranking question in Table 6.3. You can see that, although the list question asks about fruit juices and the ranking question asks about holiday destinations, only the list question allows the respondent to include another response of their choice. The list question gives the respondent the option 'other (please say)...' while the ranking question names eight holiday destinations, giving no space for the respondent to add her or his own destination. Including the 'other (please say)' option alters the data collected, something you need to beware of both when reading about others' research and designing your own questions. This is because it allows respondents to have a free choice in how they answer rather than be constrained by the options you have given them.

Now look at the two examples of rating questions. The first of these questions has an even number of possible answers (four) while the second has an odd number of possible answers (five). By giving an even number of possible answers, you are forcing your respondents to make a choice between, in the first rating question, agreeing and disagreeing. You are not allowing them to neither agree nor disagree. In contrast, in the second example the respondent is allowed to be 'not sure' being neither 'quite likely' nor 'quite unlikely'. Once again, this emphasises that you need to be clear about the precise questions asked, both when reading reports of others' research and when designing your own questionnaire.

Finally, look at the category question. A number in a smaller font size has been added next to each possible response: '1' next to 'male' and '2' next to 'female'. These numbers are the codes that will be used to represent each respondent's answer when the data are typed into a spreadsheet, such as Excel or statistical software such as IBM SPSS Statistics, for statistical analysis. Wherever possible, we suggest you add code numbers to possible question responses at the design stage. This will save you having to code the answers later! However, if you use web-based questionnaire software, such as SurveyMonkey™ or SurveyMethods™, to design your questionnaire and collect your data, codes can be added virtually automatically. Once you have collected your data via the Web, it will only take a few clicks of the mouse to save it as a spreadsheet file. This is far quicker than typing it all in yourself; it also means your data set is less likely to contain errors!

How to design the questionnaire

Your questionnaire should be pleasing to look at and, of equal importance, easy for respondents to read and fill in their answers. This means you need to tell the respondents what the questionnaire is about and why you want them to answer the questions. The order of questions needs to be logical to those answering rather than to you. Your questionnaire should be as short as possible, although you obviously need to ask enough questions to collect all the data you need to answer your own research question and meet your objectives! These design points, along with others are listed in Table 6.4.

Table 6.4 Points to remember when designing a questionnaire

Layout	Question order
• Title should be clear and a larger font size.	• At the start, ask more straightforward questions.
• Introduction should be brief and explain why the topic is important and what the respondent should do.	• At the start, ask questions that are related clearly to the stated topic of the questionnaire.
• Questions should not appear squashed on the page or computer screen.	• Ask more complex questions in the middle of the questionnaire.
• The typeface (font) should be easy to read.	• Group questions into sections that will be obvious to the respondent.
• Questions' typeface (font), font size, spacing and formatting should be consistent throughout.	• Use filter questions to stop the respondent answering questions that are not relevant.
• When printed, it should be on good quality paper/card.	• Make sure the wording of questions is consistent throughout the questionnaire.
• Include details of how to return the completed questionnaire at the end.	• At the end of the questionnaire, ask personal or sensitive questions.

If you look at Research in practice 6.2, you will see that sometimes you only need to ask a few questions. This short questionnaire is only designed to collect a limited amount of data about diners' experiences at the restaurant. Yet, despite it being short, the design includes many of the points made in Table 6.4. Starting with the layout, the questionnaire has a clear title 'How did we do?' in a larger font which also describes the topic. The brief introduction is friendly in style and explains why ('to know what you think'), and what the respondent should do ('tell us what you think') in a little more detail. The questions do not appear squashed and are printed using the same typeface throughout. Despite this, you probably think that there is not enough space for an answer to the open question at the end. We agree with you! We are told that the questionnaire is printed on card, hopefully good quality, and that the return postal address is printed on the other side. It would also have been helpful if respondents were told there was a box for completed questionnaires to be put in, perhaps by the till.

If you now look at the actual questions, you will see that these are both straightforward to answer and, other than the 'Date of visit', relate clearly to the stated topic. It may be that this is filled in by the waiter or waitress before the questionnaire is given to the customer. The first three questions are grouped as a matrix into one section and are phrased consistently: 'What was the... like?' However, the last open question has a problem: it should say 'us' rather than 'use'. Unlike the designer of this questionnaire, you need to proofread your questionnaire very carefully, remembering that a spell check will not pick up mistypes that result in the wrong word being included!

Research in Practice 6.2 does not include any sensitive questions or filter questions. Whether or not a question is sensitive will depend on what is being asked and the person who is answering it. It will therefore be a matter of judgement. Fortunately, as you will see later, this can be checked as part of pilot testing. Filter

Research in practice 6.2

Questionnaire design

Often when you visit a restaurant, you are given a 'comment card' with your bill similar to the one below. This is usually printed on card rather than paper. After a short introduction asking you to respond, there are a few questions about your experiences in the restaurant and some space for you to add your own comments and feedback. You are then expected to either place the card in a box as you leave or, alternatively, post the card to the restaurant. The postal address is printed on the other side of the card and usually the postage has been prepaid to encourage you to send it back.

How did we do?

At Mark 'n Phil's restaurant we're always keen to know what you think... so if you've got any comments about your visit we'd like you to tell us.

Date of visit? dd............. mmm.......... yy......

	Excellent	Good	Average	Poor	Awful
What was the quality of your food like?	☐	☐	☐	☐	☐
What was the service you received like?	☐	☐	☐	☐	☐
What was your overall experience like?	☐	☐	☐	☐	☐

If you have anything else you would like to tell use, please do so below...

---

questions are used to route your respondents through your questionnaire so they miss out questions that are not relevant. Let's say you have a questionnaire that includes some questions that are only relevant to respondents who are members of a professional body. Your filter question is:

22. Are you a member of a professional body?	Yes ☐
(If no, go to question 30)	No ☐

The following (open) question is then only answered if the respondent has answered 'yes'. It asks:

23. Please name your professional body: ....

Questions 24 to 29 are also about the respondent's membership of a professional body.

If you are using web-based questionnaire software, answering the filter question will, as far as the respondent is concerned, just take them to the next relevant question, in our example question 23 if they answered 'yes' and question 30 if they answered 'no'. However, if you are using a paper questionnaire in which answers are filled in by the respondent, she or he will have to find the next relevant question. Unfortunately, some respondents will not follow your filter question's instructions and will try and answer the following questions whether they are relevant or not! You therefore need to use filter questions sparingly in paper questionnaires.

What to write in the covering letter or email

In Research in practice Box 6.2 the purpose of the questionnaire was only explained briefly to potential respondents. When you distribute a questionnaire by post or the Web, you will need a more detailed covering letter or email to explain the purpose of your questionnaire. The structure and contents of your covering letter are summarised in Table 6.5. You will often be expected to put a copy of your covering letter and a blank questionnaire as appendices in your project report.

Table 6.5 Structure of a covering letter or email

Section	Contents
Letter/email head	Official, with a logo, address, telephone number and email address. On good quality white paper if for a paper questionnaire.
Name and address of potential respondent	Use name and full postal address for personal approach if for paper, otherwise just name.
Date	In full, e.g. 20th March 2011.
Greeting	Use title and name if possible, e.g. Dear Mr Penny.
Heading or email subject	Brief descriptive title of questionnaire.
1st paragraph	What research is about, why it is useful, how respondent's time is needed and their answers are of value.
2nd paragraph	Whether responses will be confidential and/or anonymous.
3rd paragraph	How results will be used. Whom to contact if there are any questions, with telephone number and/or email contact details. Explanation of how to return the questionnaire, to whom and by when.
Closing remarks	Thank recipient in advance for help.
Signature and name	Sign by hand if letter. Also put sender's title, forename and surname.

Why pilot testing is important

Before distributing your questionnaire to potential respondents, you need to check that it will work; that your respondents will have no problems in answering the questions and that their responses will be recorded correctly. This is important for both web and paper-based questionnaires. Even if you are really short of time, you still need to try out your questionnaire and covering letter with a small number of people who are like those who will answer it in your research. This is known as **pilot testing** and will also help to confirm that your actual respondents will understand the meaning of your questions and will be able to follow the instructions on the questionnaire. Remember, it is far easier to correct mistakes in your questionnaire at the pilot stage than to have to recollect your data because mistakes had been overlooked.

Definition

pilot test: the trying out of a questionnaire, interview schedule or other method of data collection with a small group of respondents who are similar to those who will be used in the actual research to see if it works. Any problems that arise in the pilot test can then be sorted out before the actual research is undertaken.

How to distribute the questionnaire

At the start of this section (6.3) we listed five ways in which you might distribute your questionnaire to potential respondents and so collect data from your sample. Whichever way you are using, you are trying to get as many completed questionnaires returned to you as possible. Although response rates from questionnaires vary considerably, research by Baruch and Holtom (2008) based on looking at 490 academic studies using questionnaires provides a clear indication of the rate you might expect. The average response for studies where data were collected from individuals was 52.7 per cent, while that for questionnaires to organisations was lower, being an average of 35.7 per cent. Studies using web-based and telephone distribution reported higher response rates than traditional paper-based questionnaire distribution.

Distributing web questionnaires

Web questionnaires are normally distributed using an email with a hyperlink to the actual questionnaire or using a link to a website that has a hyperlink to the questionnaire. For the first, this means you need to have a complete and up-to-date list of your sample's email addresses. For the second, you will need to invite people to contribute and direct them to your website and your questionnaire. If you choose to do this, you must follow the general guidelines for using the Internet. This is called netiquette and means you should do the following:

- Only send emails and posting to relevant user groups.
- Remember that postings to more than 20 user groups at once are unacceptable to many web users.
- Avoid sending junk emails or spam.
- Avoid emailing multiple mail lists as this will mean some people will get more than one copy.
- Avoid using email attachments as these may be thought to contain viruses.

To distribute a web questionnaire, you need to observe the following:

1 Ensure the web questionnaire is set up, works as you wish, the data set is generated automatically and that you have noted the direct hyperlink to include in your accompanying email or on your website.

2 If you are emailing potential respondents, let them know in advance that you will be emailing a hyperlink to a questionnaire or to a website that has a hyperlink to the questionnaire.

3 Email potential respondents with your covering email and the hyperlink to the questionnaire or advertise your website widely, highlighting the closing date.

4 If you are emailing potential respondents with the hyperlink, email them again a week after the questionnaire has been distributed, thanking those who have returned the questionnaire and encouraging others to respond.

Distributing postal, or delivery and collection questionnaires

The distribution of postal questionnaires and delivery and collection questionnaires is very similar. As you will have worked out from their names, the only real difference is that the former is delivered and returned by post, while the latter is delivered and collected in person. To distribute a questionnaire using either of these ways you need to observe the following steps:

1 Ensure that the questionnaires and accompanying letters are printed and the envelopes addressed.

2 Contact potential respondents to let them know in advance that you will be posting/delivering by hand a questionnaire to them.

3 Post or deliver by hand the questionnaire.

4 Contact potential respondents a week after the questionnaire is posted/delivered by hand, thanking those who have returned the questionnaire and encouraging others to respond.

Conducting telephone or face-to-face structured interviews

The quality of your structured interviews, whether conducted using a telephone or face to face will depend on your interviewing ability. For telephone-structured interviews, the clarity and tone of voice with which you read the questionnaire questions will be crucial, while for face-to-face structured interviews your appearance will also be important. To conduct a telephone or face-to-face structured interview using a questionnaire you need to pay attention to the following points:

1 Ensure that the questionnaires are printed.

2 Where possible and resources allow, contact potential respondents to let them know in advance that you will be telephoning/visiting them within the next week to conduct a structured interview.

3 Try and contact each potential respondent in person, noting down the date and time of contact and whether or not the structured interview took place. If you arrange an alternative appointment, note it down and visit then!

4 Try and contact each potential respondent at least twice more, each at a different time and on a different day, noting down the same information.

6.4 Collecting data using semi-structured or unstructured interviews

Every day of your life you read about, listen to and watch interviews. Journalists interview politicians and business leaders, chat show hosts interview celebrities of all kinds, and business investors known as 'dragons' interview entrepreneurs with new business ideas. All these interviews have one thing in common: they are purposeful discussions between two or more people. Although you might argue that the purpose of some of these interviews is to entertain rather than gather data for research, they still give you a real insight into the process of asking questions and the preparation and skills you need to interview people.

In the previous section (6.3) we talked about the structured interview; when each respondent is asked the same standard questions from a questionnaire by an interviewer, either by telephone or face to face. In this section we will look at two other forms of interview: semi-structured and unstructured interviews. These are sometimes also referred to as qualitative research interviews, the person answering your semi-structured or unstructured interview questions being called the **participant**. Like other researchers, you will find these types of interview particularly useful where:

● you are unsure of the answers respondents will give;

● your questions are complicated;

● you need to vary the order of questions or the actual questions asked.

In a **semi-structured interview** you (or the researcher) will have a list of topics to be covered and questions to be asked, although the order in which you ask them will vary from interview to interview depending on the responses from the participant. For some semi-structured interviews, you may decide not to ask some of your questions or not to cover one or two topics if they are not relevant to that participant. You may also decide to ask additional questions to find out further details and

Definitions

participant: the person who answers the questions in a semi-structured or unstructured interview.

semi-structured interview: a method of data collection in which the interviewer asks about a set of themes using some predetermined questions, but varies the order in which the themes are covered and questions asked. The interviewer may choose to omit some topics and questions and ask additional questions as appropriate.

explore your objectives in more depth or, alternatively, to check that your understanding of what the participant is telling you is correct. **Unstructured interviews** are more informal and are used to explore a general topic in which you (or the researcher) are interested in more depth. Unlike semi-structured interviews, you do not have a list of questions to ask, although you still need to be clear about the topics you wish to talk about. In unstructured interviews, you want your participants to talk openly and widely about the topic with as little direction from you as interviewer as possible. For this reason they are sometimes called non-directive interviews.

As you have read academic journal articles you will have found out about research that has used semi- and unstructured interviews. In many of these articles such interviews will have been used to collect data which was analysed qualitatively (section 7.4). These data will have been used to either explore what is happening and gain new insights or describe what is happening and identify general patterns. Semi- and unstructured interviews may also have been used along with other data collection techniques. For topics where little is known, the researcher may start by using unstructured interviews to explore what is happening. More often, researchers start by collecting data using a questionnaire, analyse these data statistically, and then use semi-structured interviews subsequently to understand the statistical relationships their analysis has revealed. Some years ago we, along with another colleague, used a questionnaire to collect data from a manufacturing company about employees' use of and feelings about different communication methods. Our statistical analysis showed that office employees looked at the company's noticeboards to find out what was happening, while production employees rarely looked at these noticeboards. The reasons for this difference were unclear from our questionnaire data. In our subsequent semi-structured interviews with both office and production employees, we probed for reasons why this happened. The office employees did not know why. However, the production employees we interviewed all provided a compelling reason. The noticeboards were in the main entrance hall where office employees entered each day. In contrast, the production employees used a different entrance where there were no noticeboards. Not surprisingly, we recommended the company put up noticeboards at the entrance used by the production employees.

If you are going to use semi- or unstructured interviews, you need to prepare for the actual interview. As part of your preparation, you will need to be clear about the topics you are going to cover to collect the data you need to answer your research question and meet your objectives, the location of the interview and your appearance. Next, you will need to think carefully about how you might ask questions about these topics. Following a pilot test, you will have to conduct the interviews, making sure that you test your understanding when necessary, show that you are

---

Definition

unstructured interview: a method of data collection in which the participant talks openly and widely about the topic with as little direction from the interviewer as possible. Although there is no predetermined list of questions, the interviewer will have a clear idea of the topics to explore.

listening at the same time as taking notes or audio recording the conversations. We will now look at each of these.

How to prepare for semi- and unstructured interviews

Imagine you have a meeting with an important client of the public relations company for whom you work. Before going to this meeting you would prepare carefully. You would make sure you knew about the client you were meeting and their organisation so that you were credible. You would also think carefully about the likely conversation you would have, the questions you would ask and the likely questions you would be asked and how you would answer them. Preparing for a semi-structured or unstructured interview involves thinking about similar things. In particular you need to pay attention to the following:

- Make sure you have found out as much as possible about the person you are going to interview and, where appropriate, the organisation where they work.
- Develop an interview guide, listing the topics you want to discuss and initial questions you will ask.
- Choose a location that is convenient for your participant, where she or he will feel comfortable and you will not be disturbed.
- Make sure your clothing and appearance is appropriate for the interview.
- Work out how you will use your body language to show your interest and that you are listening attentively.

These are illustrated in Research in practice 6.3. However, as well as these, to prepare for an interview you will also need to:

- develop a consent form;
- think how you are going to record the data: if you are going to audio record the interview, make sure that your audio recorder works, has sufficient memory to store a day's interviews and you have spare batteries.

Research in practice 6.3

Preparing for the interview

Céline was preparing to interview accountants in a major City firm about the impact of changes to pension regulations that had recently been introduced. She had obtained permission from a senior partner to conduct her interviews and had been offered the use of a small 'interview room' in the firm's headquarters. The partner's personal assistant had assured her that this room would be quiet and contained a low table and two comfortable chairs. Céline prepared a notice for the room's door which said 'Interview in progress. Please do not disturb'.

Céline was pleased the room had a low table as this meant there would not be a physical barrier between her and the accountants she was interviewing. She was more

→

worried about the comfortable chairs as she knew that, if she sat back and relaxed, her body language might suggest she was not interested. Céline therefore decided she would lean forward attentively and ensure she maintained eye contact with each interviewee. She also thought it was important she dressed formally for the interviews as all her participants would be wearing suits.

As her first interview was in a few days' time, she began to develop her interview guide:

Impact of changes to pension regulations research

- Thank person for attending.
- Explain purpose of research and interview, emphasising that it is participant's own opinions that are important.
- Ask if willing to be interviewed and stress this is their decision.
- If willing, ask then to sign the consent form; if not, thank them for their time and close the interview.

Interview

1 To what extent have the changes to pension regulations impacted on your work?

   (a) *Probe*: In what ways? (ask for examples)

   (b) *Probe*: Can you give me an example (if possible) of how you think these changes will improve things?

   (c) *Probe*: Can you give me an example (if possible) of how you think these changes will make things worse?

2 Do you think the government have provided sufficient guidance regarding the changes to the pension regulations?

   (a) *Probe*: How has this guidance been provided?

   (b) *Probe (if insufficient guidance)*: What extra guidance is needed?

In section 3.8 We talked about the importance of getting participants' consent for your research. Many universities expect you to ask each interview participant if they are willing to take part in the research and, if they are, to sign a consent form like that in Figure 6.1. This is important as participants have the right to refuse to take part in your research or withdraw from the interview whenever they wish.

As you can see from the consent form (Figure 6.1), the choice of whether or not to audio record the interview is the participant's, not yours! Although audio recordings provide an accurate and unbiased record and allow you to listen again to the interview, if the participant does not wish you to record the interview, then you will have to take notes. This is not easy to do at the same time as interviewing, so we suggest you practise beforehand. As well as noting what the participant says, you will need to note where and when the interview was held, and relevant background information about the participant. After each interview we suggest you word process your

Consent form

Title of the research project

Researcher's name, Final year student at University of Anycity

Please initial box

1. I confirm that I understand what the research is about and have had the opportunity to ask questions.

2. I understand that my participation is voluntary and that I can withdraw at any time without giving a reason.

2. I agree to take part in the research.

Please initial box

Yes   No

4. I agree to my interview being audio recorded.

5. I agree to the use of anonymised quotations in publications.

Name of participant: ....   Signature: ....

Researcher's name: ....   Signature: ....

Date: ....

Figure 6.1 Participant consent form
Source: Developed from Saunders et al. (2009).

notes immediately. Leaving your notes for a few days means you are less likely to be able to read what you wrote!

How to ask questions in semi- and unstructured interviews

In both semi-structured and unstructured interviews, you will have to ask questions carefully and listen attentively to answers given. As in designing a questionnaire, you will need to make sure the questions you ask are worded clearly using appropriate and unbiased language. However, unlike when using a questionnaire, you will be able to test your interpretation by asking, summarising the response and, where necessary, asking further questions. Kvale and Brinkmann (2009) identify a number of types of questions to use in interviews. We have listed those our students have found most useful in Table 6.6, along with a brief description of when to use them, and examples.

Table 6.6 Types of question for use in interviews

Type	Use when...	Examples
Introductory	... you are starting a new topic.	Could you tell me about...?
Probing	... you want to find out more detail, but without saying what.	Can you say a bit more about that? Could you let me have a bit more detail?
Specifying	... you want to find out more detail about a specific aspect already discussed.	Can you say a bit more about why you purchased a diesel car rather than a petrol car? How did you feel when your 91-year-old mother was sent home from the hospital to an empty cold house?
Direct	... you want answers about a topic introduced by the interviewer to apply to the participant.	Have you ever received a bonus for good performance? Have you used a consultant in the past?
Indirect questions	... you want answers about a topic introduced by the interviewer to apply to others.	How do other patients feel about their treatment at this hospital?
Structuring	... you want to show questions on a theme have been completed.	I would now like to ask you about another topic. Is that all right?
Interpreting	... you want to check interpretation of the participant's response is correct.	You mean that...? Is it correct that...? So what you are saying is...?

If you look at Research in practice 6.4, you will see that the types of question you use and the order in which you use them depends on the responses you receive from the participant during the interview. This means that, unlike with a structured interview, it is not possible to work out all the questions you will ask or the order in which you will ask them. This makes semi-structured and unstructured interviews difficult to conduct. In the short extract in Research in practice 6.4, the interviewer (James Caan) opens the interview with the introductory question 'Just give me a little bit of an idea on...' Without giving participants time to answer, this is followed with the specifying question, 'What's the financial model around that?' The participant's response is vague, not providing sufficient detail. Two further specifying questions are therefore asked together: 'So what is the commission and what has it generated with the 15,000 orders?' Although two questions have been asked, only the first is answered. This illustrates clearly how participants often fail to answer all questions if more than one is asked at the same time. It is therefore better to only ask one question at a time.

As only the first of the specifying questions asked together was answered, the second is rephrased as another specifying question: 'OK, so those orders at 9 per

Research in practice 6.4

Interviewing

In the BBC reality business show *Dragons' Den*, entrepreneurs present their business ideas to a group of investors (Dragons) in the hope of getting investment capital in return for a stake in their business. After their presentations entrepreneurs are interviewed about their business ideas by the Dragons.

A few years ago, Shane Lake and Tony Charles asked the Dragons for an investment of £100,000 in their takeaway food ordering online portal HungryHouse.co.uk. After the presentation they were interviewed by the five Dragons, which included the entrepreneur and investor James Caan. An extract from a transcript of the televised interview shows some of the questions asked by James Caan and the responses from Shane Lake and Tony Charles.

Caan: Hello Tony, hello Shane, I'm James Caan. Good presentation. Couple of financial questions. Just give me a little bit of idea on the 15,000 orders you've taken so far. What's the financial model around that?

Lake: Well, we charge a commission on each order that we send.

Caan: So what is the commission and what has it generated with the 15,000 orders?

Charles: We're charging the restaurants 9 per cent.

Caan: OK, so those orders at 9 per cent equates to how much?

Lake: This year we've turned over £24,000.

Caan: And what's your projection going forward?

Lake: Well, our projection is, um, turnover for Year 1, we're looking at £430,000. Expenses of that, we're looking at expenses of 400,000. Turnover in Year 2 will be £2m with expenditure of 1m, and Year 3 turnover will be 3.2m with a net profit of £2m.

Caan: OK.

At the end of the televised interview two of the Dragons, Duncan Bannatyne and James Caan agreed a joint investment of £100,000 in HungryHouse.co.uk in return for a 25 per cent stake in the company. This they agreed to drop to 15 per cent if targets were met.

Sources: *Dragons' Den* (2007), Hill (2009).

cent equates to how much?' This allows James Caan to find out further details. The next direct question to the participants, 'And what's your projection going forward?' introduces a new topic. Following the answer, it appears that these participants have now provided sufficient detail through their answers; James Caan's final structuring comment 'OK' suggests he has finished asking questions.

Why a pilot test is important

Before conducting your interview with selected participants, you need to pilot-test your interview and technique and check that your questions are likely to be understood, are not leading and will provide you with the data you need. This will give you an idea of possible problems with questions as well as how long each interview is likely to take. You also need to be sure that your audio recorder works properly, or you can take sufficient notes while interviewing. This is important for both semi-structured and unstructured interviews. Even if you are really short of time, you still need to pilot-test your interview with a small number of people who are like those who will be participating in your research. It is worth remembering that, unlike with questionnaires, it may be possible to partially overcome mistakes made in early interviews, such as missing out a topic that later appears to be important, by amending later interviews.

How to conduct semi- and unstructured interviews

Semi-structured and unstructured interviews can be conducted face to face, by telephone and by web; either by chat rooms, email or Internet forums. For such interviews the crucial issue is the number of participants you will need to interview before data saturation is reached; each additional interview provides no new insights. This depends on the nature of your population. Many texts recommend you establish the number of interviews you need inductively, simply continuing to conduct interviews until **data saturation** is reached. While this is good advice, it is not particularly helpful when you are assessing research undertaken by others using semi-structured and unstructured interviews, or when you are planning your own interviews. When assessing research undertaken by others, you need to be sure that data saturation was reached. When planning your own interviews, use the suggestion in section 6.2 that for homogeneous populations the sample size is likely to need to be about 10, while for heterogeneous populations the sample size will need to be larger, say between 15 and 25. Although this does not remove the need for you to ensure data saturation has been reached, it provides an idea of the likely number of interviews needed.

> **Definition**
>
> **data saturation**: the stage where additional data collection provides few if any new insights into the research question and objectives.

Conducting semi-structured and unstructured interviews face to face

Conducting semi-structured and unstructured interviews face to face makes full use of your interviewing skills. The clarity and tone with which you ask questions will be crucial, as will your appearance and body language. To conduct these interviews face to face you need to take the following steps:

1 Ensure that your interview checklists and consent forms are printed.

2 Contact potential participants, explain the purpose of your research and invite them to take part, providing a clear indication of the likely amount of time the interview will take.

3 If they agree to take part, arrange a mutually convenient appointment and place to conduct the interview.

4 Arrive for your interview early and make sure the room is set as you wish.

5 Conduct the interview making sure you also:

   (a) thank the participant for attending;

   (b) explain the purpose of the research, offering assurances of anonymity and confidentiality as appropriate and explain that they can withdraw at any time;

   (c) ask for permission to record the interview, if using an audio recorder;

   (d) ask participant to sign the consent form;

   (e) remember to take notes.

6 At the end, thank the participant for their time.

7 Word process your notes as soon as possible.

At the end of the interview some researchers suggest it is a good idea to offer participants a summary of the findings or a copy of your notes of their interview. This is up to you. We would, however, stress that, if you do make an offer, it is essential that you actually do provide your participants with the summary of the findings or a copy of the interview notes. If you do not, they will be less willing to participate in research in the future.

Conducting semi-structured and unstructured interviews by telephone

The process of conducting semi-structured and unstructured interviews by telephone appears very similar to conducting them face to face, although without the visual contact! This lack of visual contact means conducting such interviews by telephone is not easy. Remember, the purpose of semi- and unstructured interviews is to explore your participants' responses in detail. You will be unlikely to be able to do this unless you have gained their trust, something that is often difficult to do if you have only talked on the telephone. You will also not be able to see your participants' body language, meaning you may interpret some of their answers incorrectly. We therefore recommend that you only use a telephone for these forms of interview either where you already have met the participant face to face and gained her or his trust, or you have already established a trusting relationship.

To conduct a semi-structured or unstructured interview by telephone you need to pay attention to the following:

1 Ensure that your interview checklists are printed.

2 Contact potential participants by telephone, explain the purpose of your research and invite them to take part, providing a clear indication of the likely amount of time the interview will take.

3 If they agree to take part, arrange a mutually convenient time to telephone and conduct the interview.

4 Telephone and conduct the interview, making sure you also:

   (a) thank the participant for their time;

(b) explain the purpose of the research, offering assurances of anonymity and confidentiality as appropriate and explain that they can withdraw at any time;

(c) ask for their consent and permission to record the interview (if using an audio recorder);

(d) remember to take notes.

5 At the end, thank the participant for their time.

6 Word process your notes as soon as possible.

Conducting semi-structured and unstructured interviews using the Web

Web-based interviews can be divided into two groups: those that are conducted in real time (synchronous) and those that are, in effect, conducted offline (asynchronous). Providing your participants are IT-literate and have good access to the Internet, both groups have two advantages:

- You can interview participants who are geographically dispersed.
- Your questions and your participants' responses are recorded automatically as they are typed.

You will already be familiar with synchronous interviewing software through your use of MSN Messenger™. This and other instant messaging software can be used to undertake real-time semi-structured interviews, providing netiquette (section 6.3) is observed. Similarly, you will also be familiar with asynchronous interviewing software through your use of Internet forums, blogs and email. Internet forums or discussion groups and blogs usually deal with one topic and need to remain open for at least a few weeks if they are to generate sufficient post (data). Participants can read and comment on each others' posts, but cannot edit them. Posts are normally made by a variety of participants and so they are really group interviews. In contrast, email interviews consist of a series of email exchanges between the interviewer and a participant, each consisting of a small number of questions and the associated answers. Although it is possible to email one long list of questions, this is really just a questionnaire and means you will not be able to adapt later questions depending on participants' responses to earlier ones. Because of the delay between questions being asked and them being answered such interviews can often take more than a week.

To conduct semi-structured and unstructured interviews using the Web you need to remember the following:

1 Ensure that your synchronous or asynchronous means of asking questions is set up and works as you wish.

2 If you are using:

(a) Email or instant messaging for your interview – contact potential participants by email, explain the purpose of your research and invite them to take part, providing a clear indication of the likely amount of time the interview will take.

(b) Internet forums or blogs – invite people to join your discussion.

3 If you are using:

(a) Email for your interview and those invited agree to take part – ask a few questions at a time rather than all together.

(b) Instant messaging and those invited agree to take part – arrange a mutually convenient time to conduct the interview.

4 Conduct the interview making sure you:

(a) thank the participant for their time;

(b) explain the purpose of the research, offering assurances of anonymity and confidentiality as appropriate and explain that they can withdraw at any time;

(c) ask for their consent and permission to use the interview transcript for research purposes;

(d) remember to save the interview transcript.

5 At the end, thank the participant for their time.

Summary

- Your choice of sampling technique depends on whether or not you can obtain a complete list of the population (sampling frame), your research question and your objectives.

  - If you can obtain a sampling frame, you can use probability sampling techniques such as simple random, systematic random and stratified random sampling. You use probability samples if you want to estimate statistically the characteristics of the population.

  - If you cannot obtain a sampling frame, you must use non-probability sampling techniques such as quota, purposive, snowball, self-selection sampling. We recommend you do not use convenience sampling. You use non-probability samples when you want to make logical generalisations about the population.

- Questionnaires are used when you want to collect data by asking each person to answer the same set of questions in the same order.

- Before designing your questionnaire, you need to know what data you need to collect to answer your research question and meet your objectives. Individual questions should then be designed before putting the questionnaire together. In designing your questionnaire, use as few open questions as possible. Remember to lay the questionnaire out so it is easy to read and response to questions easy to fill in.

- Questionnaires can be distributed face to face by an interviewer, by telephone, by hand, by post and using the Web.

- Semi-structured and unstructured interviews are used when you are unsure of the answers respondents will give, your questions are complicated or you need to vary the order of questions or the actual questions asked.

- In semi-structured interviews, you ask about a set of themes, only some questions being predetermined. The order in which the themes are covered and questions asked can be varied. You can choose to omit some topics and questions and ask additional questions as appropriate.

- In unstructured interviews, the participant talks openly and widely about the topic with as little direction from you as possible. Although there is no predetermined list of questions, you will have a clear idea of the topics to explore.

- To prepare for semi-structured and unstructured interviews, you need to be clear about the topics you are going to discuss, the questions you are going to ask, the location of the interview and your appearance. When you conduct the interviews, you need to test your understanding as necessary, show that you are listening and make a record of the conversation.

- Semi-structured and unstructured interviews can be conducted face to face, by telephone and using the Web.

Thinking about collecting data

→ As you continue to read and note the literature, use your knowledge about samples, questionnaires and interviews to help you assess the appropriateness of the methods used by other researchers and the value of their research findings (section 2.7).

→ Think about the data you will need to answer your research question and meet your objectives.

→ If you are going to use secondary data, use your knowledge about samples, questionnaires and interviews to help you assess the suitability of the secondary data for your own research (section 4.5). Make notes about this, as you will need this level of detail to write the method section of your project report.

→ If you are going to collect your own (primary) data, use your knowledge about samples, questionnaires and interviews to help you choose the most appropriate data collection methods (Chapter 6).

→ If you are going to collect your own (primary) data, make notes about the reasons for your choices about selecting your sample and the method or methods you will use to collect your data. Also, make notes explaining why you need to collect the data you wish to collect, linking these data explicitly to your objectives. You will need this level of detail to write the method section of your project report.

References

Baruch, Y. and Holtom, B.C. (2008) Survey response rate levels and trends in organizational research, *Human Relations*, 61(8): 1139–60.

Dragons' Den (2007) *Shane Lake and Tony Charles: Hungry House*. Available at: *www.bbc.co.uk/dragonsden/entrepreneurs/shanelake.shtml* [Accessed 16 Dec. 2010].

Hill, J. (2009) *Dragons' Den Hungry House transcript.* Available at: *http://jeffreyhill.typepad.com/english/2009/03/dragons-den-hungry-house.html* [Accessed 16 Dec. 2010].

Kvale, S. and Brinkmann, S. (2009) *InterViews: Learning the Craft of Qualitative Research Interviewing*, 2nd edn, Los Angeles, CA: Sage.

Saunders, M.N.K. (2011) 'Choosing research participants', in C. Cassell and G. Symons (eds), *The Practice of Qualitative Organizational Research: Core Methods and Current Challenges*, London: Sage.

Saunders, M., Lewis, P. and Thornhill, A. (2009) *Research Methods for Business Students*, 5th edn, Harlow: FT Prentice Hall.

Wells, A. and Twyman, J. (2010) *2010: Did online polling come of age?* PowerPoint Presentation. Available at: *eprints.ncrm.ac.uk/1585/1/wells_twyman_online_polling.ppt* [Accessed 10 Dec. 2010].

Chapter 7

Analysing data

7.1 Why you should read this chapter

In the previous chapter, we noted how it was important to know about and understand different methods of collecting data, even if you were not collecting data yourself for your research project. We now make similar comments about analysing data. Obviously, if you collect your own data you will need to analyse these data to answer your research question and meet your objectives. Similarly, if you're using secondary data (Chapter 4) for your own research project, you will still have to analyse these data. However, even if your project is an extended essay or literature review, you will still need to know about different techniques for analysing data. Without this knowledge, you will not be able to understand or evaluate fully the journal articles, reports and book chapters you review. If you only understand partially how the data were analysed and are unclear about the reasons why particular techniques were used, your ability to assess the quality of analysis, understand the research findings or follow the discussion of these findings will be reduced. In addition, a reasonable understanding of techniques for analysing data will help you to be clear about the value of research reported in the literature to your own project.

So what do you need to know about analysing data to help you do your project and write the project report? Well, whether you're collecting your own data, using secondary data or basing your project entirely on the literature, you still need to know the same things. You need to know how to get data ready for analysis, when to use different analysis techniques, and how to interpret the results of these different analysis techniques. In addition, you need to know a bit about different types of data and the analysis techniques you should use depending on the type of data you have.

The first section of this chapter is about the different types of data you might be analysing or reading about. As you would expect from reading about collecting data (Chapter 6), this section looks at both quantitative and qualitative data. Following a similar structure to Chapter 6, the next section looks at how to analyse data quantitatively. Within this, we look at how to prepare your data for quantitative analysis using a spreadsheet such as Microsoft Excel or statistical analysis software such as IBM SPSS Statistics. We also look at when you should use different tables, graphs and statistics as well as what the results of your analysis mean. Our final section looks at how to analyse data qualitatively. Once again we will look at how to prepare your data for analysis, this time looking mainly at manual analysis. Within this, we talk about ways of coding and analysing your data as well as what the results of your analysis mean.

7.2　What are different types of data?

In section 4.2 we talked about data being split into two types: quantitative data that were numerical or whose values had been measured in some way, and qualitative data that were not numerical and had not been measured in some way. As we saw in section 6.3, quantitative data are collected in a standardised way, such as by using questionnaires. These data are collected about different variables (we defined this term in section 1.6!), which are the building blocks of quantitative analysis. Your variables are usually described using numbers and analysed using diagrams and statistics.

In contrast, qualitative data are collected in a non-standardised way, such as interviews (section 6.4). These data are analysed by developing and testing propositions, which are described using words. To be able to analyse both quantitative and qualitative data, you need to know more about each of these types, as they will dictate the analyses you can do.

Quantitative data

As you can see in Figure 7.1, quantitative data are split into two main types: categorical and numerical data. Categorical data, as the name suggests, are data that have been grouped into a descriptive set or put in rank order. Let's say you have collected

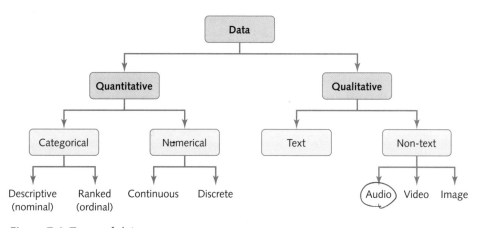

Figure 7.1 Types of data

data from a sample of students at your university using, among others, the category question:

In which faculty are you studying?	Arts and Humanities	$\square_1$
	Business and Law	$\square_2$
	Physical Sciences	$\square_3$
	Social Sciences	$\square_4$

The data you get from this category question will be descriptive, your variable 'faculty in which studying' being made up of a descriptive set of categories that are the four faculties in your university. Although these data are coded using numbers, the numbers do not mean that the Arts and Humanities faculty is first, Business and Law second and so on; they are just codes and there is no relevance to the number order. In contrast, **ranked data** are categorical data that have been put into rank or definite order. These are often called **ordinal data**. In your questionnaire, the next question is one that also appeared in Table 6.3:

How likely do you believe it is that you will pay off your overdraft within a year of graduation?	Very likely	$\square_1$
	Quite likely	$\square_2$
	Unsure	$\square_3$
	Quite unlikely	$\square_4$
	Very unlikely	$\square_5$

This rating question collects data on the variable 'likelihood of paying off overdraft within a year of graduation'. The responses are in ranked order, 'very likely' being ranked first, 'quite likely' second and so on.

Numerical data are where the data are measured using numbers. They are either data that are measured in discrete units (**discrete data**), or data that can take on any value (**continuous data**). If we return to your student questionnaire, we can again use questions to illustrate these two types of numerical data. In your questionnaire, the next question is:

On how many days did you visit the library last week?	[ ]
(For example, for 2 write: [2] *)*	

Definitions

continuous data: numerical data whose values are measured numerically as quantities and can theoretically take any value, depending on the level of accuracy with which they are measured.

discrete data: numerical data whose values are measured numerically as quantities in discrete units and can therefore only take a finite number of values.

ranked or ordinal data: categorical data that are put into a definite order.

This quantity question collects discrete numerical data on the variable 'number of days visited the library last week'. The values for this variable can only be 0, 1, 2, 3, 4, 5, 6 or 7, depending on the number of days a respondent visited the library last week. In contrast, your next quantity question collects continuous data for the variable 'time spent studying last week'. Although this variable is measured to the nearest hour, these data could theoretically take any value, depending on the level of accuracy used:

How much time did you spend studying last week to the nearest hour?   [ ] [ ] hours

(For example, for 2 hours, 15 minutes write: [ ] [2] hours)

You will notice from the key definitions above that **descriptive data** are sometimes called **nominal data**, and ranked data are sometimes called ordinal data. Where these terms are used, you will find that numerical data has been divided into interval and ratio data rather than continuous and discrete data. Don't worry; it's just a different way of grouping data variables! For **interval data**, you can state the difference between any two data values: such as, the difference between 3° Celsius and 9° Celsius is 6° Celsius. However, you can't say that 9° Celsius is three times as hot as 3° Celsius! For **ratio data**, you can say what the actual difference and what the relative difference are between two values. For example, if one student's overdraft is £15,000 and another student's overdraft is £30,000 you can say that the difference between them is £15,000, the second student having twice as large an overdraft.

Qualitative data

Looking again at Figure 7.1, you can see that qualitative data are also split into two main types: text and non-text. Text data, as the name suggests, are data in the form of words that have been recorded as text and are usually word-processed. They therefore include written answers to requests such as, 'If there are any other areas or issues that concern you please feel free to comment below', in Table 6.3. The majority of audio recordings, and the audio parts of video recordings, are transcribed and word-processed and then analysed as text data. As we discovered in Research in practice 6.4 these are known as interview transcripts and contain both the questions asked by the interviewer and the participant's answers. These transcripts often also record details about the research setting as well as the interviewer's and the participant's non-verbal behaviour. In contrast, although methods of analysing actual visual data such as video and other images are developing, they are not yet in widespread use and consequently are outside the scope of this book.

Definitions

descriptive or nominal data: categorical data that are grouped into sets (categories) that have no obvious rank order.

interval data: numerical data whose values are measured numerically so that the numerical difference between two values can be stated, but not the relative difference.

ratio data: numerical data whose values are measured numerically so that both the numerical and the relative difference between two values can be stated.

7.3   Analysing data quantitatively

How to prepare your data

If you're analysing your sample data quantitatively, you will almost certainly be using either a spreadsheet or statistical analysis software. These software require your data to be in the format of a **data matrix**. Look at Figure 7.2. This extract from a spreadsheet data matrix has one column for each variable, representing questions in your student questionnaire (section 7.2). The first row in the spreadsheet contains a short description of each data variable. Each of the remaining rows contains the data for all these variables for one student, each cell containing the code representing a student's response for a particular variable.

The codes for each variable mean different things. If you look at the first row of data (row 2 in the spreadsheet), you can translate the codes. The first cell in the row contains the student identifier. This is not to identify the student by name! Rather, by writing this number on the questionnaire containing these data, you can link the questionnaire to your data matrix. This makes it much easier for you to check your data for possible typing errors. Student 1 is studying in the 'Faculty of Business and Law' (code 2). The likelihood of this student's overdraft being paid off within one year of graduation is 'quite likely' (code 2). This student visited the library three times last week and spent 28 hours studying. Numeric codes have been used because they make subsequent analysis more straightforward. In addition, numbers are quicker to type in and you're less likely to make errors.

	A	B	C	D	E
	Student identifier	Faculty in which studying	Likelihood of paying off overdraft within year of graduation	Days visted library last week	Hours spent studying last week
1					
2	1	2	2	3	28
3	2	2	5	4	34
4	3	2	5	3	57
5	4	3	5	2	34
6	5	1	5	0	8

Figure 7.2 Data matrix in Excel

Definition

data matrix: the table format in which data are typed into spreadsheets or statistical analysis software. Each column represents a separate data variable, and in each row a separate member about who data have been obtained.

If you have collected your own data, you will need to code it and type it into your analysis software as a data matrix. To do this you will need to do the following:

1 Work out the number of variables and give them clear names.

2 For each variable, work out a coding scheme (if you collected your data using a questionnaire, you should have already done this for most variables; see section 6.4).

3 Code each variable, leaving variables with no data blank.

4 Set up your data matrix as in Figure 7.2.

5 Type in your data, saving your file regularly and also making a back-up copy.

6 Check your data for typing errors.

No matter how carefully you type in your data, you're almost certain to make a few errors. You should always check your data for errors before starting your analysis. This will save time as it prevents you having to redo analyses because your data were wrong. Two common errors you should look for are:

● *Illegitimate codes* – these are code numbers which appear in a data variable which you have not used for that data variable.

● *Illogical relationships* – these are relationships that are very unlikely to occur in your data, such as a person aged 91 who is still in full-time work.

As we pointed out in section 4.2, secondary data are increasingly available from the Internet in formats that can be read directly into your data analysis software as a data matrix. These data have already been checked for errors and, as you will not have to type the data in yourself, you will save time. However, don't forget to download the codebook and list of definitions so you know exactly what everything means and can interpret the data correctly!

How to present data

Your first stage of any quantitative data analysis is to explore and understand your data. The easiest way to do this, and we believe a most helpful way, is by presenting your data as tables and graphs. Those that are most useful in helping you answer your research question and meet your objectives will also appear in your project report. However, before you start designing tables and graphs, you need to be aware of the following:

● Particular tables or graphs are better than others for highlighting certain aspects of your data (Saunders et al., 2009).

● Categorical and numerical data often require different tables and graphs.

● All tables and graphs must be labelled clearly and designed so as not to distort the data.

In this section, we look at how to highlight different aspects of your quantitative data using tables and graphs. Within this we talk about those tables and graphs which are used to present categorical data and those which are used to present numerical data, also looking at the importance of clear design and labelling. These are summarised in Table 7.1.

Table 7.1 Presenting data using tables and graphs

For...	use a...	to present...	which allows the...
categorical data	table	a summary	individual values to be read
categorical data	bar graph	values for each category	highest and lowest values for a variable to be seen[2]
numerical data[1]	histogram	values for data grouped in categories	highest and lowest values for a variable to be seen
categorical data[1]	pie chart	proportions in each category	relative proportions in each of a variable's categories to be seen
numerical data	line graph	values for a variable over time	trend over time to be seen[2]
numerical data	scatter graph	a relationship	relationship between two variables to be seen

[1] Numerical data will need to be grouped into categories.
[2] To also compare variables, use a multiple bar chart or a multiple line graph.

How to summarise data so individual values can be read

Tables are used when you want to summarise data so that individual values can be read easily. When your table summarises the data for one variable, such as the number in each category for a question such as 'In which faculty are you studying?' it is sometimes called a frequency table or frequency distribution.

Now read Research in practice 7.1. The table Harry pasted into his project report summarises the number of hectares used for organic farming in each member of the European Union's 27 member states. Each European Union member state is represented by a separate row. The table contains data for more than one variable. The total number of hectares used for organic farming in 2008 for each member state is represented by the first column of data. A further variable, represented by the second column of data, has been included. This has been calculated using the first column of data and data for 2007, not included in the table. This is not unusual as, like most tables, it is summarising a far larger amount of data.

While the individual values in this table are easy to read, their meaning is less easy to understand. This is because Harry has simply cut and pasted this table into his project report rather than thinking! He needs, as pointed out by his supervisor, to make sure the table has a clear title, states the source of the data and that the various abbreviations and notes are explained more fully.

Research in practice 7.1

Designing and labelling tables

As part of his research project on the market for organic food, Harry decided to present some of the secondary data on the growth of organic farming, using a table he had found on the European Commission's (2010) website. He cut the table from the web page and pasted it into his chapter, which he later emailed to his project supervisor for comments. The extract below includes his supervisor's comments.

Do you mean 'member state' or 'country'? Use clear labels for all column and row headings

A useful table that seems to support your arguments. Please see my other comments to improve it

	Organic area (ha) (1) 2008	% changes 2007–2008
EU-27	7 764 722	7.4
BE	36 153	10.8
BG	16 663	22.1
CZ	320 311	9.1
DK	150 104	8.7
DE	907 786	4.9
EE	87 346	9.8
IE	42 816	4.1
EL	317 824	13.6
ES	1 317 539	33.3
FR	583 799	4.8
IT	1 002 414	−12.9
CY	2 323	:
LV	161 624	9.1
LT	122 200	1.5
LU	3 535	5.0
HU	122 817	15.0
MT	20	:
NL	50 434	7.3
AT	447 678	0.6
PL	313 944	8.5
PT	233 475	:
RO	140 132	6.6
SI	29 836	1.8
SK	140 755	19.4
FI	150 374	1.1
SE	336 439	9.1
UK	726 381	10.0
NO	52 248	6.9

(1) MT data 2006, CY, PT data 2007

Units of measurement are clear – good

I think I can work most of these country name abbreviations out. However, you really need to put these in full or provide a key for abbreviations

Does this mean these data are missing?

You MUST state the source of the data clearly. I presume it is the European Commission. Don't forget to put the full reference in your list of references

Why is this surrounded by lines? It makes it look like a total

There is no table number or title! Make sure the title is clear and describes contents of table

What does this mean? Ensure notes are clear and easy to understand

Source of table: © European Communities (2010).

How to present data so the highest and lowest values can be seen

As you can see from Research in practice 7.1, tables do not emphasise any particular values. If you wish to do this, you need to use a bar graph (sometimes called a bar chart) for categorical data or a histogram for numerical data. The bar graph in Figure 7.3 shows visually the organic farming area for each European Union member state: Spain has the largest area of organic farming area, while Cyprus, Luxembourg and Malta have the smallest areas of organic farming. Because of the scale at which the graph is drawn, it is not possible to be sure which of these three countries has the smallest area. However, if you look at the specific values in the table in Research in practice 7.1, you will find out that the lowest member state is Malta (MT), with only 20 hectares of organic farming.

More complicated forms of bar graphs can be used to compare the highest and lowest values for two or more variables. These are known as multiple bar graphs. When you draw these, you need to make sure the data you want to compare are represented by bars that are next to each other. So, if Harry wished to compare the total organic farming area in each European Union member state between 2007 and 2008 (and was able to obtain the data for 2007!), he would draw the two bars for each member state next to each other. For each member state, the first bar would represent the total organic farming area for 2007 and the second the total area for 2008.

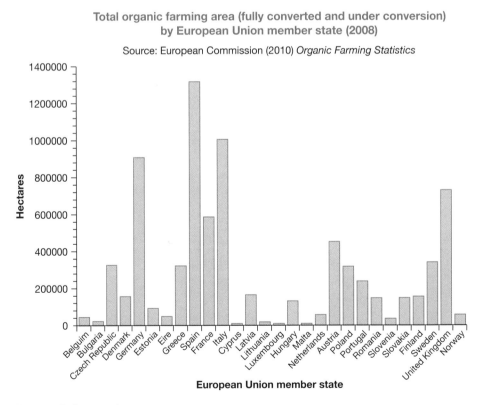

Figure 7.3 Bar graph

Histograms are the numerical data equivalent of bar graphs. In a histogram, the continuous nature of the data on the horizontal access is shown by there being no gaps between the bars. Let's look at numerical data you collected from students using the question:

How much time did you spend studying last week to the nearest hour?   [ ] [ ] hours

(For example, for 2 hours, 15 minutes write: [ ] [2] hours)

These data would consist of a series of numbers, such as 23, 34, 8, 14, 46..., each number being the number of hours a student had spent studying last week. To draw a histogram, you could place these data into a series of equal width categories such as:

less than 5 hours	25 to less than 30 hours
5 to less than 10 hours	30 to less than 35 hours
10 to less than 15 hours	35 to less than 40 hours
15 to less than 20 hours	40 to less than 45 hours
20 to less than 25 hours	45 hours or more

As one of these categories ends the next starts, the lack of a gap between the categories reflecting that your data are continuous. Your histogram would consist of ten bars, the area of each bar representing the total number of students whose time was spent studying last week for a five-hour time period (Figure 7.4). Because there is no gap between each of your categories, there is no gap between each of the bars in your histogram (Figure 7.4). Once again, the highest and lowest values are easy to see: the most frequent amount of time spent studying last week by students was 20 to less than 25 hours, the least frequent being 45 hours or more.

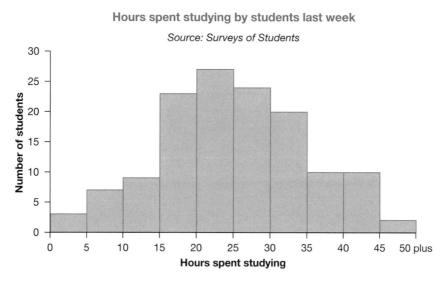

Figure 7.4 Histogram

How to present data so that proportions can be seen

As we are sure you already know, pie charts are useful if you want to show the proportions in different categories for a variable. As with histograms, if you're using
numerical data, you need to put these data into categories. The pie chart in Figure
7.5 has been drawn using categorical data collected from your student questionnaire
which used responses to the question, 'In which faculty are you studying?' The largest
segment, Business and Law, represents the faculty that had the greatest proportion of
students responding. We've added the annotations to remind you how to design and
label graphs, whatever type you're using. You will notice that one annotation states
'(Two-dimensional graph used so as not to distort or misrepresent the data)'. While
it is fun to draw three-dimensional graphs using multiple colours viewed from weird
angles, a quick look at some of graphs in newspapers shows how easy it is to use them
to misrepresent data. You should not do this in your project report.

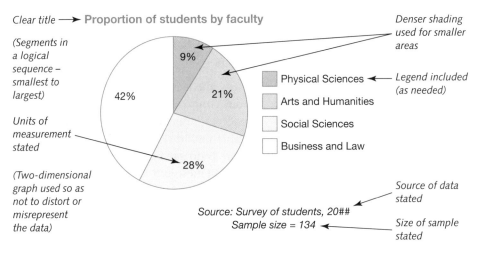

Figure 7.5 Annotated pie chart

How to present data so that a trend can be seen

You should use line graphs to highlight changes in numerical data over time (Table
7.1). For most research projects, your line graphs will be drawn using secondary data
such as that available from government websites (Research in practice 7.2, page 175)
or company reports. If you want to compare trends over time for two or more variables, you simply draw an additional line for each variable, adding a legend so you
know what each line represents!

How to present data so relationships between two variables can be seen

Relationships between two numerical variables are best shown using a scatter graph,
sometimes called a scatter plot (Table 7.1). Let's say an organisation has asked you
to find out if there is any relationship between how well its 30 sales employees performed in an aptitude test and their sales performance. The first of your variables

Research in practice 7.2

Presenting a trend

Ahmed's research project was looking at long-term economic trends. In particular, he was interested in changes in countries' balance of payments since the end of the Second World War and the relative importance of different goods and services over the years. Using the UK Government's website *www.statistics.gov.uk* as one of his sources of secondary data, he downloaded 11 balance of payments data sets free of charge. These included a set titled 'Balance of Payments – Trade in Goods'. This contained a summary of the UK's trade in goods recording the value of imports, exports and the balance of trade for the years 1946–2009. To show the trend in the balance of payments for trade in goods, he used a line graph. This showed a clear decline over time, this decline being most rapid between 1997 and 2006.

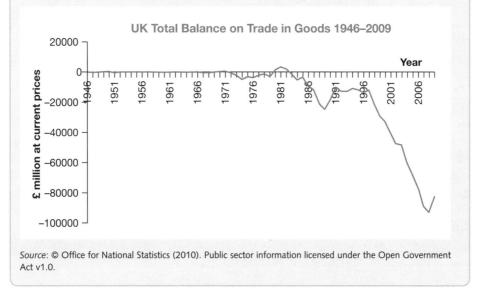

Source: © Office for National Statistics (2010). Public sector information licensed under the Open Government Act v1.0.

is each employee's aptitude test score out of 100. The second is the value of each employee's total sales for the past month recorded in pounds sterling. As you feel that sales performance is likely to be affected by aptitude, you decide that sales performance is your dependent variable and so should be plotted against the vertical axis of your scatter graph. Aptitude is the independent variable and so you plot this on the horizontal axis (Figure 7.6). Each point (cross) on your scatter graph represents an employee. The closer these points on your scatter graph are to an imaginary straight line (not shown on Figure 7.6 as it is imaginary!), the stronger the relationship between the two variables. Looking at your graph, you decide that there appears to be a strong relationship between an employee's aptitude test result and their sales performance. As we will see later, you decide to explain this cause and effect relationship statistically.

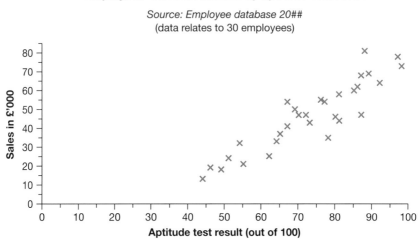

Figure 7.6 Scatter graph

How to describe data using statistics

We're sure that you've already studied statistics at some time in the past. However, we wouldn't be surprised if you had forgotten at least some things. We don't intend to give you a lecture on how to calculate lots of different statistics in this section. After all, there is no real need to do this as you will be using either a spreadsheet or some other statistics software to calculate the statistics for you. Rather, what we will do is talk about which statistics you should use to describe different types of data and, when you have calculated the statistics using your computer, what each one actually means. The statistics we will look at are summarised in Table 7.2.

Let's start by looking at the statistics you can use to describe a data variable. When you do this, you're describing one of three things:

● The **central tendency**, which is the common, middle or average value.

● The **dispersion**, which is how the data values are spread, or dispersed, around the central tendency.

● The **trend**, which is how the data values change or move in one direction over time.

Definitions

central tendency: the value for a variable that represents the common, middle or average. Statistics that describe data in this way are called 'central tendency measures'.

dispersion: the value for a variable that represents how the data are spread or dispersed around the central tendency. Statistics that describe data in this way are called 'dispersion measures'.

trend: the movement or change in one direction of the values for a variable over a period of time.

How to describe the central tendency and dispersion

As you can see from Table 7.2, if you have categorical data variables, such as the answer to your student questionnaire question 'In which faculty are you studying?' the only statistic you can use to describe the central tendency is the mode. This describes the category that occurs most often, for this question the Faculty of Business and Law. You can't describe the dispersion or the trend for categorical data.

Table 7.2 **Describing a variable using statistics**

For...	use the...	to describe the...	which represents the...
categorical data	mode	central tendency	category that occurs most often
numerical data	mode *or the*		value that occurs most often
	median *or the*		middle value when all the data values are put in rank order
	mean		average value
numerical data	range *or the*	dispersion	difference between the highest and lowest data values when they are put in rank order
	inter-quartile range *or the*		difference within the middle 50 per cent of data values when they are put in rank order
	standard deviation[1]		extent the data values differ from the mean (95 per cent of data will lie with plus or minus 1.96 standard deviations of the mean)
numerical data	index number[2]	trend	relative change in a series of data values over time

[1] only use if the data are normally distributed.
[2] only use if the data have been collected over time.

For numerical data, you can describe the central tendency, the dispersion and, where the data have been collected over time, the trend. Although you might use the mode to describe the most common value, the mean and the median are used more often by researchers with quantitative data. Let's use statistics to describe the variable 'employee sales last month' which we used for the scatter graph in Figure 7.6. Table 7.2 tells you that you can calculate the mode, median, mean, range, inter-quartile range and standard deviation for this numerical data variable. You decide to do this using IBM SPSS Statistics and get the output shown in Figure 7.7. Although your output does not give you the inter-quartile range, you could easily work it out by subtracting the 25th percentile from the 75th percentile. You use the output to describe employee sales in your project report:

Definition

normal distribution: the symmetrical distribution of data values around the mean for a quantitative variable forming a bell-shaped curve. In a normal distribution the values of the mean, median and mode are the same.

Mean sales last month for the organisation's 30 employees were £46,600. As the mean, median and mode are virtually the same, this suggests these data are **normally distributed**. Consequently the standard deviation of 18.46 indicates that 95 per cent of sales fell within the range £10,318 to £82,682, the complete range being £68,000.

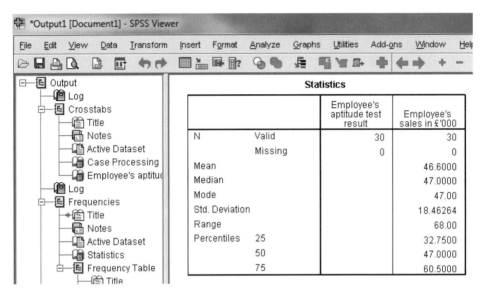

Figure 7.7 Descriptive statistics output in IBM SPSS Statistics

Source: SPSS, © 2011 International Business Machines Corporation. Reproduced courtesy of IBM.

How to describe the trend

You will have seen that the IBM SPSS Statistics output did not calculate any index numbers for the variable 'Employee's sales in £'000'. This is because these data were not collected over time and so can't be used to show a trend. However, we can do this for the data used to draw the line graph in Research in practice 7.2. Let's say Ahmed is now focusing his research on the trend for the 'Balance of payments – trade in goods' since 1981. Ahmed represents the value of his data for this starting date, known as the base year, on his spreadsheet using the number 100 (Figure 7.8). Increases in subsequent years would be represented by positive index numbers greater than 100 and decreases by positive index numbers less than 100, providing the balance of payments was in surplus. As you can see in Figure 7.8, this was not the case for the years 2000 onwards. For these years the deficit in the balance of payments is represented by a negative index number. As the deficit is greater than the initial surplus in the base year (1981), the negative index numbers are greater than 100. Concentrating on the last ten years, Ahmed interprets the index numbers in his project report:

Using 1981 as the base year it can be seen that the balance of trade went into deficit increasing rapidly up to 2008, the index number of –2875.73 in 2008 indicating the deficit for this year was over 28 times the surplus in 1981. The index number of –2543.33 in 2009 indicates a decline in the deficit from the previous year.

	A	B	C
1	Year	Balance of payments - trade in goods	Index number (1981 = 100)
2	1981	3238	100
23	2001	-41212	-1272.76
24	2002	-47705	-1473.29
25	2003	-48607	-1501.14
26	2004	-60900	-1880.79
27	2005	-68589	-2118.25
28	2006	-76312	-2356.76
29	2007	-89754	-2771.90
30	2008	-93116	-2875.73
31	2009	-82353	-2543.33

Figure 7.8 Describing a trend using index numbers

Source: SPSS, © 2011 International Business Machines Corporation. Reproduced courtesy of IBM.

How to examine relationships using statistics

We will now look at the statistics you can use to examine relationships between two or more data variables. When examining relationships using statistics, you're looking at one of five things:

- The association between two variables.
- The correlation between two variables.
- The difference between two or more variables.
- The explanation of one (dependent) variable by one or more other (independent) variables.
- The prediction of one (dependent) variable by one or more other (independent) variables.

When you do this you're also seeing how likely the relationship between your variables is to have occurred by chance. This is called significance testing and means you have to work out both a statistic and the probability (likelihood) of this statistic occurring by chance. If this probability is small (usually 0.05 or lower), then you can say your relationship is statistically significant. Statisticians refer to this as 'rejecting the null hypothesis and accepting the hypothesis'. When you reject a null hypothesis, you're rejecting a statement such as 'There is no significant association between...' and accepting a hypothesis such as 'There is a significant association between...'

As you can see in Table 7.3, different statistics are used to test each of the five things we listed above. You will also see that the statistic you use depends on the data you have, and that there are far more statistics to choose from for numerical data than for categorical data. This means you need to think carefully about which statistic you use and why. Table 7.3 should help you in this!

Table 7.3 Examining relationships between variables using statistics

For ...	use ... (symbol in brackets)	to examine ...	which represents the ...
categorical data	chi-square test (χ^2)	association	probability of the association between two variables occurring by chance
categorical ranked data	Spearman's rank correlation coefficient (ρ) or	correlation	strength of the relationship between two variables and the probability of this occurring by chance
	Kendal's rank correlation coefficient (τ)	correlation (when data contains tied ranks)	strength of the relationship between two variables and the probability of this occurring by chance
numerical data split into two groups using a categorical variable	independent groups t-test (t)	difference	probability of the differences between the values in the two groups occurring by chance
numerical data split into three-plus groups using a categorical variable	Analysis of variance (ANOVA) (F)	difference	probability of the differences between the values in the groups occurring by chance
pairs of numerical data for two variables measuring the same feature under different conditions	paired t-test (t)	difference	probability of the differences between each half of the pair (the two variables) occurring by chance

Table 7.3 Examining relationships between variables using statistics (*continued*)

For . . .	use . . . (symbol in brackets)	to examine . . .	which represents the . . .
numerical data	Pearson's product moment correlation coefficient (*r*)	correlation	strength of the relationship between two variables and the probability of this occurring by chance
	Regression coefficient (coefficient of determination) (r^2)	explanation	strength of a cause and effect relationship between a dependent and one or more independent variables and the probability of this occurring by chance
	Regression equation ($y = a + b x$)	prediction	formula to predict the values of a dependent variable, given the values of one or more independent variables

How to examine associations

Let's say you, in your questionnaire to a sample of students, collected data on each student's gender (male or female) as well as the faculty in which she or he was studying. These are both categorical data variables. You look at Table 7.3 and see that, as these data are not ranked, the only statistic you can use to examine the association between gender and faculty is the chi-square test. You use this statistic to test the null hypothesis 'There is no significant association between the faculty in which students are studying and their gender' using IBM SPSS Statistics. Your output is shown in Figure 7.9.

Figure 7.9 Examining the association between variables using a chi-square test

Source: SPSS, © 2011 International Business Machines Corporation. Reproduced courtesy of IBM.

Your output gives you both a crosstabulation of the data and another table headed 'Chi-square Tests'. The first row of the 'Chi-square Tests' table contains the (Pearson) chi-square statistic and the probability (Asymp. Sig.) of this occurring by chance. Next to the chi-square value is a reference to a footnote which states '0 cells (.0%) have expected counts of less than 5...' This is important as, for the statistic to give correct results, no more than 25 per cent of cells can have expected values of less than five. Fortunately this is not the case and, since the probability is less than 0.05, you can reject your null hypothesis: 'There is no significant association between the faculty in which students are studying and their gender', and accept the hypothesis: 'There is a significant association between the faculty in which students are studying and their gender'. You use the table and the chi-square statistic to interpret the relationship between gender and faculty in your project report:

> There is a significant association between the faculty in which students are studying and their gender (chi-square = 11.716, $df = 3$, $p = 0.008$). Students in both the Arts and Humanities and Social Sciences faculties are more likely to be female, while those in the Physical Sciences faculty are more likely to be male. Students in the Business and Law faculty are divided evenly between genders.

How to examine relationships

The only other categorical data statistics we mention in Table 7.3 are for ranked data. You will see in this table that there are two possible statistics that can be used to measure the strength of the relationship between two ranked variables:

- Kendall's rank correlation coefficient
- Spearman's rank correlation coefficient.

Both these statistics assume your sample has been selected at random, but do not need your data to be normally distributed. If your data for a variable contains tied ranks, let's say two or more students came equal second in an examination, it is better to use Kendall's rank correlation coefficient. Otherwise, you should use Spearman's rank correlation coefficient.

Like all correlation coefficients, the value of both Spearman's and Kendall's rank correlation coefficients will always be somewhere between –1 and +1 (Figure 7.10). This means that if your value is outside this range an error has been made in the calculation! If your correlation coefficient has a value of +1, this means that your two variables are related perfectly, the positive value meaning that as one variable increases, so does the other. If your correlation coefficient has a value of –1, this also means your two variables are related perfectly. However, a negative value means that as the values of one variable increase, the values of the other variable decrease. Beware: it is extremely unusual to find two variables that are related perfectly. As you can see in Figure 7.10, a correlation of zero means your two variables are independent, not being related at all. You have probably worked out by now how to interpret other values of a correlation coefficient from Figure 7.10. However, to allow you to check you have got it right, let's look at two different values: a correlation coefficient of −0.23 represents a weak negative correlation; a correlation of coefficient of 0.7 represents a strong positive correlation.

When you interpret a correlation coefficient you also need to see how likely the relationship between your variables is to have occurred by chance. As in the chi-square test, this is called significance testing and represents the probability (likelihood) of your statistic occurring by chance. Once again, if this probability is small (usually 0.05 or less), then you can say your relationship is statistically significant. Statisticians refer to this as 'rejecting the null hypothesis and accepting the hypothesis'. When you reject a null hypothesis for a correlation coefficient, you're rejecting a statement such as 'There is no significant correlation between...' and accepting a hypothesis such as 'There is a significant correlation between...'

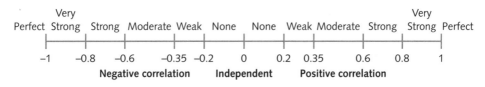

Figure 7.10 How to interpret correlation coefficients

Source: Developed from Hair et al. (2009).

Research in practice 7.3

Using *t*-tests, analysis of variance and correlation

Samantha was writing an extended essay on brand consciousness. Within her essay, she was particularly interested in the factors that influenced people's awareness of different brands and how this differed according to their demographic characteristics. During her search of the literature she had found a 2011 article by Zaharah Ghazali in the *International Journal of Management and Marketing Research*. This article used a sample of 230 students at a Malaysian university to investigate how socialisation factors such as the media, parents and peers all influenced students' brand consciousness for clothing. Within the article, Ghazali also looked at how brand consciousness differed according to the students' demographic characteristics.

Ghazali's article outlined how the data for each of the variables had been collected using a questionnaire, which Samantha considered had an excellent (88 per cent) response rate. The article also stated that the questions used to collect the data were all derived from previous questionnaires, although Samantha noted the source for some of the questions was not always referenced clearly. Variables used in the analysis included the following:

- Gender – categorised as male or female;
- Ethnicity – categorised as Malay, Chinese, Indian or other;
- Socialisation factors:
    - exposure to television media – measured on a numerical scale;
    - exposure to radio media – measured on a numerical scale;

→

- exposure to online media – measured on a numerical scale;
- exposure to movie media – measured on a numerical scale;
- exposure to parents' influences – measured on a numerical scale;
- exposure to peers' influences – measured on a numerical scale;
- Brand consciousness – measured on a numerical scale.

Ghazali had undertaken a variety of statistical analyses using these variables, such as:

- Independent sample t-tests for gender differences in brand consciousness.
- One-way analysis of variance for ethnicity differences in brand consciousness.
- Pearson's correlations for exposure to each of the six socialisation factors with brand consciousness.

Based on the first of these, Ghazali (2011) commented in her article that there was a significant difference for brand consciousness between genders stating the t-test value and its significance ($t = -2.495$, $p = 0.013$). This Ghazali interpreted as indicating that females were more likely to be highly brand-conscious than males.

Samantha felt that the t-test was the correct statistic to use. She looked at the table in the article that showed the results of the t-test and noted the mean brand consciousness score for males (2.98) and females (3.24). This provided further support for Ghazali's statement that females were more likely to be highly brand-conscious than males.

Interpreting the one-way analysis of variance statistic ($F = 8.732$, $p = 0.000$), Ghazali (2011) commented there was a significant difference in brand consciousness across ethnicity. This she interpreted as students from her category of 'other ethnic groups' (including those of Siamese, Singaporean and Indonesian origin) being more likely to be highly brand-conscious than students of Malay, Chinese and Indian origin.

Samantha felt that analysis of variance was the correct statistic to use. She looked at the table in the article showing the results of the analysis of variance. This gave the mean brand consciousness score for 'other' (3.95), as well as the Malay (3.09), Chinese (3.10) and Indian (3.13) ethnic groups. This supported Ghazali's interpretation that students in the other ethnic groups were more likely to be highly brand-conscious than Malay, Chinese and Indian students.

Finally, using Pearson's product moment correlation coefficient, Ghazali (2011) discussed the influence of brand consciousness on socialisation factors such as media socialisation, parents and peers. She noted how media influence differed between these media, movie-viewing having a negative relationship with brand conciousness ($r = -0.369$, p < 0.01), while parental influence ($r = 0.134$, $p < 0.05$) and peer influence ($r = 0.486$, $p < 0.01$) both showed positive relationships.

Samantha considered Ghazali's discussion of the findings in relation to the correlation statistics presented in the associated table in the article. She felt that the use of Pearson's correlation was right for numerical data. Although these statistics had been interpreted correctly, she felt that none of the correlations were particularly strong. She noted that, while there were significant correlations between brand consciousness and exposure to each of movie media, parents' influences and peers' influences, the correlations with exposure to television, radio and online media were not significant. Although this point was made by Ghazali in her article's discussion section, Samantha decided to note down the remaining correlation statistics with brand consciousness and their significance levels for use in her extended essay. These were exposure to television media ($r = -0.081$, $p > 0.05$), exposure to radio media ($r = -0.020$, $p > 0.05$), and exposure to online media ($r = 0.067$, $p > 0.05$).

If you haven't done so already, now read Research in practice 7.3. This looks at the use of statistics in a journal article a student is reading for her extended essay. Towards the end of this Research in practice the student, Samantha, looks at how the author of the article has used Pearson's product moment correlation coefficient. As the data used to calculate Pearson's product moment correlation coefficient are numerical, she feels rightly that the correct statistic has been used. The article's author has given both the statistic (r) and the probability (p) of a chance occurrence for possible relationships between brand consciousness and six socialisation factors. Where this was less than or equal to 0.05, the author has implicitly rejected the null hypothesis 'There is no significant relationship between...' and accepted the hypothesis 'There is a significant relationship between...'. This practice of not stating either the null hypothesis or hypothesis often happens in academic journal articles, so don't worry too much if they are not actually stated in an article you're reading. Although the article's author has not provided an indication of how to interpret the strength of the significant correlations, Samantha recognises that they are not particularly strong. If you look again at Research in practice 7.3, you will see that the negative correlation between exposure to movies and brand consciousness ($r = -0.369$, $p < 0.01$) and the positive correlation between exposure to peer influence and brand consciousness ($r = 0.486$, $p < 0.01$), although both significant, might only be interpreted as a moderate relationship. In contrast, the relationship represented by the positive correlation between exposure to parental influence and brand consciousness ($r = 0.134$, $p < 0.05$), although significant, might be interpreted as 'none', owing to the very low value of the correlation coefficient. None of the remaining correlations with brand consciousness are considered significant, the value of p for each being greater than 0.05.

How to examine differences

Research in practice 7.3 also shows how two statistics, the independent groups' t-test and the analysis of variance, can be used to analyse differences when a numerical variable is split into two or more groups. In the article Samantha is reading, the author split the numerical variable 'brand consciousness' into two groups using the categorical variable 'gender', and then used the independent groups' t-test statistic to see if there was a significant difference between males and females. The independent groups' t-test was used because the author was testing for differences between two groups. It is worth you noting here that a paired t-test was not used because the data in the two variables were not collected in pairs, one from each group. Although a paired t-test is calculated in a slightly different way, its interpretation is exactly the same. As the p value of 0.013 was less than 0.05, this shows that a null hypothesis such as 'There is no significant difference in brand values between males and females' could be rejected, and a hypothesis such as 'There is a significant difference in brand values between males and females' could be accepted. Once again, neither was stated in the article.

The author of the article also split the numeric variable 'brand consciousnesses' into four groups using the categorical variable 'ethnicity', and then used the analysis of variance statistic to see if there was a significant difference in brand consciousness between Malay, Chinese, Indian and other ethnic groups. Looking at Table 7.3, you can see that analysis of variance was used because brand consciousness was now split into more than two groups. The recorded F ratio ($F = 8.732$) had a probability of occurring by chance of less than 0.001, recorded by the author as $p = 0.000$. This shows that a null hypothesis such as 'There is no significant difference in brand values between ethnic groups' could be rejected and a hypothesis such as 'There is a significant difference in brand values between ethnic groups' could be accepted. As previously, neither was stated in the article.

How to explain and predict cause and effect relationships

You've already looked at a cause and effect relationship using a scatter graph to display the relationship between all sales employees' aptitude test results and their sales performance for the past month (Figure 7.6). When you plotted these data on your scatter graph, you plotted aptitude test result as the independent variable and sales performance in £'000 as the dependent variable. This scatter graph suggested there was a cause and effect relationship between employees' aptitude (the cause) and their sales performance (the effect). As we stated you would, you now test this statistically by calculating the regression coefficient (Figure 7.11). As your data relate to all sales employees, the population, there is no need to calculate the likelihood (probability) that this regression coefficient has occurred by chance.

Your regression coefficient of 0.83 means that 83 per cent of the variation in your dependent variable, sales in the past month, can be explained by the independent variable, aptitude test result. This means that the aptitude test is a very good predictor of sales performance for the past month as it's rare to obtain a regression coefficient larger than 0.8. Note: the value of a regression coefficient must always be between zero and one. If it is outside this range, then there has been an error in the calculation!

The regression equation you've calculated in Figure 7.11 can be used to predict the value of your dependent variable, sales for the past month, if you know the value of the independent variable, aptitude test. This means, for example, if a potential employee scores 70 in an aptitude test taken as part of the selection process, you can use the regression equation to predict what their sales in £'000 would have been for the past month:

	A	B	C	D	E	F	G	H	I	J	K
1	Aptitude t	Sales in £ '000									
2	44	13		Regression coefficient:			0.83				
3	46	19									
4	49	18		Gradient (b):			1.11				
5	51	24									
6	54	32		Intercept (a):			-34.58				
7	55	21									
8	62	25									
9	64	33		Regression equation:			Sales in £'000 = -34.58 + 1.11 Aptitude test result				
10	65	37					(y = a + b x)				

Figure 7.11 Regression coefficient and regression equation

$$\text{Sales in } £'000 = -34.58 + (1.11 \times 70)$$
$$= -34.58 + 77.7$$
$$= 43.12$$

You could therefore predict this potential employee would have made sales of £43,120 for the past month.

7.4 Analysing data qualitatively

At the start of this chapter, we said that we would focus on analysing text data quali-tatively, only talking about the analysis of non-text data such as audio recordings and the audio parts of video recordings where these have been transcribed and so can also be analysed as text data. If you're collecting your own data, perhaps by interviewing, you will probably have already begun to think about what these interviews are telling you. This is quite normal. We would expect you to begin to analyse your qualitative data before you've collected them all. Doing this will allow you to follow up initial insights suggested by early interviews in later interviews, as well as to recognise when you have reached data saturation (we talked about this in section 6.3). In this sec-tion we will start by looking at how you prepare text data so that they are suitable for qualitative analysis. As you do this, you will begin to immerse yourself in your data and so begin to understand it better. Next, we will talk about how you develop propositions and then how you use these propositions to build or test theory by look-ing for patterns in your data. Finally, we will look at how you assess the credibility and dependability of qualitative research findings reported by others.

How to prepare your data

If you're analysing your data qualitatively, you may or may not be using specialist qualitative data analysis software. It is only recently that computer-aided qualitative data analysis software (**CAQDAS**), such as QSR International's NVivo, have begun to be used by students for undergraduate and master's research projects. This means that, although you will be expected to use a spreadsheet or statistical analysis soft-ware to analyse quantitative data, you're less likely to be expected to use CAQDAS to analyse qualitative data. However, the things you need to do to prepare your text data for qualitative analysis are similar whether or not you intend to use CAQDAS.

Definition

CAQDAS: a general term for all computer-aided qualitative data analysis software such as NVivo, ATLAS.ti and MAXqda.

Research in practice 7.4

Annotated interview transcript

As part of her research project on employees' reactions to change, Xue had conducted and audio recorded semi-structured interviews with 12 participants, each of whom signed a consent form. She found the transcription of the interviews very time-consuming as, although each only lasted on average half an hour, word processing each audio recording took between three and four hours. She emailed her first transcript to her supervisor and asked him to see if there were any ways it could be improved. The extract below from the start of the interview includes her supervisor's comments relating to preparing the transcript for analysis. It does not include any of the supervisor's comments about Xue's interviewing skills.

I presume names have been changed to preserve anonymity

[Organisation Name] Interview 2

Include more details such as date, time and place of interview

XUE: *Thankyou for agreeing to be interviewed. Now, just to give a little bit of context, we're going to be talking about you in relation to your work and the changes at [organisation name] in the interview. But first, can you give me an idea of what sort of job you do? (...) Can you give me a quick overview?*

Use of italics makes questions easy to see

Use of capitals makes names easy to see

PHIL: I work in Financial Services in the payroll section and I work within the control section of the payroll section running payrolls and that sort of thing (...)

I presume dots inside the single brackets mean a pause

XUE: *So what is your job title Phil?*

I know there are no typographical errors here, but check there are none in all your transcripts

PHIL: Well (...) at the moment it is Project Officer (...) or something like that, I mean (...).

XUE: *Basically what you are doing is running the payrolls?*

I presume the double brackets means this is your description inside the brackets

PHIL: Well we've gone on to a new payroll system in the last twelve months and are also involved in setting-up (......) I WAS involved in the project setting it up (...) and NOW I have just sort of moved back into the payroll section, and running payrolls, dealing with queries, dealing with changes to the system, that sort of thing at the moment ((appears to be unhappy about this)). There is a restructuring going on in the section, so the job title and what I do could, again, be changed into something else.

I presume more dots inside the single brackets means a longer pause

I presume capitals means this word was spoken more loudly than the others

DON'T FORGET TO SAVE EACH INTERVIEW AS A SEPARATE FILE

Research in practice 7.4 examines an annotated extract from a student's interview transcripts, showing you how to prepare an audio recording as text for qualitative analysis. As you can see from how Xue has prepared her transcript, when preparing data as text for qualitative analysis you need to do the following:

- Include details of the date, time and place where the data were collected.
- Anonymise both the organisation's and the respondents' names, using the alternatives consistently.
- Consistently use *italics* to signify questions asked.
- Consistently use capitals to highlight the names of the interviewer and the respondents.
- Consistently use (...) to show a pause in speech, the number of dots showing the relative length of the pause.
- Consistently use CAPITALS within the transcript to show those words that were spoken more loudly than others.
- Consistently use (( )) to enclose your description of what is happening such as the participant's tone of voice, facial expressions or other visual cues.
- Make sure there are no typographical errors and that words are spelt consistently throughout.
- Save each interview transcript as a separate file.

Having just read this list, you will see that being consistent in your preparation of qualitative text data such as transcripts is crucial. If you're going to analyse web-based interview data where questions and responses were automatically captured as they were typed in, it is unlikely that these data will have been recorded consistently or in precisely the right format for CAQDAS. If you're going to analyse other forms of text data, including secondary data such as online business news reports, these data are also unlikely to be in quite the right format for CAQDAS. Although you will not need to anonymise secondary text data that are available publicly such as news reports, you will still need to add full details of when it was collected and the source where you found it. It is also likely that such data will contain some typographical errors and inconsistencies that you will need to correct. You will therefore need to spend time preparing your text data for qualitative analysis by following the points outlined above, whatever its source!

You only need to read this paragraph if you're going to analyse your data using CAQDAS! If you are, you need to find out the precise data format that the software you have chosen needs, as it probably will not recognise some features of your word-processing software. For example, if you're using QSR International's NVivo 9, you will find that this software does not import headers and footers from Microsoft Word documents. Other CAQDAS software, especially early versions, may require you to save each document as a text only file (.txt) or in rich text format (.rtf). This means you will lose some of your word-processing software's features. Beware!

How to develop propositions to build or test theory

We are sure that sometime in your life you have at least had a go at completing a jigsaw puzzle. When you started to make the puzzle, you probably looked first at the picture on the box lid. Let's say it was a photograph of Tower Bridge in London, although unlike Figure 7.12, in colour. You then tipped all the pieces out of the box on to a table and turned them picture side up before sorting them into different groups or categories that had similar characteristics. To help you with your sorting, you looked at the picture to get some ideas for categories. These would have included categories such as part of 'Tower Bridge', the 'sky', the 'river', 'vegetation' as well as the 'edge of the puzzle'. Inevitably, you could have put some of the puzzle pieces into more than one category such as being at the 'edge of the puzzle' and also part of the 'sky', or being part of the 'river' and part of 'Tower Bridge'. You then fitted pieces in each category together, completing different parts of the puzzle such as the sky, the river or Tower Bridge. You then used those pieces that were in more than one of your categories such as the 'sky' and 'Tower Bridge' to join together the different parts of the puzzle you had already completed, before fitting the remaining pieces. Finally, you compared the puzzle picture with that on the box lid.

You're no doubt wondering why we've spent so much time talking about completing a jigsaw puzzle. The answer is simple! Analysing qualitative data and, in particular, looking for patterns by categorising data is similar to completing a jigsaw

Figure 7.12 Tower Bridge, London
Source: © Mark Saunders, 2011.

puzzle. Let's start with the lid of the puzzle box. In addition to the picture of the completed puzzle, it normally says how many pieces there are in the puzzle and how difficult it is to complete. This is similar to your critical review of the literature (section 2.2), as the lid provides an overview of significant information about the puzzle and a clear idea of how the pieces should fit together. The information on the box lid therefore represents the existing knowledge about how the puzzle pieces relate to each other. From this existing knowledge you develop **testable propositions**. For example, looking at the picture on the box lid (Figure 7.12), a testable proposition would be that the pieces of sky are at the top of the picture. Another would be that the vegetation pieces are on the left and at the bottom of the picture. Pieces that can be put in two or more categories show the interrelationships within the theory, such as the relationship between the vegetation and the sky. You test these propositions (and others) by categorising the pieces and making the puzzle. If the picture on the box is the same as the puzzle picture you have made, then the propositions you have developed are supported!

What you have done in using the picture and other information on the puzzle box lid is analyse your data (the puzzle pieces) deductively (we've talked about both inductive and deductive approaches in more detail in section 5.3). This is because you started with what was already known about the puzzle (the picture and other information on the box) and used this as a guide to develop your series of testable propositions. You then designed your analysis (categorised your pieces and made the puzzle) to test these propositions. If you're analysing qualitative data deductively for your project report, you're looking for things in the data to answer research questions and test the propositions that you have developed using your understanding of the academic literature. Like the picture on the puzzle box lid, the literature on which your research questions and propositions are based give a clear direction of the categories that are important and, where a piece falls into two or more categories, how they should fit together. By systematically categorising your data and seeing if particular patterns occur, you're testing your propositions. Remember, as we pointed out in section 6.4, as you collect and analyse your data, you may get new insights into your testable propositions that you did not initially expect and so may need to revise them.

If your puzzle had no picture on the box lid or any other information, then you would have had to analyse your data inductively. You would have started without a clear theory from which to develop testable propositions of what the puzzle looked like, the number of pieces and how they were related. You would have done this by sorting the pieces into different categories that had similar characteristics. However, as there was no information on the box, you would have had to use ideas

---

Definition

testable proposition: an assertion that something is true that can be tested using the data available.

you generated by looking at (analysing) the puzzle pieces to decide on your categories. You would have found that some of the categories you first thought of were less useful than others and may well have decided later not to use them. If you're analysing qualitative data inductively for your project report, you do not have (or need) a clearly defined theoretical framework. Rather you're identifying possible propositions (theories) about your data and then developing questions to test them. Like a puzzle about which you have no information, your theory about how the pieces fit together will develop as you systematically analyse your data, collect more data and the most relevant patterns become clearer.

Research in practice 7.5

Developing testable propositions and categorising data

Mark was working with a group of students who, like many, found writing their project report difficult. During his preparation he used a number of academic sources on writing, including the book *Writing for Social Scientists* (Becker, 2007). Using this, he developed three testable propositions:

1 Students adopt particular habits when they write.

2 Students adopt these habits because they:
   (a) find writing difficult,
   (b) are easily distracted from writing,
   (c) are afraid that what they write will be wrong.

3 The habits students adopt differ between male and female students.

He decided to test these propositions and asked each of the students to describe in writing how he or she wrote. He explained he was not interested in the students' scholarly preparations, but the details of what they actually did when they were writing. The students' descriptions were subsequently word processed and anonymised and formed Mark's data. Mark also developed a brief set of categories to attach to this data:

Habit	*Unsure what these could be. Develop categories from the data.*
Reason	– difficult
	– distraction
	– afraid wrong
Gender	– male
	– female

The following extract of a student's description shows these categories attached to units of data, each of which is one sentence of the description.

GENDER – MALE	**Male student**
HABIT	I always compose directly into a word processor. I usually have
HABIT	hand-written notes to work from which give me an overall structure,
HABIT	but the thoughts are typed directly in. Before starting, I make sure
	that my desk is relatively clear, other than for the notes and articles
HABIT	I'm going to use. I also make sure I have a fresh cup of tea. The
	computer is in a room which I always use for writing and I feel
REASON – COMFORT/DIFFICULT	comfortable there. To be honest, I find it difficult to write
HABIT	anywhere other than this room. The word processor software is set
	to my preferences: Times New Roman 12, and no auto spell
HABIT	corrections. I've turned off the underline for misspelled words
REASON – DISTRACTION x2	because it puts me off. I don't have any distractions in the room
HABIT	where I write – no music or television, although there is a telephone.
HABIT	I nearly always start early in the morning (7.30) and work through
	until about 10.30–11.00 before I have a break. I like to have full
	days for writing as it helps me organise my thoughts...

Look at the first two paragraphs of Research in practice 7.5. In his research, Mark developed three testable propositions from the literature. Each proposition was carefully worded, often as a possible explanation, to enable it to be tested. Reread Mark's first proposition:

> 1. Students adopt particular habits when they write.

Although this proposition does not offer a possible explanation, whether or not the students adopt particular habits when they write, it can be tested by looking for patterns in the data Mark has collected.

Now look at Mark's second proposition:

> 2. Students adopt these habits because they:
>   (a) find writing difficult,
>   (b) are easily distracted from writing,
>   (c) are afraid that what they write will be wrong.

This suggests three possible explanations for students adopting particular habits when they write: (a) they find writing difficult, (b) they are easily distracted from writing and (c) they are afraid that what they write will be wrong. The data Mark collects in the form of students' descriptions of how they write will enable each possible explanation to be tested. When testing these explanations, it will be important that Mark also looks for alternative explanations, such as other reasons why students might adopt these habits. It may be that some students do not even adopt particular habits when they write! If you do not look for alternative explanations, you will probably only notice evidence that supports your own opinions, resulting in your findings being biased and subjective. By testing your own propositions and looking for alternative explanations through looking for clear patterns, you will be able to develop clearly justified credible conclusions from your data.

And finally look at Mark's third proposition:

---

3. The habits students adopt differ between male and female students.

Like Mark's first proposition, this can be tested using the data Mark has collected. As with his other propositions, he will test this by looking for patterns in the data.

How to build or test theory by looking for patterns

Our earlier jigsaw puzzle example emphasises that, whether you're using a deductive or an inductive approach to look for patterns to test your propositions, you need to take the following steps:

1 Develop meaningful **categories** or codes to describe your data.

2 Decide on the **unit of data** that is appropriate for your analysis and to which you will attach relevant categories.

3 Attach relevant categories to units (pieces) of your data.

If you using a deductive approach, your categories will be based on terms used in the literature, often being drawn from existing theory. In contrast, if you're using an inductive approach, your categories will emerge from your data. For both deductive and inductive approaches, it is likely that you will refine your categories to ensure they are meaningful as you look for patterns during your analysis to test your propositions. Your choice of the unit of data to which you will attach a relevant category or categories depends on what works! You need units of data that are large enough to highlight where there are relationships between categories, and yet not so large as to be described by all your categories. Depending on the analysis, we've found units of a line of transcript, a sentence and an individual response can all work well.

Let's now look at the categorising of the student's description in Research in practice 7.5. In this research, Mark created hierarchical categories to test three propositions he developed from the literature. However, other than the source of

---

Definitions

categorising data: developing meaningful categories and attaching those categories that are relevant to specific units of data.

unit of data: a predetermined piece of data such as a line of a transcript, sentence, paragraph, or response.

categories, the process he has used is the same for both deductive and inductive approaches. For his first category, 'habit', Mark was unsure what these might be and so decided to develop more detailed subcategories from the data. This means that for these detailed subcategories he will be working inductively. Although the extract only shows part of one student's description, it implies, as suggested in proposition one, students do have habits associated with how they write. Possible subcategories of 'habit' that Mark could use to group his data suggested by the extract include 'computer use', 'refreshment' and 'room'. If these subcategories also proved suitable for categorising other students' descriptions, they would reveal that the habits were common. It is likely that further new subcategories would be revealed by the other students' descriptions of how they write. For his second category, 'reason', Mark used the literature to provide three subcategories: 'difficult', 'distraction' and 'afraid wrong'. The first two of these have been used when categorising units of data in the extract. In addition Mark has introduced a new subcategory: 'reason – comfort' based on the data. This indicates he is looking for alternative explanations. Mark's use of the category 'gender – male' provides descriptive data about the student and will allow him to test his third proposition by looking for differences in patterns between male and female students.

We'll now look at how categorising these data has already begun to suggest a possible pattern with which to test the second proposition. Proposition two offered three reasons why students adopted these habits associated with writing. If we look at the student's description we can see that the 'reason' subcategories 'difficulty' and 'distraction' are both in close proximity to the category 'habit'. This provides Mark with an indication that there may be a pattern. Looking at the actual data, you can see that the 'reason' for the 'habit' of using a particular room is because it is 'difficult' to write anywhere else and, towards the end of the extract, because there are no 'distractions'. Obviously from such a short extract Mark can't be sure that this is a pattern. Analysis of the other students' descriptions of how they write will enable him to test the proposition further and confirm whether a similar pattern occurs.

How to assess the value of qualitative research reported by others

You're probably now thinking: this is all very well but, when I read articles reporting qualitative research, how do I know that patterns that are discussed and the insights offered are of value? Your question is a good one! As with you, the researcher's biases, preferences and so on will influence at least to some extent the way the data have been collected, analysed and interpreted. This means that when you read an article you need to carefully assess whether the author's claims are credible and dependable, being justified by methods used and supporting evidence that has been offered. To do this we suggest you use the following questions:

1 Is the method used to collect the data explained clearly (section 6.4)?

2 Is the method used to analyse the data explained clearly (section 7.4)?

3 Are the findings explained thematically?

4 Are the findings related explicitly to research objectives, questions or propositions?

5 Do the arguments made and the evidence presented support the claims made? For example:

   (a) Are the quotations used placed in context and do they support points made?

   (b) Are data included that do not support the claims made and an explanation offered as to why?

Research in practice 7.6

Assessing findings from interviews

Robin's research project was an extended literature review about how organisations used training and development. In her search of the Emerald online database, she had found an article by McDowall and Saunders (2010) that explored how managers responsible for training and development conceptualised about these activities in practice. McDowall and Saunders had analysed data from 26 telephone interviews with these managers. They stated that data saturation was reached after they had analysed 19 interviews, analysis of the remaining 7 interviews providing no further insights. Robin felt that the article described both their data collection and analysis clearly, providing sufficient detail for her to see precisely how these had been undertaken. This gave her confidence in their findings. The authors had organised on a thematic basis, considering each of their research questions explicitly in turn.

As part of the findings about how managers saw the link between training and development in practice, McDowall and Saunders (2010: 618) had written:

> Training was seen by about a quarter of managers as a means for development; in other words training was a process and one available mechanism to support an individual's development, development being the outcome and an umbrella term. Participant B commented:
>
> > Training I would see as something that FEEDS into development, I would not say that they are different (...) ultimately, training feeds into long-term development.
>
> This suggests a link between training and development, as explained by a Participant F, a senior manager from the private sector:
>
> > Development I would see as something that is a sort of on-going development, many things feed into development. One of the things that may feed into development is training. I see training as a specific thing that is done to address either a specific need or a long-term need. Whereas development is something that can be down to a person's day-to-day job, which ultimately should be developing them, if that makes sense. Training I would describe as a specific programme to address specific needs, development I would describe ultimately as the sort of long-term change in an individual as they work towards a specific target.
>
> Despite general agreement that development and training were linked, managers differentiated between them according to the practical aspects. Training was seen

as skills-based, technical and focused on the current job, whereas development was seen as wider-ranging and relating to interpersonal skills, mirroring the definitions of Warr (2002) and Laird (1985) considered earlier. There was agreement that training was always planned and formal whereas development activities could, in addition, be ad hoc, unplanned, sporadic and informal. In approximately half of interviews, development entailed a career-related element focussing upon a change in the person's duties, such as…

Source: McDowall and Saunders (2010: 618). Copyright © 2010 Emerald Group Publishing Limited (www.emeraldinsight.com/0309-0590.htm). Reproduced by permission of the publisher.

Robin felt that this extract, along with the rest of the section on the link between training and development provided credible evidence that, although managers agreed training and development were linked, there were differences of opinion regarding the use of development. She also recognised that, although the quotations used in the article provided credible supporting evidence regarding how the managers interviewed used training and development in their organisations, there was no need to include them in her extended literature review. Her supervisor agreed and suggested she just referred to the key findings, where appropriate, to particular themes in her review.

If you haven't done so already, now read Research in practice 7.6. This looks at a journal article using qualitative research a student is reading for her extended essay. The student, Robin, feels that the methods used to collect the data and to analyse the data have been explained clearly in the article (questions 1 and 2 from the list above) and we'll believe her! We're also told that the findings have been organised thematically, each of the authors' research questions being considered explicitly (questions 3 and 4 from the list above). This suggests the findings are based on a dependable method.

Using the extract from the article, we can now consider whether or not we agree with Robin's assessment that the article 'provides credible evidence' to support the claims made. To do this we'll use the final question (5) from the list above. Look at the first quotation in the extract. Although this quotation is less than five lines in length, it has been indented. If you're including quotations in your project report, check your university's regulations. Often quotations of four lines or less are just included within the main text of the paragraph. This first quotation provides credible evidence to support the authors' claim that, for about a quarter of their participants, training is one available mechanism to support an individual's development (question 5a). However, as you read on, you will see it does not appear to support the authors' later claim that training and development are different, the participant's comment 'I would not say that they are different' providing contrary evidence (question 5b). As indicated by question 5a, the quotation is attributed to a particular anonymised Participant, B, who was contextualised earlier in the article as a 'senior manager in the media industry' (McDowall and Saunders, 2010: 618).

Now look at the second quotation in the extract. Once again, this quotation is placed in context, Participant F being described as a 'senior manager from the private sector'. This quotation provides credible evidence, and explains reasons, for the link between training and development. However, in contrast to the previous quotation, it implies that this manager does believe that training and development are different. The last paragraph in the extract builds on this evidence claiming that, despite training and development being linked, managers do differentiate between them 'according to the practical aspects'. Further examples of ways in which this occurs are subsequently provided to support this claim, clear indications of where there are differences of opinion being shown by phrases such as 'In approximately half of interviews...' Later in the same section, although not included in the extract for reasons of space, as suggested by question 5b the authors offer an explanation as to why not all evidence supports the claim that training and development are different, commenting that 'training and development activities are perhaps not as clearly differentiated by managers as the literature suggests, and that individual perceptions may be organisation-dependent' (McDowall and Saunders 2010: 619). Following this discussion, we can say we agree with Robin's assessment and that the article 'provides credible evidence' to support the claims made.

Summary

- The data that you and others analyse can be divided into two types: quantitative data that are numerical or whose values had been measured in some way, and qualitative data that are not numerical and have not been measured in some way.

  - Quantitative data can be split into categorical data (descriptive and ranked) and numerical data (discrete and continuous).

  - Qualitative data can be divided into text data and non-text data (audio, video and image).

- When preparing quantitative data for computer analysis, you should enter it as a data matrix for computer analysis. Secondary data can often be downloaded in this format. You should check data for errors before undertaking analyses.

- Tables and diagrams are used to present quantitative data. The tables and diagrams you use depend on the type of data you have and what you want to show.

- Statistical analyses are used to describe data and to examine relationships. The statistics you use depend on the type of data you have, what you want to describe or examine and whether you can meet the assumptions of the test. For some statistics you will need to also work out the probability of the finding occurring by chance.

- Qualitative data are often analysed in text form. When preparing qualitative data for analysis as text, you should record it as a word-processed document, ensuring you use recording conventions consistently. You can either analyse qualitative data manually or using computer-aided qualitative analysis software.

- You can undertake the process of qualitative data analysis both deductively and inductively.

- In both inductive and deductive qualitative analysis, you can use testable propositions to build and test theory. This involves looking for patterns in your data and testing alternative explanations for these patterns using your data. To look for patterns you need to:

  - develop meaningful categories or codes to describe your data;
  - decide on the unit of data that is appropriate for your analysis and to which you will attach relevant categories;
  - attach relevant categories to units (pieces) of your data.

- It is important that, in analysing data, the arguments you offer and the findings you present support claims you're making clearly and logically.

Thinking about analysing data

→ As you continue to read and note the literature, use your knowledge about quantitative and qualitative data analysis to help you assess the value of other researchers' findings (section 2.7).

→ Think about the analyses you will need to undertake to answer your research question and meet your objectives.

→ If you're going to use or are using secondary data (Chapter 4), use your knowledge about different types of data and how to prepare data for analysis to help you assess which data analysis techniques will be most suitable. Make notes about the reasons for your choices as you will need this level of detail to write the method section of your project report.

→ If you're going to collect or have collected your own (primary) data, use your knowledge about different types of data and how to prepare data for analysis to help you assess which data analysis techniques will be most helpful. Make notes about the reasons for your choices as you will need this level of detail to write the method section of your project report. If possible, make your assessment of techniques before you collect your data. You may find you need to change parts of your collection methods, such as questionnaire questions (Chapter 6).

→ Also, make notes explaining how the analyses you have chosen will mean you can answer your objectives. You will need this level of detail to write the method section of your project report.

References

Becker, H.S. (2007) *Writing for Social Scientists*, 2nd edn, Chicago: University of Chicago.

European Commission (2010) *Organic Farming Statistics* [Accessed 21 December 2010]. Available at: *http://epp.eurostat.ec.europa.eu/statistics_explained/index.php/ Organic_farming_statistics*

Ghazali, S. (2011) The influence of socialization agents and demographic profiles on brand consciousness, *International Journal of Management and Marketing Research*, 4(1): 19–29.

Hair, J., Black, W., Babin, B. and Anderson, R. (2009) *Multivariate Data Analysis*, 7th edn, London: Pearson.

McDowall, A. and Saunders M.N.K. (2010) UK managers' conceptions of employee training and development, *Journal of European Industrial Training*, 34(7): 609–30.

Office for National Statistics (2010) *Balance of payments – Trade in goods*. Available at: *http:// www.statistics.gov.uk/statbase/tsdownload.asp?vlnk=224* [Accessed 22 December 2010].

Saunders, M., Lewis, P. and Thornhill, A. (2009) *Research Methods for Business Students*, 5th edn, Harlow: FT Prentice Hall.

Chapter 8

Writing and presenting the research proposal

8.1 Why you should read this chapter

When we sat down to plan this book we thought long and hard about the order in which the chapters should appear. The most difficult decision was where to place this chapter. It had to appear at the beginning of the book or at the end. We could have put it at the beginning. Setting out the recommended content of the research proposal could have acted as a route map from which you could plot your path through the book. This would ensure you were familiar with the role of, say, the literature review and the details you should include about your proposed methods. We decided against this. We thought that you should be familiar with the major concepts and techniques that the conduct of research involves before you think about your proposal. In short, we felt that you would be better equipped to write an effective research proposal having read and understood the previous seven chapters.

Writing an effective research proposal is a vital part of the research process. We explain the reasons for this in the first section of this chapter. Perhaps you feel it is unnecessary to elaborate on this. After all, your university may require you to produce a written research proposal as the assessment vehicle for the research methods module, so this reason is sufficient. But the research proposal is a vital document for reasons other than assessment necessity. Indeed, you may be reading this book to help you prepare a research proposal which will be a vital starting point in your research. For example, you may be embarking upon a research project required by your work organisation. Whatever the purpose, writing an effective research proposal is vital.

We then move on to consider at which point in the research process you should be writing your research proposal, before considering the most important topic which is addressed in the chapter: the content of the research proposal. The chapter ends with two discussions which we hope you will find useful. The first is on the writing style you should adopt when compiling your research proposal. This is something many of us have found difficult, and confusing, in our academic careers and is something worth thinking about. Finally we return to the subject of assessment, and ask just what is it that the assessor(s) of your research proposal will be looking for when that all-important judgement is made.

8.2   Why is the research proposal so important?

The overall purpose of the research proposal is to present and justify a research idea you have and to explain the practical way in which you think this research should be conducted. In effect it is a 'contract' between you and your reader(s) which sets out precisely what it is you aim, or would aim, to do and the way in which you will do it. You can also think about this contract as a personal document which binds you to your stated intentions in the event that you are tempted to break the contact! So think about the research proposal as an essential discipline measure in a process which has the potential to become extremely undisciplined!

Now let's look at some of the more specific reasons the research proposal is so important.

■ It clarifies your ideas and helps you organise those ideas

Another reason we decided to place this chapter at the end of the book is that you will have realised by now that assembling your research ideas is a very difficult process. Moreover, assembling them in a way that they will make sense to an audience that is far less familiar than you with those ideas is even more difficult.

We have made the point elsewhere (Saunders et al., 2009 and in Chapter 2 of this book) that writing can be the best way of clarifying our thoughts. This is a valuable purpose of the research proposal. There is nothing quite so frightening as sitting in front of a screen with just the heading 'Research proposal' to concentrate the mind. The very blankness of the screen forces you to come up with some ideas. If all else fails, we always suggest to our students to do what we do ourselves (and in fact what we did in planning this chapter): to turn to Rudyard Kipling! There is a section in one of his 1902 *Just So Stories* where Kipling wrote:

> I KEEP six honest serving-men
> (They taught me all I knew);
> Their names are What and Why and When
> And How and Where and Who.

Source: Kipling (2007).

Using Kipling to help you in framing your research proposal, you can build the content around the answers to the following:

● What are the research questions I am seeking to answer?

● What are my research objectives?

● Why is the research I propose significant?

- When are the key dates in the research process?
- How will I go about collecting the necessary data to answer the research questions?
- Where will I be conducting my research (e.g. organisation, sector, country)?
- Who are the key participants in the research process (e.g. gatekeepers, respondents)?

Not only will this technique clarify your thoughts but it will also help you to organise your ideas into a clear statement of your research intent. Clarity, in this sense, means organising your ideas in such way that they are coherent and rigorous. Coherence means that they make sense, they are plausible and can be understood easily; by rigorous we mean that the ideas will stand up to searching analysis and can be defended by you in the face of demands to justify their inclusion in your proposal. Your assessor will be looking for this standard of work in your proposal. It serves as a route map to guide you through the research process.

If you are going on to do the research that you have detailed in your research proposal, the proposal will be a very useful check for you to ensure that you are doing what you said you will do. This may sound an obvious point but some of us have had our imaginations fired by a great idea during the research process only to be deflated by a supervisor who says, 'Yes, that's a super idea but look again at your research objectives; explain to me how this new idea fits'. Too often the response is 'Mmm... I see what you mean' when it is apparent that the new idea does not fit.

We have found that some students benefit from putting up on their study wall a copy of their research question(s) and objectives in large, bold type so that they can revisit them frequently to ensure they are on the right track.

Research in practice 8.1

Defining research questions

Freya was a final-year undergraduate who had to prepare a research proposal for her research methodology module assessment. For her topic she had chosen to explore the extent to which work experience during an undergraduate course impacted on job performance in the graduate's first job. Her interest in the topic stemmed from her own time in a large non-profit organisation which she felt prepared her well for her entry into paid employment. So her overall research question was, 'To what extent and in what ways does the degree student placement affect the job performance of the newly recruited graduate?'

As a result of a lot of reading of reports, particularly in the educational media, Freya generated the following research objectives:

1 To establish whether there is a link between the experience of a placement by the undergraduate and the performance in the first career job.

2 To discover whether the type of placement (e.g. duration, amount of responsibility) is associated with level of job performance.

3 To identify the variables which may be most strongly associated with job performance (e.g. quality of experience gained, personal confidence, closeness of relationship between placement duties and first-job duties).

→

Freya's proposal went on to detail her research strategy and methods that she would adopt. Her main data collection method was that of interviews with two samples of UK students, one that had completed a work placement and one that had not done so. She also suggested interviews with managers to whom the first-job graduates were responsible.

Freya was praised for her proposal which raised an interesting question that would be of considerable use to future students. However, her assessor criticised the lack of consistency between her objectives and her data collection methods. In particular, her assessor thought that the language of her objectives was couched in precision (e.g. duration of placement, amount of responsibility, and most importantly, actual job performance), whereas Freya's data collection method was more consistent with subjective impressions. In short, there was a mismatch between her objectives and method. The overall comment of her assessor was, 'You may have been wiser to stress in your objectives the quality of experience of the graduate in the first job rather than the performance: the first suggesting subjective impressions, the second, objective measurement'.

It shows you have a good knowledge of the existing work

Your research proposal is your opportunity to demonstrate your expertise on the subject you have chosen. This will largely be a result of your close acquaintance with the relevant literature. It is from this that you will gain the insights that will help you to produce an interesting proposal. Later in this chapter we talk more about the place of the literature in the research proposal. At this stage we must stress that there is a world of difference between the proposal which merely lists some references at the end and that which clearly uses the literature to inform the choice of topic, the question(s) and objectives and the research approach, strategy and methods.

If you have read thoroughly in preparation for your research proposal, this will shine through because it will demonstrate that you are up to date with the current news and debates concerning your topic. This will be at two levels. First, the news level where the latest developments in, say, outsourced marketing are reported and, second, where academic research has been done to reach a deeper level of understanding of the topic. Of course, current knowledge of the second level means that you don't submit a research proposal which merely replicates research done by other researchers, risking quite justifiable criticism from your assessor. But even if your proposal is similar to that already done by another researcher, you can demonstrate novelty and knowledge of current literature by building on existing research and, perhaps, approaching the research from a different perspective.

It demonstrates to the assessor(s) that the research is viable

If you have to submit a research proposal without having to actually conduct the research, there is a danger that you will not give sufficient thought to the practical issues which would be faced by the researcher. The focus here is on resources.

As a management and business expert, your assessor will be mindful of the cost implications of your proposal. This relates to the direct costs involved, such as travel and possible accommodation expenses, and indirect costs, most particularly your time. You will have other things to do in your degree programme, so submitting a proposal which implies that it will take up more of your time that you can reasonably afford to devote is not a good idea. It is not only the amount of time that is important, but also the length of time of the proposed research from start to finish that you should consider. It is no good suggesting a research project which, say, plots the effect of management coaching on longer-term job performance if the timescale is longer than you have allocated.

But perhaps the most important resource of which you may underestimate the importance is data availability. There may be little point in developing a proposal which examines the importance of the vision that Sir Richard Branson brings to the Virgin Group if you cannot get access to the man himself! In the example above (Research in practice 8.1), the proposal specifies the role of job performance. This assumes that job performance data will be made available to the researcher. This is problematic, given issues of confidentiality.

Two further points about the viability of the research are relevant for those of you who are not only submitting your proposal for assessment but are also going to conduct the research you have included in that proposal. The first relates to the extent to which you indicate that you are capable of doing the research. This may be implied in all that has gone before in terms of evidence of quality of thought. But you also have the opportunity to show that you are creative and innovative, not only in the research objectives you set but also in the way in which you set out to achieve them. A genuine interest in the research you propose is something that will be clearly evident in what you have written. The second point about the viability of the research concerns the practical planning for the research from your university's perspective. A clear and timely proposal is often used to decide who would be the most suitable supervisor for you.

It ensures that your research meets the requirements of your university

It is likely that your proposal may have to contain your assurance that you have considered the requirements of your university. An example of these requirements is the university which states in its code of practice that an ethics committee needs to consider all research proposals which actively involve human participants. In another UK university, the research proposal must clarify exactly what is meant by guaranteeing anonymity and confidentiality to research participants when they participate in the research. Here, anonymity refers to concealing the identity of the participants in all documents resulting from the research. Confidentiality is concerned with the right of access to the data provided by individual participants and, in particular, the need to keep these data secret or private. In addition, researchers should clarify the steps they will take to ensure protection of respondents' identities and ensure that the information collected is stored securely. We go into the subject of research ethics in more detail in section 3.8.

For those of you who are going to conduct the research you have outlined in your proposal, you are justified in thinking that a proposal which is deemed acceptable implies that the research itself promises to be successful. Obviously this cannot be guaranteed. But it is reassuring to know that at least you started your research journey with a suitable destination and journey plan. Just make sure you stick to it!

8.3 When should I write my research proposal?

In our view, the proposal could be started at day one of your research module. At that stage it may bear little or no resemblance to the finished article, but there are enormous benefits to be gained from starting early, not the least of which is committing thoughts to writing. Once again, we make the point that writing is a great way of clarifying your thoughts. At the first stage of thinking about your research, you will probably not be able to note any more than outline topics in which you are interested. As your thoughts develop you may add some initial research questions and then follow these with research objectives. All the time, expect that you will amend what you have written. This is where the word processor is so helpful: amendment is so easy. But do keep a copy of the various main versions of your proposal document. You never know when you may need to resurrect a previous idea. Treat your proposal as work in progress rather than seeing it as a 'one off' – something which you write up and submit after your thinking, discussing and planning stage.

We have always encouraged our students to adopt this approach to the development of their research proposals. This has proved to be beneficial to us too. When we sit and discuss our students' research ideas, it is so helpful to have a shared document to form the basis of that discussion, even if it is in a very early stage of development. Also, we keep copies of earlier drafts, which show us how thoughts have developed and become more concrete. We have the ability then to look back at ideas which may have become 'lost' and may be usefully reconsidered.

The earlier the research proposal is discussed with your supervisor the better. Often she or he will suggest that the scope of what you are considering is too ambitious. This will usually be because the work proposed is not viable for one of the reasons we have explained in section 8.2. Whatever amendments you need to make, and for whatever reason, the sooner you begin preparing you research proposal the better!

8.4 What should I include in my research proposal?

To a great extent the content of your research proposal will be governed by the format required by your university and by the proposal content itself. What we offer here is a guide to the sections that it is most likely you will need to include.

Research overview

You may think of this first section as an abstract or an executive summary. As such, it is brief statement of what you intend to do for the research. It should be no more than a paragraph or two and describe the proposal content to busy readers in no more than a few words.

Title

Try here to reflect as accurately as possible the content of the proposal. The economist Adam Smith may not have written a research proposal for his famous book but it seems to us that you can't be more precise than the title he chose: *An Inquiry into the Nature and Causes of the Wealth of Nations* (1904).

You may want to leave composing the title until you have finished the body of the proposal. Alternatively, this may be your start point. If this is the case, don't be afraid to amend the title as your work progresses.

Introduction to the research

This is an important part of the proposal. You should place the proposed study in a context which will assist your assessor in understanding why it is you have chosen this particular topic. You may wish to demonstrate the topical relevance of your proposal if it is concerned with something that is generating current debate. An example here would be the way the retail banks are trying to overcome their negative public image through their marketing strategies. Alternatively, you may wish to concentrate on a problem being experienced by an organisation with which you are familiar. Here, an example may be the difficulty the organisation has with retaining key employees.

In either of these two cases, your assessor will be keen to see if you are knowledgeable about the topic and can relate it to existing theory. So in the case of the retail bank proposal you may show how this is drawn from and/or may contribute relevant marketing theory. Similarly, you may use the literature on employee retention strategy theory in the second example.

It will help persuade your assessor of the quality of your proposal if you can explain why you are interested in the topic. This may be because you have worked in the particular organisation or have studied the retail banks in another module.

If your proposal is the precursor to you going on to conduct the research, it will be helpful if you show that you are enthusiastic about the research topic. This will help convince your assessor you have sufficient commitment to sustain your effort over the life of the research.

In short, the real value of this background section is to convince the assessor that the research is worth pursuing: not just by you as part of your course, but by a competent researcher who will add to an understanding of the particular topic you are studying.

Research question(s)

In section 1.6 we explain what is meant by research questions and research objectives and the difference between the two. To recap, the research question may be one overall question, or a number of questions that the research process will address which are, often, the forerunner of research objectives. Research objectives are clear, specific statements that identify what the research process seeks to achieve as a result of doing the research. So, the movement from research questions to research objectives is a developmental one: objectives follow questions to provide precision to that which is more general.

This progression from research questions to research objectives is reflected in the order we suggest for the sections in the research proposal. We propose that the literature review section separates them. The reason for this is that we see the research question as directing and leading you into the relevant literature whereas the research objectives are developed as a result of careful consideration of the literature. Of course, the process is not this straightforward. Our model implies that reading generally on the topic of your interest may fire your imagination sufficiently to raise workable research questions, and having developed a research question(s) you then embark on more specific reading to develop your question(s) into objectives. The reality is that the three processes of reading, question development and objective development may take place in no coherent order, or, more likely, simultaneously without you really sensing that there is a particular order. There are some examples of research questions in section 1.6.

Literature review

Chapter 2 explains in detail the role of the literature review in doing research and ways in which this may be accomplished. A critical literature review is something that you would normally include in a final written project report. Here we are more concerned with that which you should include in your research proposal. It is important to show in your proposal that you are knowledgeable about the literature that relates to your research topic. More specifically, you should use this opportunity to explain how your proposal relates to the academic debate which is being conducted in the literature. You will be expected to show a clear link between the previous work that has been done in your field of research interest and the content of your proposal. Put simply, you should show in your review of the literature where your research question(s) came from and how your research objectives will move the debate forward by, say, applying a new perspective or setting your research in a new context: the literature is both a point of departure and a signpost pointing to your destination.

This all suggests that it is insufficient in your research proposal just to provide an overview of the key literature sources from which you intend to draw. Clearly, you should include references to key articles and texts, but you must show that you appreciate their relevance to your research area.

Research in practice 8.2

A research proposal about national cultures

Samit was a final-year undergraduate at a UK university. During his final year he was going to undertake a work placement in Macrohard, a large multinational IT organisation with managers in most parts of the world. He wanted to use the experience on the placement to complete the assessment for his research methods module. For this he had to submit a research proposal on a topic of his choice which related to the modules he was studying.

Since Samit was interested in both globalised organisations and the concept of national culture, he decided to link the two in his proposal. This is the section (which we have abbreviated) in Samit's proposal which dealt with the literature he would use.

This study will draw on the work of Hofstede (2002) who, in his study of national work related values, concluded that there are five dimensions of culture. Hofstede has not been without his critics, particularly McSweeny (2002) who is sceptical about the assumptions on which Hofstede bases his conclusions. Nonetheless I plan to use the dimensions developed by Hofstede. The dimensions are:

Power distance, which relates to the extent to which power is distributed unequally in organisations. In cultures with small power distance (e.g Sweden) people expect power relations to be more democratic. However, in cultures with large power distance (e.g. Thailand), the less powerful accept power relations that are autocratic or paternalistic.

Individualism vs. collectivism. In individualist cultures organisational members display their tendency to act independently of the work group whereas in collectivist cultures they identify their interests as being associated with other members of collectives such as work groups or trade unions.

Masculinity vs. femininity. This dimension refers to the difference between what in the West we see as male values such as competitiveness and assertiveness and female values, e.g. nurturing and concern for quality of life.

Uncertainty avoidance relates to the degree to which organisational members display anxiety about the unknown and cope with that anxiety by minimising uncertainty. High uncertainty avoidance is associated with a desire for formal structure and rules while low uncertainty avoidance is associated with more flexible structure and implicit rules.

Long vs. short term orientation. Cultures with a long-term orientation, such as Japan, emphasise tradition and a longer term view of business success while cultures with a short term culture are more concerned with immediate results.

This typology of five cultural dimensions will be a key axis around which this study is formed. It will provide a means of constructing a questionnaire which will be administered to a sample of approximately 200 of Macrohard's organisational members at all levels of seniority. The content of the questionnaire will reflect not only Hofstede's dimensions but the particular operating circumstances of Macrohard. Through using Hofstede's typology as a framework to analyse the data I will make the results and conclusions specific to Macrohard.

→

References

Hofstede, G. (2002) *Culture's Consequences* (2nd edition), Thousand Oaks, CA: Sage.

McSweeny, B. (2002) Hofstede's model of national cultural differences and their consequences: A triumph of faith – a failure of analysis, *Human Relations* Vol. 55, No. 1, pp. 89–118.

Research objectives

We made the point earlier in this section that the research objectives are developed as a result of careful consideration of the literature. Make sure that they:

● relate to and are developed from your research question(s);

● relate to and are developed from your review of the literature;

● are specific, measurable, achievable, realistic and timely (see section 1.6 and Table 1.6).

Method

This will be one of the more detailed sections of your research proposal. It flows directly from your research objectives and shows how you will go about achieving them. In the method section, you have the opportunity to show the assessor the extent to which you really understand the research process through ensuring this close connection between research objectives and method. For example, if one of your objectives is 'to establish the influence of price promotions on supermarket milk sales', you will need to think about ways in which you may quantify the effect price has on sales. This may be done, for example, through the examination of sales records. Whether it is possible to collect the data is an important consideration here: that is a potential assessor concern that you must address in the proposal. This example also raises the issue of validity and reliability (see section 5.6). A key question that will be going through your assessor's mind will be, 'Are the methods being proposed here likely to deliver credible results that can lead to sound, valid conclusions?' It is vital that you think this through thoroughly when preparing the method section of your proposal. You should justify your choice of methods in the light of the question about credibility. So, in defence of any questioning of your research methods, you can answer, 'I chose to collect data this way because I feel this will provide valid and reliable data'.

Your method section can be divided into two parts: research design and data collection. In the research design part of the section, you should explain two aspects of your research design. First, the location of your research and, second, the research population from which you will select your sample (section 6.2). If your research is to be carried out in one organisation, then the location is straightforward and needs no further elaboration. However, if your research topic is not concentrated in one organisation, then you will need to detail the locations. So, for example, a study of the introduction of a new distribution strategy by Internet retailers may mean choosing a sample of retailers among whom you are carrying out a comparative study. In this case you would need to explain why you chose the participant organisations. Your reasoning here will be judged against the extent to which your choice of organisations is consistent with your research objective and the need to provide credible data. You may be proposing a project which is even more generic, say, a study of the effect of changing consumer preferences for downloading on the music industry. Here you would need to explain why you chose this sector.

Secondly, in this part of the section on research method, you will need to describe and justify the population from which you propose to collect data. This may be a small sample of employees that you propose to interview, a large sample that will receive a questionnaire (Chapter 6) or a number of companies about which you can access secondary data (Chapter 4).

The method section should also include an explanation of the way in which you intend to carry out the research. It could involve, say, questionnaires, semi-structured or unstructured interviews, examination of secondary data or use a combination of data collection techniques. Again, it is essential to explain why you have chosen your approach. Once again, this explanation should reflect upon whether this is the most effective way of meeting your research objectives and providing credible data. The data collection section should be much more detailed about how specifically the data are to be collected (Chapter 6). For example, if you are using questionnaires, you should specify your population and sample size, and how your sample will be collected. You should also clarify how the questionnaires will be distributed, the likely response rate, and how the data will be analysed. If you are using interviews, you should explain how many interviews will be conducted, how long they will last, whether they will be audio recorded, and how they will be analysed. You should show your assessor that you have thought carefully about all the issues regarding your method and their relationship to your research objectives and data credibility. Don't worry about the necessity to be too detailed. It is normally not necessary in the proposal to include precise detail of the method you will employ, for example the content of an observation schedule or questionnaire questions. In this section you will also need to include a statement about how you are going to adhere to your university's ethical code (see section 3.8).

Timescale

This is a useful part of your research proposal. Clearly breaking down the research process into a series of steps will show you whether it is reasonable to expect the various tasks to be done within the timescale. For example, it is no good taking three months to do your literature research if your project has to be submitted in two months. More importantly, it will show clearly how much time is to be made available for data collection and analysis. The time required here is often far more than anticipated. This is for a number of reasons, not the least of which is the degree of dependence that you may have upon your respondents from whom you are collecting your data. Analysing the data also often takes far more time that anticipated (Chapter 7). This is particularly so if you have a limited amount of experience with any software that is being used for analysis.

Devising a timescale is also an important part of the research proposal because it enables your assessor to assess the variability of the work you propose. You can follow all the advice in this chapter, and in this book, and produce a beautifully crafted, intellectually coherent research proposal only to be marked down with the damning comment, 'An excellent proposal but one which proposes research that could not possibly be done within the timescale'. Discussing your plans with your supervisor should avoid this happening. Experience of reading many proposals usually gives supervisors a good idea of what is practicable in a given timescale.

Table 8.1 An example timescale for a research project

Task	To be completed by:
Begin research idea formulation and first coverage of literature	1/10/2011
Main part of literature research completed, research questions and objectives defined	20/11/2011
Research proposal submitted	30/11/2011
Make arrangements for data collection	31/12/2011
Literature research finished and review written	31/12/2011
Secondary data research	31/12/2011
Primary research and analysis	20/2/2012
Draft written report	31/3/2012
Revised draft written report	15/05/2012
Final submission of written report	30/5/2012

Resources

It may be that you are asked to list the resources required for the completion of the project you propose. This will also assist your assessor in considering the viability of your proposal. We explained in section 8.2 that you should detail direct costs involved, such as travel and possible accommodation expenses, and indirect costs, most particularly your time.

We also mentioned in section 8.2 the importance of data availability. Your assessor will be concerned about approval from any organisations in which you are planning to conduct your research and may well require written evidence of this. You will also need to convince your assessor that the response rate to any questionnaire that you send is likely to be satisfactory.

You should also be able to convince your assessor that you can undertake the analysis of your data satisfactorily. This is often an aspect of the research process that is ignored when the proposal is submitted. It is important that you describe the resources you have available for data analysis purposes. This may include computer software and the appropriate skills to perform the analysis, or help in learning these skills in an appropriate time.

References

You may be tempted to impress your assessor (and fellow students!) with a long list of references at the end of your proposal. This is not necessary. Do bear in mind the point we made in section 8.2 that simply listing references to those sources which you have consulted is not what is required. You should only list those references that clearly use the literature to inform the choice of topic, the question(s) and objectives and the research approach, strategy and methods.

We end this section on the content of the research proposal with the first of two complete proposals (Research in practice 8.3 and 8.4) for you to consider. Neither of these should be seen as ideal. Indeed, you should review their content in the light of the points made in this chapter to conduct your own assessment.

Research in practice 8.3

Research proposal

Research proposal
Ms A.S. See, BA (Hons) Business and Management

An exploration of learning in alliances between organisations in the Information and Communication Technology sector in the UK

1. BACKGROUND AND ACADEMIC CONTEXT

Introduction

My two principal interests are firstly the learning organisation, and secondly working with teams to improve their effectiveness. These teams could be formal in the line management sense, or virtual teams such as project teams or alliances.

I propose to conduct my research into alliances in the Information and Communication Technology (ICT) sector in the UK.

Research question

To what extent do UK-based businesses of global organisations in the ICT sector plan to learn from and with their alliance partners within the same sector?

Alliances

Yin and Stanley (2008) define an alliance in terms of an agreement between two or more firms with a view to jointly manage assets and achieve objectives. The amount of

→

alliances appears to be increasing (Qui, 2010). But the dominant view in the literature is that the majority of these alliances fail (Dyer et al., 2001). The research that has been published on alliances concentrates upon the criteria for selecting alliance partners (Pidduck, 2006), identifying critical success factors (Stanek, 2004) and selecting the appropriate contractual vehicle (Pett and Dibrell, 2001).

Learning in alliances

A learning organisation is one that facilitates the learning of its members and continuously transforms itself. It needs to maintain knowledge about new products and processes, understand what is happening in the external environment and produce creative solutions utilising the knowledge and skills of all within the organisation. Such creativity demands co-operation between individuals and groups, effective communication, and a culture of trust (Argyris, 1999).

Such research that has been done on learning in alliances (e.g. Das et al., 2003) suggests that the dominant mode of organisational learning is single loop: the examination of processes and organisational relationships to identify areas for improvement. Argyris recommends that double loop learning is necessary for real improvements to occur. This learning mode challenges the organisation's values and norms (Örtenblad, 2010).

Research objectives

Alliances are widespread in the UK (ICT) sector. This sector has undergone rapid consolidation through mergers and acquisitions in recent years, bringing together significantly different practices and cultures to the management of their alliances.

This research sets out to explore the extent to which the UK-based global ICT organisations plan to learn from and/or with their alliance partners within the same sector. The research objectives are:

1 to establish the performance characteristics regarded as important by each party to an alliance;
2 to examine the degree to which both parties to an alliance agree on the important performance characteristics;
3 to explore the extent to which organisations within an alliance set out to learn from each other;
4 to discover how organisations share and learn from their collective experiences and the topics of that learning;
5 to analyse the extent of double loop learning in the alliances studied.

Research methods

Research context
I propose to use two case study organisations for this research: ABC and DEF. Both organisations have formed alliances with other organisations in the ICT sector. ABC has an alliance with GHI and DEF with JKL. I have contacts in ABC and DEF and will use these contacts to arrange the data collection.

Both ABC and DEF are UK-based subsidiaries of global companies with long-term experience of forming and managing alliances. Each has significant numbers of alliances.

Data collection and analysis

I plan to collect data by interviewing employees in each organisation. Participants will include the alliance managers and key operational staff from each organisation. Between six and ten people will be interviewed individually in each organisation. As this research is focused on the nature of the relationship, the number of participants per organisation is not critical.

Interviewing will take place in two stages. Stage one treats each of the four organisations separately, concentrating on the employees in each of those individual organisations. The second stage combines organisations ABC and GHI, and, separately, DEF with JKL. Interviews will be with pairs (where possible) of employees, each pair comprising an employee from each of the organisations.

The interviews will concentrate on discussions based on the five research objectives. They will be unstructured and led by me. I will seek permission to audio-record the interviews and then make notes of the key points following each interview. Each interview will take a maximum of one hour.

I will analyse the data manually by sifting through the data and finding key themes which will respond to the five research objectives.

Research ethics

I will guarantee confidentiality to each organisation in that I will not disclose any information which I receive which may be commercially sensitive. In addition, I will guarantee anonymity to all participants. Neither the participating organisations nor individuals will be named in the research project.

Timescale

It is my intention to complete the research in three stages. Stage one consists of writing the introduction, literature review and method chapters of the final report. This will be completed by December 2010. The second stage will be the data collection and analysis stage. All data will be collected and analysed by the end of March 2011. Stage three is the preparation of the final report. This will be completed by 20th May 2011.

Resources

No significant resources are needed for this research. The participant organisations are near my home and I will use the time I have allocated as part of my coursework. The four participant organisations have granted access for this research.

References

Argyris, C. (1999) *On Organizational Learning*, 2nd edn, Oxford: Blackwell Publishing.

Das, S., Sen, P.K. and Sengupta, S. (2003) Strategic alliances: a valuable way to manage intellectual capital, *Journal of Intellectual Capital*, Vol. 4, No. 1, pp. 10–19.

Dyer, J., Kale, P. and Singh, H. (2001) How to make strategic alliances work, *Sloan Management Review*, Vol. 42, pp. 37–43.

Örtenblad, A. (2010) Odd couples or perfect matches? On the development of management knowledge packaged in the form of labels, *Management Learning*, Vol. 41, No. 4, pp. 443–52.

→

Pett, T.L. and Dibrell, C.C. (2001) A process model of global strategic alliance formation, *Business Process Management Journal*, Vol. 7, No. 4, pp. 349–64.

Pidduck, A.B. (2006) Issues in supplier partner selection, *Journal of Enterprise Information Management,* Vol. 19, No. 3, pp. 262–76.

Qui, L.D. (2010) Cross-border mergers and strategic alliances, *European Economic Review,* Vol. 54, No. 6, pp. 818–31.

Stanek, M.B. (2004) Measuring alliance value and risk, *Management Decision,* Vol. 42, No. 2, pp. 182–204.

Yin, X. and Stanley, M. (2008) Industry determinants of the 'merger versus alliance' decision, *Academy of Management Review,* Vol. 33, No. 2, pp. 473–91.

8.5 In what style should my research proposal be written?

We have included a section on a number of dos and don'ts on writing style in this chapter. It will obviously be very relevant to those who are writing the project report. We hope it will also help those of you who are doing the research proposal without progressing to the full project report following the conduct of the research. The points we make in this section are sufficiently generalised to meet all research writing needs.

Do write clearly and simply

You are unusual if you enjoy the style in which much of the material you have to read for your university work has been written. We hope you find the content interesting (it would be worrying if you didn't!) but the style, well that's a different matter. We agree with the American academic C. Wright Mills who you can see from the quote below was unimpressed by the writing of many of his academic colleagues.

> The . . . lack of ready intelligibility [in scholarly writing], I believe, usually has little or nothing to do with the complexity of the subject matter, and nothing at all to do with profundity of thought. It has to do almost entirely with certain confusions of the academic writer about his own status . . . To overcome the academic prose you first of all have to overcome the academic pose . . .   Wright Mills (1970: 239–40).

This is not to say that you should trivialise what you write in your research proposal or report. Far from it. You will be dealing with a serious subject for a serious purpose so your writing should reflect this. But you can be serious and clear at the same time!

An example will illustrate our point. Consider the following two statements.

> The research proposed here is seeking to gain an understanding of the ways in which those factors which are closely associated with the relationship between consumer preferences for security and economy are reconciled when the consumer purchasing decision for delivery is made in the Internet seller auction sector.

> When sellers on Internet auction sites decide which carrier to use they consider both security and cost. In this research I aim to establish how these two factors influence the purchasing decision.

Both statements say the same thing, but the second uses 34 words rather than 50. This is 32 per cent less words! So the 'wordy' research proposal which takes 1,000 words could do the same job for 660. Just consider the benefit to you of asking the assessor to do 32 per cent less work! In addition to this obvious advantage, you will be conveying the same meaning in a much clearer way, so your assessor will not only have to read fewer words but also digest much more easily those that are read.

Do write simple sentences

Not only does the second statement in the example above use fewer words while conveying the same meaning but it also uses two short sentences rather than one long one. Look at your writing and break up those long sentences. Use the simple rule: one idea – one sentence.

Research writing is often difficult because you are writing about ideas and facts and usually working out relationships between the two. Long, complicated sentences usually mean that you aren't sure about what you want to say. This is quite understandable. Shorter sentences are much better for explaining complex information because they break the information up into smaller chunks which are easier to follow.

One more golden rule: *avoid the embedded clause!* Consider these two sentences.

> While confidentiality is of the utmost importance, it is necessary to bear in mind the practicalities of organisational life, therefore respondents will be interviewed individually insofar as this is possible, although privacy may not always be possible for the same reasons of practicality.

> I plan to interview the respondents individually in a setting which will be private and therefore conducive to confidentiality. This depends upon the availability of suitable rooms.

Sentences with lots of clauses and exceptions confuse the audience by losing the main idea in a jungle of words. Don't put all your ideas in one sentence; separate your ideas and make each one the subject of its own sentence, like in sentence 2 above.

Do be careful with spelling and grammar

Spelling and grammatical errors detract from the quality of your work and make it look less credible and authoritative. It's too easy to say that the word processor you use will do this job for you. It won't tell you that you have used 'practice' and 'practise' or 'moral' and 'morale' in the wrong context. Try to get a friend who is a good speller to check your work so you don't make these errors.

Common grammatical errors can irritate the assessor. All assessors have their pet hates! So avoid simple mistakes, such as referring to one interviewee as 'they'; calling lots of data 'it' rather than 'they' (a single piece is 'datum'); using clichés such as 'the real world' to refer to that which exists outside the university. Again, persuade a critical reader to check your writing for you. You may not avoid all the grammatical pitfalls, but at least you may not fall into the obvious ones.

Don't use jargon

All disciplines have their jargon, and business is as guilty as most. The meaning of terms like 'buy-in' are clear enough to us but nonetheless they have the potential to irritate your assessor. There are perfectly good words to use which are correct English and the irritated assessor may ask, 'What is wrong with 'gain agreement'?'

Jargon should not be confused with technical terms. Some technical terms are perfectly valid. Here it is useful to put a glossary of technical terms in the appendices. However, do not assume that your assessor will have your level of knowledge of the subject and, in particular, the context. Try to put yourself in the position of the assessor. As part of a research writing workshop, we ask students to assess research proposals. Some of these are written by students who use their own organisation as a context for the research. The students assessing these proposals are usually amazed at the assumptions that their fellow students make about the assessor's prior knowledge.

Do beware of using large numbers of quotations from the literature

In your research proposal you are unlikely to use many quotations from your literature sources. Yet, one or two may lend authority. However, it is important that you use these to illustrate or emphasise a point that you are making rather than insert it to make your proposal 'look good'. We should stress here that the point that you are making must be your point. If you are using a quotation that is largely unexplained, it is that author's point alone. In general, it is better to explain other people's ideas in your own words. In that way you can really gain an understanding of what the author means, and convince your assessor of your understanding.

When it comes to the project report we feel that quotations from the literature should be used sparingly. Sometimes we read draft projects that consist of little more than a series of quotations from books and journal articles that a student has linked together with a few sentences of her or his own. This is unacceptable. It tells us very little about the student's understanding of the concepts within the quotations. All it shows is that he or she has looked at the book or journal article and (hopefully!) acknowledged sources correctly! Using quotations in this way means that the line of argument becomes disjointed and difficult to follow. That doesn't mean that you should never use quotations. But we advise you to use them in moderation to create maximum impact in supporting your storyline.

Do be careful when using personal pronouns

Often project reports are written in a rather dry and unexciting style. This is partly because the convention has been to write impersonally (e.g. it was decided to interview a small sample…). Here, the writer is distanced from the text. Some writers anonymise themselves by referring to themselves as 'the author' or 'the researcher'. Our view is that, where appropriate, your writing is much livelier if you use the first person (I decided to interview a small sample…). We say 'where appropriate' because your research strategy and methods may dictate your choice of personal pronoun. It may be useful to ask yourself, 'Am I inside or outside the data collection process?' By 'inside' we mean that the researcher is an intrinsic part of the data collection. This may be the case with interviews. However, with questionnaires the researcher is 'outside' the data collection process. As a broad rule, only if you are inside the data collection process is it appropriate to use the personal pronoun.

Do check this with your supervisor. There may be conventions which you are expected to observe. Some researchers think that excessive use of 'I' and 'we' casts doubt on your ability to stand outside your data and to be objective.

Do be careful when using tense

Rather like the use of personal pronouns, there are no clear rules about the correct use of tense in academic writing. We usually recommend that you use the present tense when referring to previously published work (e.g. Smith notes in his earlier article…) and the past tense when referring to your present results (e.g. I found that…). Although there are exceptions to this rule, it serves as a useful guide.

Do be careful when using gender

No doubt you will already have been warned about use of language that assumes the gender of a classification of people. In business and management, the most obvious example is the constant reference to managers as 'he'. This is not only inaccurate in many organisations, but it also gives offence to many people of both sexes. It is easy to avoid falling into this trap. Instead of 'I propose to interview each senior manager in his office', it is more appropriate to write 'I propose that each senior manager's office will be the setting for the interview'. (In an early draft of another book we have written, we referred to a particular writer as a 'master craftsman' before deciding it would be more suitable to change this to 'an expert in the field'!)

In the event of your research having an international dimension, it is a good idea to be aware of any country-specific or national guidelines on the non-discriminatory use of language.

Do preserve anonymity

It is likely that you have given your participants (and the organisations) from whom you collected data an undertaking that you would not disclose their identity in your written work. You will need to conceal their identity in your research proposal or report. Normally you can do this by inventing pseudonyms for organisations (as in Research in practice 8.3 where ABC, DEF was used) and not to name individual participants. It may make your work a little less interesting to read, but in such cases you have no choice. Anonymising may also allow you do be rather more critically evaluative than you could have been with named participants.

Do successive drafts of your work

In section 8.3 we recommended that you continually revise your research proposal, keep each successive draft and treat the report as 'work in progress'. This point applies to all your writing. Your style and content will be refined, sharpened and clarified with each successive version.

8.6   How will my research proposal be judged?

Your module guidelines should make clear the assessment criteria against which your research proposal will be judged. In this final section we offer three guidelines. These may be in your published assessment criteria, and they summarise much of the material already covered in this chapter in particular, and this book in general. We offer them here to emphasise their importance.

The extent to which the components of the proposal fit together

The main components of your research proposal should fit together in one coherent and seamless whole. These are the following:

1 The introduction, which should include an explanation of the reasons for conducting your research, a summary of the previous published research and relevant theories in the topic area.

2 Your research question(s) and objectives, which should be based on the material in the introduction.

3 Your proposed method, which should flow directly from these research question(s) and objectives.

4 The time that you have allocated, which should be a direct reflection of the methods you employ.

5 The resources that you need, which should be a direct reflection of the methods you employ.

The absence of preconceived ideas

Your research should be a voyage of discovery. As a broad rule: if you know the answer to the research question already, look for another topic! Having preconceived ideas will stunt your creativity and lessen the enjoyment you derive from the research process.

The viability of the proposal

This is the answer to the question: 'Can this research be carried out satisfactorily within the timescale and with the available resources?'

Research in practice 8.4

Research proposal

Research proposal
Mr C.D. Eff, MBA (part-time)

Knowledge management in high-technology manufacturing SMEs:
key strategies to maintain competitive advantage

Research question

This research is designed to answer the question 'What are the key features of a knowledge management strategy which can contribute to competitive advantage for UK knowledge-based small and medium sized enterprises (SMEs) in the high-technology manufacturing sector?'

Knowledge management

Growth of the field of knowledge management (KM) began in the 1990s and has been ongoing (Hislop, 2009). This has been driven by the evolution of a 'knowledge economy' where businesses must continually adapt and use their knowledge effectively to maintain competitive advantage. Teece (2001) attributes superior performance to the ability of firms to be good at innovating, protecting intangible and difficult to imitate knowledge assets and using those assets effectively.

The field of KM has two distinct processes (Tidd et al., 2001). The first has its basis in investment in IT (i.e. intranet) and the second in people and processes encouraging employees to 'identify, store, share and use' knowledge throughout the organisation. It is clear that the organisational aspects of KM must be addressed to fully realise the benefits of the technology. Tidd et al. state there are five main types of KM strategy. These are ripple (bottom-up continuous improvement), integration (functional knowledge into processes), embedding (coupling systems, products and services), bridge (novel combination of existing competencies) and transfer (existing knowledge in new context). The optimum knowledge strategy is likely to be a mix of these and will depend on the structure and culture of the organisation, the market environment and the availability of resources.

Knowledge sharing and organisational memory in high-tech SMEs

For large organisations, organisational design and formal procedures form the basis for knowledge integration. In contrast, for high-technology SMEs, the role of senior management is far more important in the integration of technological knowledge and devising strategies to exploit knowledge competencies. Tidd et al. (2001: 56) state that it is the manager's 'level of technical and organisational skills' which determine whether

→

they 'will be able to develop and commercially exploit a firm-specific technological advantage'. As firms grow, it is clear that organisational design, processes and culture need to be developed to maintain and foster the environment of knowledge sharing which was inherent in the smaller organisation.

The five main learning activities described by Garvin (1993) are 'systematic problem solving, experimentation, learning from experience, learning from others and transfer of knowledge quickly and efficiently throughout the organisation'. For high-technology SMEs, practice is often lacking in the application of past experience and the systematic recording and sharing of often tacit knowledge throughout the business. Rather, as suggested by Hutchinson and Quintas (2008), these firms manage knowledge in informal ways which are both structured and deliberate.

Swart and Kinnie (2003) used a case study approach to examine organisational structure and processes which successfully promote knowledge sharing in a knowledge-intensive high-tech SME. They conclude that organisational size is not necessarily an obstacle to knowledge integration; however, people and KM policies are critical for success.

Research objectives

The aim of this research is to understand the characteristics of the firms and their products which determine the success of different types of KM strategy. The research objectives are:

1 To identify KM strategies in operation in SMEs in the high-technology manufacturing sector.
2 To analyse the importance of KM and understand how the strategies and practices in operation contribute positively or negatively to competitive advantage.
3 To understand the practices which enable the development of organisational memory.
4 To understand the characteristics, structure and products of a firm which determine the success of different types of KM strategy.
5 To develop a list of key practices and a route for implementation of a successful KM strategy for an SME in the high-technology manufacturing sector.

Research methods

Research approach and design
The analysis of the research will be largely quantitative, highlighting patterns. The findings will be compared to theory in order to describe the patterns which exist. An inductive approach will be used in order to develop theory as a result of the research findings, although there will be an element of deduction in that the structure of the research will be based on the academic literature.

The research will be based on a series of case studies using:

1 structured interviews with a senior manager in each of the case study organisations;
2 questionnaires to all employees in each of the case study organisations.

The cases chosen all have the following characteristics: located in the SME high-technology manufacturing sector, possessing a significant R&D function as a basis for product development and are UK-based. The method of selection of case studies was through personal networking and sampling to find a number of organisations with the required characteristics. Effort was also made to select a range of organisations with different characteristics such as markets, sizes and life-spans. Within the case studies the respondents will be senior managers who understand the KM practices and business environment. I intend to interview one management participant from each organisation. The questionnaire respondents will be either all, or at least 10, of the employees working in research or related areas, depending on the size of the company.

A structured interview will be held with a senior manager in each case study organisation to gain company information such as number of employees, number of research staff, annual turnover, market sector and products. The interviews will include open-ended questions to discuss the KM practices in order to gain an understanding of the approach taken, the structure and effectiveness of the KM practices and how and why certain strategies work while others are less effective. Each respondent will be asked to answer identical questions.

The questionnaire delivered to employees in each organisation will be used to establish the practices and individual perceptions in the organisation. The aim is to gain an understanding of how the KM strategies work through gaining the opinions and understanding of the employees. The questionnaire will have closed questions with set responses in order to map the KM characteristics of the organisation. There will also be a few open questions for participants to make comments on the various aspects of KM in their organisation.

My approach to the design of the questionnaire is as follows:

- Preliminary framework built on the review of theory from academic literature prior to design of questionnaires and structured interviews.
- Pilot interview – restructure the questions as necessary.
- Pilot use of questionnaire – restructure the questions as necessary.
- Structured interviews – notes taken during interview and audio-recording to produce a full record immediately after interview.
- Questionnaire explained and handed out/collected during session.

Data collection and analysis
I intend to perform research in my own organisation, for which I have been granted access to carry out the interviews and questionnaire. In addition, I believe that I require at least four further organisations to make a comparison of the KM practices and their effectiveness. I have contacted nine organisations and have obtained a verbal agreement for access from three of them so far. I am confident that I will be able to gain the required number of participating organisations; however, if I have fewer participants I can modify my research approach and increase the number of interview and survey participants at each organisation and complete a more in-depth study.

In order to make the process run smoothly and to obtain a speedy and efficient response to the questionnaires, I intend to run one or two sessions in the organisation where all of the participants will be present and during which I will hand out and collect the questionnaires. This will both ensure a high response rate and that the correct participants answer the survey. In addition, it will enable me to explain clearly the aims

→

of the research, control how the survey is administered and make clear the type of information required for the open-ended part of the questionnaires.

Analysis of the structured interviews will be mostly qualitative, with the interviews used to understand the business environment, characterise knowledge strategies and canvas individual opinion on their effectiveness. Quantitative analysis of the questionnaires will be used to map the characteristics of the organisations and discover patterns in the responses within organisations. Consideration of the data and patterns found in all of the organisations will be used in conjunction with academic theory to try to explain the findings and answer the research objectives.

Validity and reliability

I will attempt to achieve internal validity through the use of multiple sources of evidence, structured interviews and questionnaires. The design of questions will be based on understanding of the theory from the literature, and pilot testing of the interview and questionnaire will be used to make sure questions are understood as intended.

I have ensured external validity through the use of multiple cases to examine whether findings can be generalised over a number of organisations. There is no requirement to make a statistical analysis of the results for generalisation here as the approach chosen examines practices and their effectiveness. The aim is to explain the findings and explore generalisability through a comparison of findings with theory.

Reliability is pursued through structured interviews with questions derived from the literature in order to examine cases in the same way. In addition, the surveys reinforce the interviews and obtain views from a wider group. The questionnaires will all be administered at the same time and in controlled manner, with explanation to ensure participants all understand the research in the same way.

Research ethics

Respondents will be given a clear written description of the purpose, scope and intended outcomes of the research. The type of information required for the research will be clearly stated, as will the policy for anonymity and confidentiality.

The research will be carried out in a way that will ensure confidentiality of the participant organisations and the individual participants in the surveys. The organisations which participate in the research will not be named in the project, nor will the interviewees, and the questionnaires will be anonymous.

The interview questions and questionnaire will be designed to examine only the practices of KM; no confidential product or customer information will be required.

Timescale and resources

The plan for the research project timescales is shown below.

- Literature review. I have already performed a background literature search to help formulate research ideas. I plan a further extensive period of research before writing the literature review. This will be completed by December 2010.

- Questionnaire/interview design. I have a questionnaire which needs adapting for use. I intend to design the structured interview and questionnaire after the majority of the literature review is complete; they will both be piloted and their design reviewed. This will be completed by December 2010.
- Interviews and questionnaires. I plan to visit participant organisations to carry out data collection during January and February 2011.
- Data analysis. This will be completed by the end of March 2011.
- Project draft completed by end of April 2011. Final submission end of May 2011.

The main resource required to carry out the research is my time; I have the support of my employers to carry out this research and I will be able to take days out of work to visit the participant organisations. I have the means to visit the participants and also to analyse the data and write up the project report.

References

Garvin, D. A. (1993) Building a learning organization, *Harvard Business Review*, Vol. 71, No. 4, pp. 78–91.

Hislop, D. (2009) *Knowledge Management in Organisations,* 2nd edn, Oxford: Oxford University Press.

Hutchinson V. and Quintas, P. (2008) Do SMEs do knowledge management?: or simply manage what they know? *International Small Business Journal*, Vol. 26, No. 2, pp. 131–54.

Teece, D. J. (2001) Strategies for managing knowledge assets: the role of the firm in structure and industrial context, in Nonaka, I. and Teece D.J. (eds) *Managing Industrial Knowledge: Creation Transfer and Utilization*, London: Sage.

Tidd, J., Bessant, J. and Pavitt, K. (2001) *Managing Innovation: Integrating Technological, Market and Organizational Change*, Chichester: Wiley.

Swart, J. and Kinnie, N. (2003) Sharing knowledge in knowledge-intensive firms, *Human Resource Management Journal*, Vol. 13, No. 2, pp. 60–75.

Summary

- Writing a research proposal is important because: it clarifies your ideas and helps you organise those ideas; it shows you have a good knowledge of the existing work; it demonstrates to the assessor(s) that the research is viable; it ensures that your research meets the requirements of the university's research committee.
- It may helpful to begin your research proposal at the start of the research process and treat it as a 'work in progress' by amending it as you progress through the process of preparing the proposal.
- The content of the research proposal is likely to be: research overview; title; introduction to research; research questions(s); literature review; research objectives;

method; timescale; resources required and literature references. The main points to consider when writing the research proposal or report are: to write clearly and simply; to use short, simple sentences; exercise care in spelling and the use of grammar; avoid jargon; beware of using large numbers of quotations from the literature; the use of personal pronouns, tense and gender and the preservation of confidentiality and anonymity.

● Among the criteria against which your research proposal will be assessed will be the extent to which the various components of the research fit together and the absence of preconceived ideas.

Thinking about your research proposal

→ Look again at the idea of the six honest serving-men (section 8.2) to generate some initial headings for your research proposal. Your headings may respond to the following 'prompt questions': What are the research questions I am seeking to answer? What are my research objectives? Why is the research I propose significant? When are the key dates in the research process? How will I go about collecting the necessary data to answer the research questions? Who are the key participants in the research process (e.g. gatekeepers, respondents)?

→ Study the brief given to you detailing your university's requirements for the research proposal and note the key sections that you should include in your proposal.

→ Look again at the brief given to you specifying your university's requirements for the research proposal and ensure that you are aware of the assessment criteria that will be used to grade your proposal.

→ Consider the advice given in section 8.5 on the use of personal pronouns in your writing. In the light of this advice and that from your supervisor, decide which person is appropriate for you to use.

References

Hofstede, G. (2002) *Culture's Consequences*, 2nd edn, Thousand Oaks, CA: Sage.

Kipling, Rudyard (2007) *A Collection of Rudyard Kipling's Just So Stories*, London: Walker Books.

McSweeny, B. (2002) Hofstede's model of national cultural differences and their consequences: A triumph of faith – a failure of analysis, *Human Relations*, 55(1): 89–118.

Saunders M., Lewis, P. and Thornhill, A. (2009) *Research Methods for Business Students*, 5th edn, Harlow: FT Prentice Hall.

Smith, A. (1904) *An Inquiry into the Nature and Causes of the Wealth of Nations*, 5th edn, London: Methuen and Co.

Wright Mills, C. (1970) On intellectual craftsmanship, in *The Sociological Imagination*, London: Pelican.

Bibliography

Baruch, Y. and Holtom, B.C. (2008) Survey response rate levels and trends in organizational research, *Human Relations*, 61(8): 1139–60.

BBC News Online (2010) *Google 'may pull out of China after GMail cyber attack'*, 13 January. Available at: *http://news.bbc.co.uk/1/hi/business/8455712.stm* [Accessed 14 January 2010].

Becker, H.S. (2007) *Writing for Social Scientists*, 2nd edn, Chicago: University of Chicago.

Beynon, H. (1973) *Working for Ford*, London: Allen Lane.

Clough, P. and Nutbrown, C. (2008) *A Student's Guide to Methodology*, 2nd edn, London: Sage.

Collard, S. and Breuer, Z. (2009) *Attitudes towards investment choice and risk within the personal accounts scheme: Report of a qualitative study*. Department for Work and Pensions, Research Report No. 565, London.

Corbin, J. and Strauss, A. (2008) *Basics of Qualitative Research: Techniques and Procedures for Developing Grounded Theory*, 3rd edn, London: Sage.

Creswell, J. (2008) *Qualitative, Quantitative, and Mixed Methods Approaches*, 3rd edn, Thousand Oaks, CA.: Sage.

Dimitrakopoulou, C. (2010) Winter season tourism trends 2009/2010 *Eurostat Data in Focus 41/2010*. Available at *http://epp.eurostat.ec.europa.eu/cache/ITY_OFFPUB/KS-QA-10-041/EN/KS-QA-10-041-EN.PDF* [Accessed 12 October 2010].

DirectGov (2010) *Data protection*. Available at: *www.direct.gov.uk/en/Governmentcitizensandrights/Yourrightsandresponsibilities/DG_10031451* [Accessed 20 January 2011].

Dragons' Den (2007) *Shane Lake and Tony Charles: Hungry House*. Available at: *www.bbc.co.uk/dragonsden/entrepreneurs/shanelake.shtml* [Accessed 16 December 2010].

European Commission (2010) *Organic Farming Statistics*. Available at: *http://epp.eurostat.ec.europa.eu/statistics_explained/index.php/Organic_farming_statistics* [Accessed 21 December 2010].

Family Expenditure Survey (2009) ESDS Government. Available at: *www.esds.ac.uk/Government/fes/* [Accessed 27 November 2010].

Fenwick, D. and Denman, J. (1995) The monthly unemployment count: change and consistency, *Labour Market Trends*, November: 397–400.

Ghazali, S. (2011) The influence of socialization agents and demographic profiles on brand consciousness, *International Journal of Management and Marketing Research*, 4(1): 19–29.

Hair, J., Black, W., Babin, B. and Anderson, R. (2009) *Multivariate Data Analysis*, 7th edn, London: Pearson.

Harvard College Library (2006) *Interrogating texts: 6 reading habits to develop in your first year at Harvard*. Available at: *http://hcl.harvard.edu/research/guides/lamont_handouts/interrogatingtexts.html* [Accessed 27 November 2010].

Hill, J. (2009) *Dragons' Den Hungry House Transcript*. Available at: *http://jeffreyhill.typepad.com/english/2009/03/dragons-den-hungry-house.html* [Accessed 16 December 2010].

Hofstede, G. (2002) *Culture's Consequences*, 2nd edn, Thousand Oaks, CA: Sage.

Institute of Leadership and Management and Management Today (2010) *Index of Leadership Trust 2010*. Available at: *www.i-l-m.com/downloads/ILM_Index_Leadership_Trust_2010_Report.pdf* [Accessed 12 October 2010].

Kipling, Rudyard (2007) *A Collection of Rudyard Kipling's Just So Stories*, London: Walker Books.

Kvale, S. and Brinkmann, S. (2009) *InterViews: Learning the Craft of Qualitative Research Interviewing*, 2nd edn, Los Angeles, CA: Sage.

Levitas, R. (1996) *Interpreting Official Statistics*, London: Routledge.

Lewin K. (1945) The Research Centre for Group Dynamics at Massachusetts Institute of Technology, *Sociometry*, 8(2): 126–36.

McDowall, A. and Saunders M.N.K. (2010) UK managers' conceptions of employee training and development, *Journal of European Industrial Training*, 34(7): 609–30.

McSweeny, B. (2002) Hofstede's model of national cultural differences and their consequences: A triumph of faith – a failure of analysis, *Human Relations*, 55(1): 89–118.

Office for National Statistics (2010) *Economy: Retail Sales – Growth slows in August*. Available at: *www.statistics.gov.uk/CCI/nugget.asp?ID=256&Pos=1&ColRank=1&Rank=374* [Accessed 12 October 2010].

Office for National Statistics (2010) *Balance of payments – Trade in goods*. Available at: *www.statistics.gov.uk/statbase/tsdownload.asp?vlnk=224* [Accessed 22 December 2010].

Oxford Brookes University (2010) *Ethical standards for research involving human participants: code of practice*. Available at: *www.brookes.ac.uk/res/ethics/ethics_codeofpractice.pdf* [Accessed 20 January 2011].

Pavlov, I.P. (1927) *Conditioned Reflexes*, London: Oxford University Press.

Pirto, J. (ed.) (2010) *Europe in Figures: Eurostat Yearbook 2010*, Luxemburg: European Union.

Raimond, P. (1993) *Management Projects*, London: Chapman & Hall.

Saunders, M., Lewis, P. and Thornhill, A. (2009) *Research Methods for Business Students*, 5th edn, Harlow: FT Prentice Hall.

Saunders, M.N.K. (2011) Choosing research participants, in C. Cassell and G. Symons (eds) *The Practice of Qualitative Organizational Research: Core Methods and Current Challenges*, London: Sage.

Saunders, M.N.K. (2012) Web versus mail: The influence of survey distribution mode on employees' response, *Field Methods*, 24(1).

Smith, A. (1904) *An Inquiry into the Nature and Causes of the Wealth of Nations*, 5th edn, London: Methuen and Co.

Sutton, R. and Staw, B. (1995) What theory is not, *Administrative Science Quarterly*, 40(3): 371–84.

UK Children's Media Literacy (2009) London: OFCOM.

University of Greenwich (2009) *Dissertation Handbook*. Available at: *www.gre.ac.uk/__data/assets/pdf_file/0006/342951/UG-Dissertation-Handbook-for-BUIL-0015-09-10.pdf* [Accessed 20 January 2011].

Wallace, M. and Wray, A. (2011) *Critical Reading and Writing for Postgraduates*, 2nd edn, London: Sage.

Wang, C.L., Indridason, T. and Saunders, M.N.K. (2010) Affective and continuance commitment in public private partnership, *Employee Relations*, 32(4): 396–417.

Wells, A. and Twyman, J. (2010) *2010: Did online polling come of age?* PowerPoint Presentation. Available at *eprints.ncrm.ac.uk/1585/1/wells_twyman_online_polling.ppt* [Accessed 10 December 2010].

Wright Mills, C. (1970) On intellectual craftsmanship, in *The Sociological Imagination*, London: Pelican.

Index

abstracts 42–4
academic writing *see* articles; journals
action research 117–19
  definition of 117
Adobe Reader 43
analysis of variance *see* variance, analysis of
anonymity for research subjects 81, 205
anthropological studies 119
archival research, definition of 121
articles 31, 34–5, 37
  abstracts of 42–4
  full texts of 43
  peer review of 36, 54
assessment criteria for research 17, 220–5
association, statistical examination of 181
author-date referencing systems 49, 55

background thought 6
Bannatyne, Duncan 157
bar graphs 172
Beynon, Huw 120
bibliographies 48
Bing search engine 30, 38–9
Blackwell Reference Online database 40
Boolean operators 41–2
brainstorming 9–10, 39
Branson, Richard 205
Breuer, Z. 22
Brinkman, S. 155–6
British Airways 106
Business Source Complete online database
  38, 40–1, 3

Caan, James 156–7
CAQDAS (computer aided qualitative data
  analysis software) 187, 189
case studies 116–17
categorical data 165–6, 169, 177, 180, 198
categorisation of data 194–5
category questions 143, 145
cause and effect
  law of 105
  statistical examination of 186–8

central tendency 176–7
Charles, Tony 157
charts *see* tables, charts and graphs
chi-square tests 180–2
clarity in research 18
Clough, P. 20
codes of practice 75
Collard, S. 22
computer aided qualitative data analysis
      software *see* CAQDAS
concept mapping 10, 39
conference proceedings 37
confidentiality 77–8, 81, 205
confidentiality agreements 66
construct validity 142
consumer focus groups 110
contacts, use of 61–2
content validity 142
continuous data 165–6
convenience sampling 140
Corbin, J. 119
correlation 180, 182–4
Cresswell, J. 26–7
critical realism 105
criticism, receipt of 72
cross-sectional studies 123–4

data
  access to 16
  categorisation of 194–5
  consistency in 126
  definition of 24
  dispersion of 176–7
  preparation errors in 169
  processing of 3–4
  reliability of 18
  sensitivity of 59
  and theory 24
  types of 77, 138, 165–7
  units of 194–5
  validity of 18
data analysis 5, 35–6, 164–7
  qualitative 134, 187–98
  quantitative 168–88, 198

data collection 131–2
  combining methods of 122–3
  harm caused by 78–9
  honesty in 79
  plausibility of methods 126
  sample selection 132–41
  techniques of 34–5
  using the Internet 79
  see also interviews for data collection;
    questionnaires
data matrices 168–9
data presentation
  display of extreme values 172
  display of proportions 174
  display of relationships between
    variables 174–6
  display of trends 174–5
  for puposes of description 176–9
  for puposes of summarisation 170–1
  see also statistics, use of; tables, charts
    and graphs
Data Protection Act (1998) 79–80
deadlines 72
decision-making processes 26
deduction 108–10
  definition of 108
deductive analysis 194–5, 199
Delphi Technique 13–15
descriptive data 165–7
descriptive studies 111–14
direct realism 105
discrete data 165–7
discussion of ideas 11, 13
dispersion of data 176–7
Dragons' Den 157

EBSCO *see* Business Source Complete
    online database
elimination of research ideas 1–5
Emerald online database 38, 40–3
employee surveys 12
employers, production of reports for 11–12
enthusiasm for a research topic 15
ethical standards in research 74–82
  breaching of 77
  definition of 74
ethnography 119–20
Excel software 135
experiments 114–15

explanatory studies 113–14
exploratory studies 110–11, 114
external organisations 13
  assurances of confidentiality given to 66
  establishment of credibility with 66–7
  gaining access to 58–60
  procrastination by 59–60
  reluctance to participate on the part of 59

filter questions 147
flexibility in research 16–17
footnotes, use of 49
Ford Motor Company 120
fresh insight 18

gatekeepers 75, 81
  definition of 60
Ghazali, Zaharah 183–4
Goldilocks test 20
Google search engine 30–1, 38–9
  Google Scholar 40
grand theories 26–27
graphs *see* tables, charts and graphs
grounded theory 119

Harvard College Library 47
Harvard style of referencing 49
Heathrow Airport 106
histograms 172–4
HungryHouse.co.uk 157
hypotheses 25, 182, 185; *see also* null
    hypotheses

illegitimate data codes 169
illogical data relationships 169
induction and inductive analysis 109–10,
    194–5, 199
information overload 4
informed consent 75–6
Internet
  as a source of information 36, 38–9, 54
  used for data collection 79, 160–1
interpretivism 106–7
interval data 167
interviews for data collection 112
  participants in 75–6, 151–2, 154–5
  semi-structured 151, 152–62
  structured 141, 151–62
  unstructured 152–62

jargon, avoidance of 218
journals 8, 34
   peer review of 36, 54
JSTOR online database 40

Kendal's rank correlation coefficient 180,
   182–3
keyword searches 38
Kipling, Rudyard 202
Kvale, S. 155–6

Lake, Shane 127
learning objectives 23
learning outcomes, statements of 73
lecture notes 7
Lewin, Kurt, 26
Lewis, Philip J. *xv*, 27, 46, 48, 103, 118,
   134, 143, 155
libraries, 13, 30, 36, 54
line graphs 175
list questions 143, 145
literature
   obtaining of 38–45
   types of 36–7
   usefulness of 45–6
literature reviews 7–8, 13, 30–1
   and accreditation of sources 46–50
   and choice of research topic 33–4
   definition and purpose of 31–2
   downloading of articles and abstracts 43
   and identification of research techniques
     34–5
   importance of 33–6
   keywords and phrases in 39, 54
   and online databases 39–41 , 55
   research projects based on 33
   search techniques 38, 41–4, 54
   'shopping catalogue' reviews 52–4
   structure of 51–2
longitudinal studies 124–5

McDowell, A. 196–7
marking scheme guides 74
matrix questions 144
methodology of research 34, 126, 210–11
middle-range theories 26–7
Mills, C. Wright 216
motivation for research, maintenance of
   69–70

news media, use of 8–9, 12
   newspapers 37
Nexis online database 40
nominal data *see* descriptive data
non-directive interviews *see* unstructured
   interviews
non-probability sampling
   definition of 134
   techniques of 137–40
non-text data 165, 198
noting of ideas 10–11
null hypotheses 181–2, 185–6
numerical data 166–7, 169, 177, 180–1, 198
Nutbrown, C. 20

observer bias 128
observer error 128
Ofcom (Office of Communications) 112–13
online databases 31, 36, 38–44
open questions 143–4
ordinal data *see* ranked data
organisational skills, development of 57
Oxford Brookes University 75

paired *t*-tests 180
participants in research 151–2
   anonymity of 81, 205
   confidentiality for 77–8, 81, 205
   consent from 75–6, 154–5
   definition of 151
past projects, use of 6–7, 13, 39
Pavlov, Ivan (and Pavlov's dogs) 105
PDF files *see* Portable Document Format
Pearson's product moment correlation
   coefficient 181, 184–5
peer review 36
personal experience 3
pie charts 174
pilot testing 148–9
   definition of 149
   for interviews 152, 157–8
plagiarism 31, 47–8, 54
populations for sampling 132–5, 161
Portable Document Format (PDF) files 43
positivism 104–5
pragmatism 107
preliminary studies 12–13
primary data
   availability of 16
   harm caused by collection of 78–9

probability sampling
    definition of 133
    techniques of 135–7
progress reports 72
project literature
    links to 17
    use of 12
project objectives 18
project standards and specification 17
proposition development 190–4
purposive sampling 138–9
    definition of 138
    varieties of 139

QSR International NVivo 9 software 188–9
qualitative data 187–98
    confidentiality of 77
    and purposive sampling 138
    types of 165–6
    and non-probability sampling 134
quantitative data 77, 198
    analysis of 168–87
    preparation of 168–9, 198
    presentation of data 169–76
    types of 165–6
    and use of statistics 176–88
quantity questions 144
questionnaire design 3–4, 142–8, 161
questionnaires 3–4, 34–5, 112, 115–16,
        122, 161
    definition of 141
    distribution of 149–51
    pilot testing of 148–9, 152
    potential respondents to 148
    types of question in 143–4
    web-based software for 145, 148
quota sampling 137–8
quotations from literature 218

ranked data 165–6, 180
ranking questions 143, 145
rating questions 144–5
ratio data 167
reactivity 78
realism 105–6; see also critical realism;
        direct realism
referencing 48–50, 213
regression 181, 186
relationships. statistical examination of
        182–5

reliability, definition of 128
research
    approaches to 107–110
    clarity of 18
    elimination of ideas for 1–5
    motivation for 69–70
    noting ideas for 10–11
    professionalism in 64–5
    scope of 16–17
    sources for 46–7
    validity of 127–8
research findings
    believability of 125–8
    consistency with data 126
    logical flow of 125
    reliability of 128
research ideas, generation of 5–11
research objectives 18–27, 126–7
'research onion' 103
research overviews 207
research philosophies 103–7
research process, management of 57–60,
        68–82
    by self-management 68–70
    in universities 73–4
    use of supervisors 70–3
research projects 1, 4–5, 16–18, 33, 68
research proposals 201–6, 216–25
research questions 18–20, 23–7, 126–7
research resources 3–4, 15, 212–13
research strategies, types of 124–7
research topics, selection of 10–27
    characteristics of good topics 15–18
    difficulties in 4–5
    importance of 2–4
    role of literature review in 33–4, 208
respondents
    definition of 141
    vulnerability of 77

sample selection 132–41, 161
    non-probability-based techniques 137–40
    probability-based techniques 134–7
samples and sampling, definition of 112,
        132
sampling frames 136–7, 161
    definition of 133
Saunders, Mark N.K. xv, 27, 35, 46, 48, 103,
        118, 134, 143, 155, 196–7

scatter graphs 174–6, 186
search engines 30–1, 38–9
search term, definition of 39
search terms 38, 39, 41
secondary data
    harm caused by use of 79
    and literature reviews 34, 54
    qualitative analysis of 189
    reanalysis of 112
    relevance of 16
self-selection sampling 140
semi-structured interviews 151–62
simple random sampling 135
skills of researchers 3
SMART test 23–4
Smith, Adam 207
snowball sampling 139–40
Spearman's rank correlation coefficient
        180, 182–3
specialist knowledge 3
SPSS software 36, 177–8, 181
statistical analyses, types of 180–7
statistics, use of 176–88
stratified random sampling 136–7
Strauss, A. 119
Staw, B. 24
structured interviews 141
subject bias 128
subject error 128
substantive theories 26–7
supervisors 5, 70–3
SurveyMethods software 145
SurveyMonkey software 145
surveys 12, 115–17
Sutton, R. 24
systematic sampling 136

t-tests 180, 183–5
tables, charts and graphs 169–76, 186, 198

testable propositions 191–4
text data 165, 198
textbooks 7, 36–7, 54
theory
    definition and types of 24–7
    development of 107–8
    as an element of research 5
    logical flow from research findings 125
Thornhill, A. 27, 46, 48, 103, 118, 134,
        143, 155
timescales 68–9, 211–12
topicality of research 16
trade magazines 34
trends in data 176–9
triangulation process 122–3
Twyman, J. 138

units of data 194–5
University of Greenwich 73–4
unstructured interviews 62, 152, 161–2
useful sources 46–7

validity of research 127–8
Vancouver style of referencing 49
variables 25, 104–5, 177
variance, analysis of 180, 183–4
Virgin Group 205

Wallace, M. 48
Wells, A. 138
Wikipedia 31, 39, 41
Wiley Online database 40
Wray, A. 48
writing style 216–20

YouGov 138